P9-BYB-249

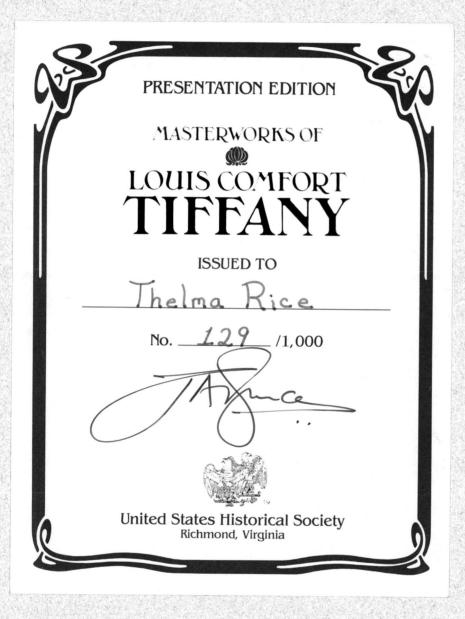

PRESENTATION EDITION

MASTERWORKS OF

LOUIS COMFORT
TIFFANY

ISSUED TO

Thelma Rice

No. _129_ /1,000

United States Historical Society
Richmond, Virginia

MASTERWORKS OF
LOUIS COMFORT
**TIFFANY**

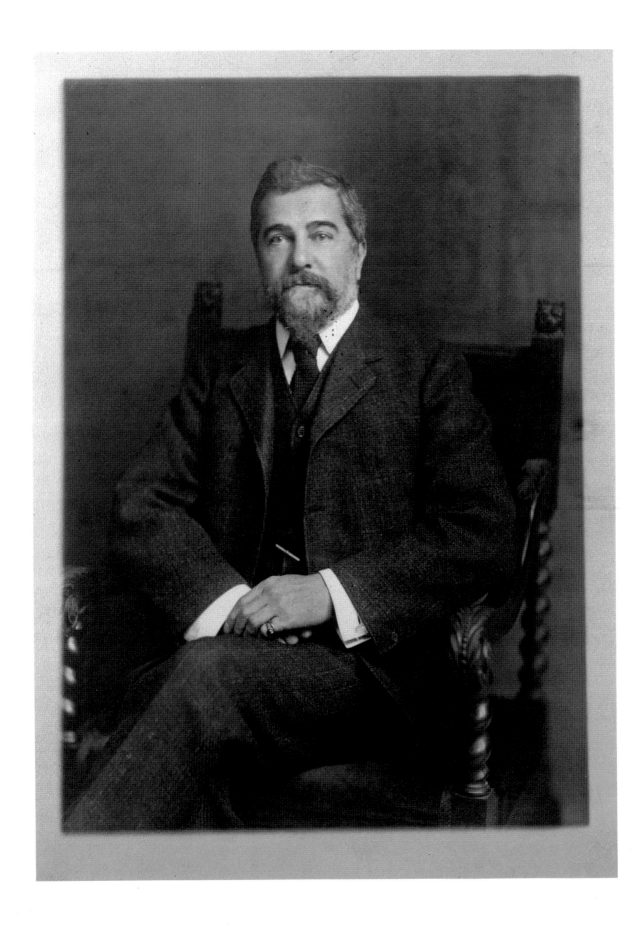

# MASTERWORKS OF LOUIS COMFORT TIFFANY

Alastair Duncan

Martin Eidelberg

Neil Harris

HARRY N. ABRAMS, INC., PUBLISHERS, NEW YORK

Library of Congress Cataloging-in-Publication Data

Duncan, Alastair, 1942—
    Masterworks of Louis Comfort Tiffany / Alastair Duncan, Martin
Eidelberg, Neil Harris : foreword by Alastair Duncan.
        p.   cm.
    Catalogue of an exhibition to be held at the Renwick Gallery,
Washington, D.C. in Oct. 1989 and at the National Academy of Design,
New York, in 1990.
    ISBN 0-8109-1537-5
    1. Tiffany, Louis Comfort, 1848-1933—Exhibitions.    I. Tiffany,
Louis Comfort, 1848-1933.    II. Eidelberg, Martin P.    III. Harris,
Neil, 1938-    .   IV. Renwick Gallery.    V. National Academy of Design
(U.S.)   VI. Title.
N6537.T5A4    1989
709'.2'4—dc19                                                    89-422
ISBN 0-8109-2440-4 (pbk.)                                        CIP

Copyright © 1989 Thames and Hudson Ltd, London

Published in 1989 by Harry N. Abrams, Incorporated, New York
All rights reserved. No part of the contents of this book may be
reproduced without the written permission of the publisher

A Times Mirror Company

Printed and bound in Japan

# CONTENTS

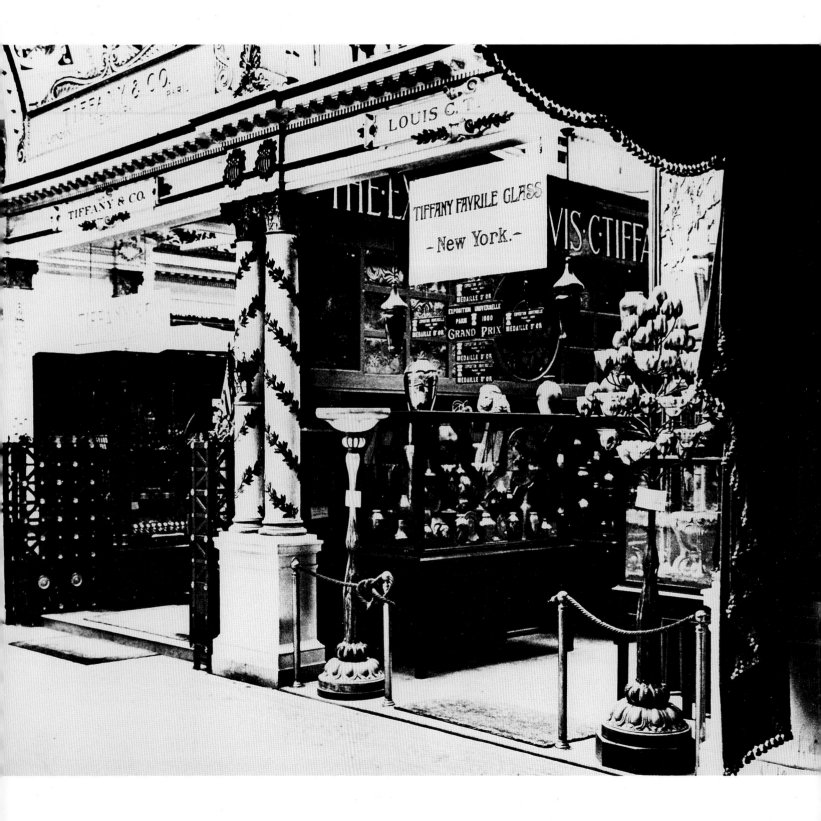

# INTRODUCTION

## Alastair Duncan

his book accompanies the exhibition *Masterworks of Louis Comfort Tiffany*, organized by the Smithsonian Institution under the sponsorship of Tiffany & Company. The exhibition provides the first opportunity in nearly one hundred years, from the time Tiffany rose to public eminence at the 1893 Columbian Exposition in Chicago, to measure his achievements through the display of a selection of his finest works. Two previous retrospective shows — those at the Museum of Contemporary Crafts in New York in 1958, and at the Heckscher Museum in Huntington, Long Island, in 1967 — were restricted in their selection by the fact that they preceded the art market surge of the late 1970s and early 1980s which helped to coax many of the items included in this exhibition from their original homes. For a brief moment at least, the whereabouts of most of Tiffany's surviving masterpieces are now known. This has provided the Smithsonian Institution with the forum by which the public can reassess Tiffany's individual genius before some of the items are dispersed into new collections, some of which, from recent market trends, will almost certainly be overseas.

### "A Dumbfounding Versatility"

Full comprehension of Tiffany's achievements as an artist has largely been blurred by his other role, that of the owner and director of a firm which mass-produced household and liturgical objects such as lamps, memorials, miscellaneous glassware, and bronze candlesticks and desk top items. The sheer volume of products generated by the Tiffany Studios for so many years has overwhelmed the public's perception of the man at the heart of this giant commercial enterprise; one of prodigious individual talent who for more than fifty years wrestled with the dilemma of how to juggle the dual role of individual and industrial artist. The latter has persistently veiled attempts to analyze Tiffany the artist, whose unswerving quest of beauty led him into the fields of painting, glass (not only the manufacture of the material itself, but its selection for windows, lamps, mosaics, and decorative glassware), bronzes, enamels, ceramics, and jewelry, and, on occasion, photography, architecture, textile design, and interior decoration, to all of which he applied himself with surpassing ability and imagination.

Contemporary critics understood the breadth of Tiffany's artistry, although they differed on the respective merits of his achievements in each discipline. An editorial in the *Baltimore Evening Sun* (October 19, 1910), provided a summary of the high respect Tiffany enjoyed among most critics: "it is doubtful if another can be mentioned who has contributed more substance to art in all its phases and embraced a wider range of expression in the interpretation of all things beautiful." The German Otto von Bentheim provided the most succinct assessment of Tiffany's work in his review of the Studios' exhibit at the 1900 Exposition Universelle in Paris, which he judged to be of "a dumbfounding versatility."

The Tiffany Studios exhibit at the Paris Exposition Universelle, 1900. In the right-hand vitrine is the punch bowl of Favrile glass and gilded silver designed for Mr. Henry O. Havemeyer.

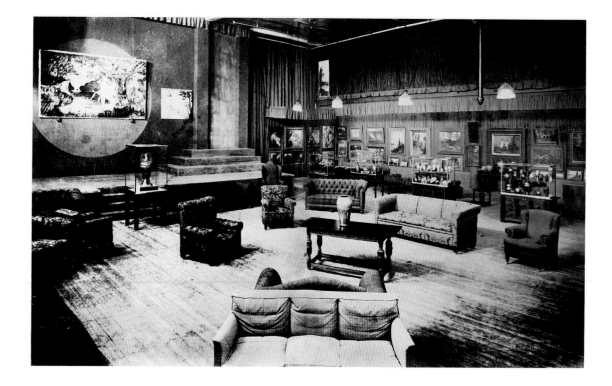

Our analysis of Tiffany today varies in several important aspects from the way he was perceived at the height of his career and, incidentally, from the way he intended himself to be judged by posterity. There remains no serious dispute on the fundamental talents which governed his energies — those of a colorist and naturalist — nor of his spectacular innovations as a glassmaker, a thirty-year odyssey which reached fruition in his mastery of the most intoxicating range of blended colors and techniques attained in the annals of the craft. Time has afforded a different view, however, of the relative strengths and weaknesses of what he created in so many artistic media. Not surprisingly, he did not excel all the time, nor was he equally excellent at everything he attempted. But he was, at his height, a decorative artist of unparalleled ability, vision, and accomplishment, whose achievement will probably never be surpassed; one who through a felicitous blend of intelligence, ambition, wealth, creativity, and boundless energy seized the unique opportunities afforded him by the extraordinary expansion and prosperity which America enjoyed at the turn of the century. It was the nation's first Gilded Age, and Tiffany was perfectly placed to act as its most fashionable purveyor of taste, not only within the home, but in every type of public and private institution, including places of worship, hotels, clubs, libraries, hospitals, and even ferry boats.

Tiffany considered the production of windows as his most prestigious pursuit as the medium was, in his opinion, the most exalted of all decorative art forms. Yet in this he was continually thwarted by the insistence of his major client, the church, for ecclesiastical figural compositions, a style in which his designs were far from unique. The body of his religious work was, in fact, saved from banality only by his inimitable glass. Today his figural church commissions appear, if anything, less distinguished than they were considered at the time, in sharp contrast to his landscape and floral panels, which, although far fewer in number, must in their juxtaposition of glorious hues have occasionally exceeded even Tiffany's own aspirations as a colorist.

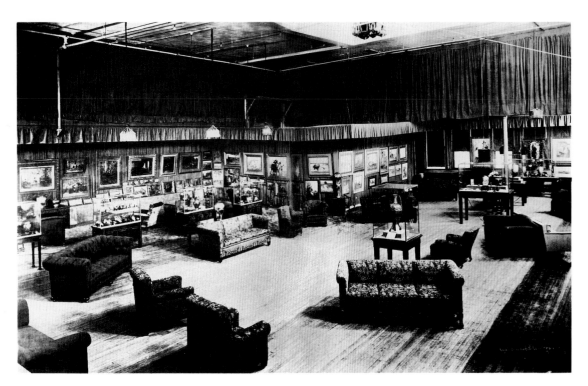

Two views of the exhibition staged in 1916 by L.C. Tiffany at the Tiffany Studios showrooms to celebrate his sixty-eighth birthday. Over 150 paintings and decorative objects were included.

It is ironic that posterity has perceived Tiffany primarily as a maker of leaded glass lamps; this would have frustrated him greatly for their rank commerciality caused him to feel less satisfaction than in any other of his artistic endeavors. Even his biographer, Charles de Kay, in his 1914 volume, which examined in detail Tiffany's multifaceted abilities (including his relatively obscure achievements in textile and furniture design, and architecture), studiously avoided any reference whatever to the Studios' glass lamp operation. This, coming at the moment when Tiffany's leaded lamps had been produced for a seemingly insatiable market for fifteen years, is astonishing. Such an obvious omission must be ascribed to the insistence of Tiffany himself, either directly or via his children, for whom the book was commissioned. In addition, there is no surviving literature in which Tiffany refers to his lamps, although he eagerly expatiated on his philosophy of color, light, nature, and glass in numerous speeches and articles. In the exhibition which he staged at the firm's showroom in 1916 to celebrate his 68th birthday, there was only one lamp – the unique peacock model which he designed for Charles Gould and which had a hand-blown, rather than leaded, shade – among over 160 paintings and cabinets crammed with examples of his Favrile glassware, enameled pieces, and jewelry. The fact that the lamps were produced in multiple, unlike his windows, enamels, and hand-blown glassware – which were each unique works of art – was no doubt in conflict with the image that he had of himself as an artist. That the lamp manufacturing process was initiated by the need to utilize the fragments of sheet glass which had accumulated through years of window production, and that there was therefore a lingering stigma – one of expediency and commercialism – associated with their origin, was another factor that kept Tiffany from acknowledging his lamps as an integral part of his artistic repertoire. Yet they have regained their initial popularity for the same reason they were first successful: their three-dimensionality provides the perfect vehicle by which a collector can enjoy the spectacular kaleidoscope qualities of Tiffany's glass at the mere turn of a switch within the confines of his own home. Even their uncountable numbers cannot obliterate the fact that they remain at their finest a uniquely Tiffany form of artistic expression and, as such, easily identifiable and fashionable artefacts of interior decoration. And even if Tiffany did not himself invent the concept of leaded glass lamps (there is no evidence in contemporary literature to prove whether he did or not) – that of using pieces of *flat* glass contained within a delicate web of soldered strips of copper foil to create a curved lampshade – his perfection of the process warrants our recognition that it was in itself a measure of his ingenuity.

No discussion of Tiffany's lamps can exclude consideration of his bronze bases. Missing from the literature of the Studios was any reference to the quality of casting of its bronzeware, which it described only as "metal." Yet the crisp chased detailing and unwavering excellence of the firm's patinas matched the quality of anything produced by the foremost foundries in the United States – the Roman Bronze Works, Gorham, and Henry Bonnard – at the time.

Contemporary critics were lavish in their praise of the shimmering spectral qualities of Tiffany's Favrile glassware, which made its debut in 1893. This enthusiasm has been retained by today's collectors, although there is no consensus, as there is among Tiffany lamp collectors concerning the most important lamp models, as to which of his technical processes is the most successful, and therefore the most desirable. At times perceived as secondary to his lamps (measured in part by their relative inexpensiveness), Favrile vases have recently elicited fresh appreciation, and growing competition among collectors, for their fluid organic forms and unique surface iridescence and texturing.

Beyond his glass windows, lamps and vases, Tiffany brought significant technical innovations to the related fields of mosaics – in which he rejected the medium's conventional grid-pattern form of assembly for his domestic commissions – and enamel-on-copper, in which he developed shaded translucent enamels under which light-reflective particles of metallic foil were placed to heighten significantly their naturalistic effects. In his experimentation with ceramics, Tiffany's achievements were likewise distinguished, although more modest in his application to vessels of organic form of a single colored glaze, a technique made fashionable by other potteries at the time.

In his jewelry, to which Tiffany applied an enchanting range of botanical and entomological motifs, the full extent of his achievements remains obscure, as his experimentation, even more than that involved in his enamels and ceramics, was swathed in secrecy. Surviving pieces, frequently in handwrought gold enriched with *champlevé* enamels, show his facility with the medium, and even drew the praise of a French critic who, in what he erroneously presumed would be taken as a compliment, described Tiffany's brooches at the 1905 Paris Salon as "worthy of an amateur Lalique." The obvious advantages provided by Tiffany's association with Tiffany & Company, of which he was the Artistic Director from the time of his father's death in 1902 until his own in 1933, afforded him endless opportunities for experimentation and innovation. Several of the firm's pieces of jewelry from the period, especially between 1908 and 1914, indicate his influence in their floral designs and delicate summer palette.

In only one category, painting, has today's audience been less charitable to Tiffany in its judgment than his peers were. The problem is twofold: on the one hand, as his involvement in other areas of the arts grew in the 1870s – specifically interior design and glass experimentation – Tiffany had fewer opportunities to paint professionally. Most of his surviving canvases

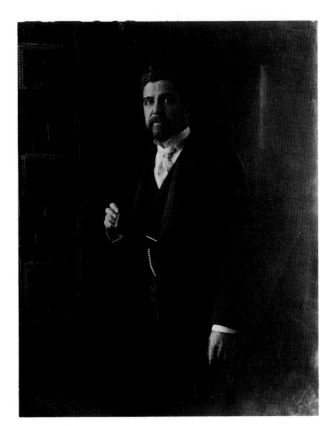

Louis Comfort Tiffany at the height of his career.

therefore appear unfinished – which both these and many of his cartoons for windows in fact were. The second problem is that the majority of his finest paintings have been passed down within his family, which has slowed appreciation of his painterly skills by the public at large. Tiffany would not have risen to the top rank as a painter, but he was considerably more gifted, when he allotted himself sufficient time, than he is often now given credit for from the dreary selection of landscapes and Arab bazaar studies that appear intermittently in the market place.

*"Infinite, Endless Labor Makes the Masterpiece"*

The man behind these spectacular objects remains an enigma, one who, when pressed on his accomplishments, spoke with diffidence of his continuing role as a student of art, as in a 1916 speech: "If I may be forgiven a word about my own work, I would merely say that I have always striven to fix beauty in wood or stone or glass or pottery, in oil or water color, by using whatever seemed fittest by the expression of beauty; that has been my creed, and I see no reason to change it." On other occasions he spoke expansively *around* the objects he had created – on the aesthetic concepts which motivated him – but not specifically about them. The observations of his contemporaries tell far more about him. Critics and friends spoke always of his boundless energy, which acted as the catalyst in unifying his other talents. Rene Quelin, for example, in a 1922 article on Tiffany entitled *A Many-sided Creator of the Beautiful* (*Arts & Decoration*, July 1922, p. 176), wrote, "This no doubt has been the secret of his success and renown – work, work, everlasting work – like the Old Masters of the Middle Ages, the times when artists were also true craftsmen, preparing all their materials and tools themselves . . ." Charles de Kay provided a similar testimonial: "Infinite, endless labor makes the masterpiece".

Inextricably bound to this voracious appetite for work was Tiffany's preoccupation with perfection. Stories have survived of him as an old man walking through the Corona factory and striking pieces from the work bench which did not meet his artistic or technical standards of the moment. Other anecdotes passed down through the families of his top employees – such as Joseph Briggs and Frederick Wilson – corroborate this image of a man obsessed with excellence, which on occasion manifested itself negatively in his relationship with his staff. Tiffany could be an arbitrary, high-handed, and uncompromising employer, who was equally prepared to overrule his clients on artistic issues. An article in the *New York Tribune* of June, 1901, which described progress on the Wade Memorial Chapel in the Lakeview Cemetery, Cleveland, shows how Tiffany set standards for himself above and beyond the comprehension of others: "Tiffany, who is considered the most clever and at the same time the most erratic maker of stained glass in America, has probably taken his last look at the windows in the memorial for the present, and in consequence architects Hubbell & Benes and Mr. Wade are breathing sighs of relief. Mr. Wade said last night that Tiffany had torn the magnificent windows he had placed in the structure to pieces, on the occasion of each of his previous visits of inspection, and he was fearful that Tiffany might still be dissatisfied with his work. 'The great artist goes after a certain effect,' said Mr. Wade, 'he is never satisfied until he gets it, and frequently destroys costly creations of his own because he does not like the effects of certain portions of his work.'"

Other facts support the vision of an artist imbued with a divine mission: that of the beautification of everything within his reach. That Tiffany Studios recorded a loss from year to year – the firm's treasurer, Mr. Fielding, noted that Tiffany invariably wrote a check at the close of the financial year to offset the outstanding debt – shows a man blinded to the economic realities of the business world, whose father's largesse subsidized his ambitions. Today we need not concern ourselves with the non-profitability of Tiffany Studios, and can be grateful, rather, that if additional funding was required to balance the books, it prevented the diminution of Tiffany's unwavering artistic standards.

*The Masterworks of Louis Comfort Tiffany* exhibition provides the public with the opportunity to appreciate Tiffany's accomplishments through a selection of objects of which he would presumably have approved, as most of those chosen were included in his displays at international expositions or illustrated in literature published by the Tiffany Studios as representative of its finest work. He would also no doubt welcome a retrospective exhibition which attempts to show that, beyond the lamps which he so deprecated, he produced art of a stupefying beauty and artistic sensibility in a host of other media. Many observers will also realize for the first time that, although he worked for fully one half of his fifty-odd year career in this century, Tiffany's style remained firmly entrenched in the nineteenth century in its embrace of nature as a decorative theme and in its preoccupation with superlative handcraftsmanship.

# LOUIS COMFORT TIFFANY:
# THE SEARCH FOR INFLUENCE

## Neil Harris

he Tiffany legend is alive and well. The return of the brilliant lamps, glass, and windows to popular favor, the fabulous sums they now command at auction, and the resurgence of Art Nouveau in this country and abroad together have reasserted the power of the Tiffany name. Indeed, it is hard to understand how it was so placidly understated for so long.

But there are still some who confuse Louis Tiffany with his jeweler father, Charles. And others who mistake Tiffany for any maker of stained glass in turn-of-century America. Despite the new attention and respect, Louis Comfort Tiffany remains for many a rather vague and somewhat distant figure, a curious mixture of impulses and influences: artist, businessman, inventor, promoter, socialite, philosopher, teacher. This may be partly a function of his longevity, for he spanned the period between the Mexican War of 1847-48 and the election of Franklin Delano Roosevelt in 1932. More likely it has resulted from the extraordinary variety of his interests and decorative art exploits. In fact, Tiffany's eighty-five years encompassed not one but several careers, each of them concerned with special expressive problems, each developing its own strategies of persuasion and exemplification. No phase of his life, of course, was absolutely separate from any other. His commitments and experiences transcended specific periods of his work. But in making sense of Tiffany's remarkable blend of inventiveness, salesmanship, and aesthetic passion, it might be useful to distinguish three large responses he made to some very different challenges. First, the initial need to establish a personal and professional reputation by providing arresting and integrated interiors for both individuals and institutions. Second, the desire to shape mass taste by producing and then selling products of his workshops, marketing a variety of goods that reflected his preferences and technical experiments. And third, the attempt to provide a legacy, to establish a permanent mark of his personality on the art life of his country by training a corps of artists who would share with him the ideal world of Laurelton Hall.

It is impossible to do equal justice to all these phases of his career, and this essay will concentrate on the earlier years. But it may be helpful in gauging the scope of the man to realize how numerous his innovations were.

Perhaps Louis Tiffany's greatest achievement was to propound a philosophy of decoration that accepted the supremacy of aesthetic effect as its primary justification. While he preached a religion of beauty through his lifetime, Tiffany avoided most of the respectful moralisms that had flavored the domestic guidebooks of earlier generations. In forming the Associated Artists in 1879 with Samuel Colman, Lockwood De Forest, and Candace Wheeler, Tiffany advanced a view of interior spaces that reoriented — in at least two fundamental ways — the preferences of his day. One was literally a reorientation, a turn to the East, to Persia, India, Byzantium, Japan, North Africa. And the other, a candid embrace of lushness, illusion, exotic naturalism, and artistic virtuosity. Both met the ambitions of clients eager to break with the more formal eclecticism favored by the rich business class, and eager to explore the fabulous on a global level. In this first career, moreover, Louis Tiffany and his partners gave some of their attention to a newly evolving set of interiors, simultaneously public and private, civic and domestic. Their very existence revealed the changing character of American society, the dismantling of boundaries separating the sacred and the profane, the commercial and the artistic, the familial and the theatrical. In obtaining these early jobs and defining a group of patrons Tiffany, even more than most of his generation, suggested the skillful and aggressive approach to marketing that would be a permanent part of a successful career in the decorative arts.[1]

"Is it not almost time to rebel against the professors of household art?" asked the *New York Times* in 1877. "They are so numerous, persistent and dogmatic that they make life a burden. . . . No man or woman dares any longer to be comfortable in his or her own house. We must be artistic first and comfortable afterward – if possible."[2]

Long before the Civil War interior spaces, public and private, had captured the attention of American moralists. Their design was invested with high ethical aims. Domestic settings seemed especially vital. These arenas in which to rear the young, protect femininity, and provide a family retreat from the harassing pressures of the outside world were rhetorical fodder for architects, ministers, educators, landscape gardeners, social reformers, and feminists alike. In dozens of texts published in the 1840s, '50s, and '60s, they indicated how color, pattern, light, furniture, and efficient planning could be used to promote domestic health, personal comfort, rational beauty, and spiritual safety. Their readers were expected to apply these lessons toward furthering the American family's stability and happiness.[3]

Typically, these authors did not themselves manufacture the objects they described, although a few owned patents for individual innovations, and several were architects. They concentrated instead on proposing general principles, guiding novice homemakers through the maze of existing alternatives. But their specific advice radiated ethical imperatives. The consequences of showy, ugly, or inappropriate domestic spaces were so painful that it was impossible to avoid the moral dimension. Philosophers of art who worked with ethical vocabularies – John Ruskin, Charles Eastlake, Andrew Jackson Downing – found in America enthusiastic audiences.[4]

So the complaints of newspapers like the *Times* came only after the alternating spasms of advice and counter-advice had turned the middle-class American home into a battlefield between dogmatists of different persuasions. Although the *Times* was most exercised about eclectic variety (a man must "hang his hat on a Queen Anne hook, put his cane in a mediaeval rack . . . die on a Louis XIV bedstead. . . ."), the "aesthetic trials" of house planning also had included periods of enforced simplicity, of "artistic" furniture meant to discipline flights of fancy in the interests of restraint and consistency.[5]

By the 1870s many books surveyed existing American houses, and either praised or criticized their presentations of self. Despite what was often fairly expensive advice, most critics continued to relate room interiors to a middle-class version of national life, projecting older ideals of democratic simplicity and egalitarianism, or at least resting their aesthetic objectives on these assumptions.

The rooms they addressed were in large part the work of architects rather than interior designers. And they were linked to appropriate behavior patterns. The library of a house should be its "most interesting, stimulating, and useful room," urged Charles Wyllys Elliott in his *Book of American Interiors*. "Here the family should gather in the evening for talk, for work, for reading; here should come friendly people. . . ."[6] Americans seldom gave dinner parties, observed another writer in Samuel Sloan's *Architectural Review and American Builders' Journal*, and when they did there was, thankfully, no male withdrawal for drinking or carousing. The company more properly retreated to the parlors. Only palaces used drawing rooms as reception halls or salons, "and to set apart such a room for the reception of guests by a republican people is at best but a paltry effort at copying a part of a whole system which we nationally decry."[7]

Avoidance of vulgarity, control over extensive display, and reassertion of domestic values were of special concern to a group of self-taught women writers, who published their suggestions for room-decorating primarily in the 1870s. While exterior domestic designs were reserved to male architects, women could step into the vacuum left by male indifference or insecurity, and assess the merits of various wallpapers, carpets, door moldings, and draperies. Their readers were more frequently concerned with small economies and countering the deficits of size and shape than were the upper-middle-class builders of libraries and dining rooms.[8]

The newly rich of the post-Civil War years did not feel obliged to use these books as their guides. Breaking with traditions of self-denial or affirmations avowing the value of inconspicuous consumption, they went to furniture designers like Herter Brothers, who arranged the spaces for their custom pieces and procured complementary accessories. Or they left such matters in the hands of their architects. These clients were neither interested in moralizing advice nor in need of thrifty pointers. Increasingly the great urban home builders of the 1870s and '80s sought fashionable acclaim and impressive effect; for their houses were not so much domestic retreats as social centers for the dinner parties, concerts, dances, and civic receptions that were becoming a part of metropolitan life. No philosophy of action was necessary for these undertakings; they required buying experience, craftsmanship, and coordination.[9]

Such wealthy clients did not always know what they wanted or even, necessarily, what they liked. But they expected value for money, and usually involved themselves in some of the choices being made. Richard Morris Hunt, Stanford White, Herter Brothers, Pottier & Stymus, along with other decorators and architects, grew affluent serving their needs.[10]

Why would such clients come to Tiffany and his associates with a decorating commission? How could a young, little-known artist succeed in competing with established architects or large furniture-makers? Other scholars have asked this question, and their answers seem reasonable: through a combination of design originality, extensive promotion, and personal connections. And also, to be sure, by addressing an apparently intense need. The distinction of their first customers suggested how clearly Associated Artists had gauged their market, and how shrewd Louis Tiffany had been in determining that there was a great deal of money to be made in servicing such clients.[11]

The young Tiffany had impressive advantages. His father was already servicing the display needs of the wealthy through his jewelry and silver. Louis Tiffany himself, the child of a successful businessman, began as a painter, but resembled more nearly in background and aspiration some of the successful architects of his day, inevitably dependent on the good will of prospective clients for major commissions. The position and the social skills necessary for participation in the clubs, the dinners, the parties and other social functions organized by potential patrons helped greatly. Personable, articulate, and socially respectable, Louis Tiffany had the further advantage of artistic training and cosmopolitan experience. His studies abroad and voyages of discovery in North Africa demonstrated his seriousness; by the time he turned to decorating he had gained some little attention as an exhibited painter. Intense as well as handsome, well traveled, and opinionated, he owned the necessary credentials for persuasive salesmanship.

Unlike the architect, the interior designer required no technical knowledge of building methods or building laws. Nor did he need any license. The expenditures he consumed were

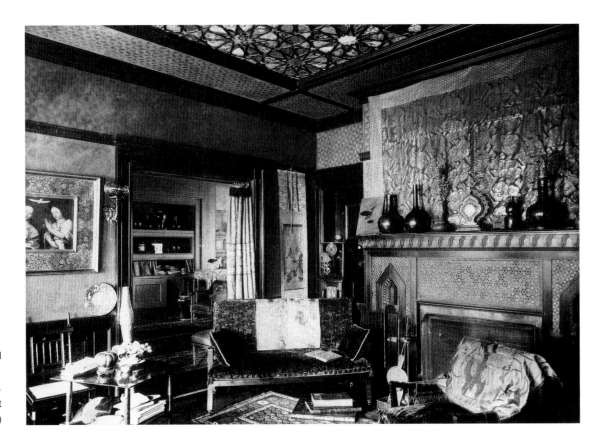

The library of the Samuel
Colman house in Newport,
Rhode Island, in the 1880s.
(Photo courtesy of the Art
Institute of Chicago)

much smaller than the architect's, and the preparation period much briefer. The decorator's requirements were imagination, judgment about color, texture, and scale, a broad knowledge of stylistic vocabularies, and access to craftsmen who could translate his ideas into reality. Most of all, the interior designer was in need of a signature, a distinctive approach, to rise above competitors. Tiffany's enthusiasm for eastern themes and materials, and his fascination with light and color provided an immediate signature.[12] His connections with Candace Wheeler, Samuel Colman, and Lockwood De Forest opened up the craft world. And his personal background reassured those entrusting him with special commissions, either from architectural firms like McKim, Mead and White, or from individual clients.[13]

But these advantages aside, the rise to celebrity remains astonishing in its speed. Before 1879 Tiffany had done no interior designs at all. Within three years he was taking orders for the White House. In between he had designed or redesigned homes for several of America's best known millionaires, as well as its most celebrated writer. In this process Tiffany's name, breeding, and appearance were enablements permitting the pursuit of commissions. But they were certainly not sufficient. The margin of difference may well have been the dazzling impact his first interiors produced on clients and architects bored by the well-managed repetition they encountered everywhere else, and ready to take a chance. Selecting Associated Artists, in the early '80s, represented something of a calculated risk. The gamble was taken either by the adventurous, or by those already so secure they were unworried by the possibility of failure. Any anxieties, to be sure, were lubricated by the personal associations that held designer and customer together.

Tiffany understood the value of promotion and the importance of demonstration from the very beginning. And he quickly benefited from the attention of friends and relations. One of the first critics to define his characteristic approach to interior design was a well-known New England architect, author, and agriculturist, Donald Grant Mitchell, who had achieved a journalistic reputation by writing for New York newspapers under the name of Ik Marvel. Books of humorous essays, a popular 1850 novel, *Reveries of a Bachelor*, and foreign correspondence helped support his later efforts at farming and town planning. By the 1870s Mitchell was eminent enough to serve on decorative art commissions, and as architect of Connecticut's building for the Philadelphia Centennial of 1876.[14]

He was also connected to Louis Tiffany through the marriage of his brother to Tiffany's sister. Indeed it was in Donald Grant Mitchell's house that Tiffany met his first wife, Mary Woodbridge. Ten years later Mitchell wrote a series of articles on the Tiffany quarters in the Bella Apartments on East 26th Street, New York City. Tiffany had moved his family there in 1878 and remained until moving into the house Stanford White built for them on Madison Avenue.

Mitchell's articles appeared in a new popular illustrated journal in 1882, and gained much attention.[15] Yet Tiffany was obtaining major commissions even before their publication. His first big job came from a sixty-three year old pharmaceutical millionaire, George Kemp, who was building a house on Upper Fifth Avenue. Apparently Kemp knew Charles Tiffany, and this may explain why he was willing to take a chance on his son.

The Kemp commission reaped almost immediate celebrity. At just about the same time that Donald Mitchell was describing the Bella Apartments, A. F. Oakey depicted in *Harper's Monthly* the work of Associated Artists for the Seventh Regimental Armory's Veterans Room, and an unnamed residence which was illustrated in the essay, and is clearly the Kemp House.[16] We don't know Kemp's reaction to the publicity, but presumably it was not unwelcome.

It was also not unprecedented. During the 1880s and '90s, as a result of advances in printing technique and development of the halftone process, both popular and professional journals enjoyed featuring domestic interiors as part of their programs of illustration. They shared space with many other kinds of images: natural disasters, battle scenes, election rallies, holiday celebrations, theatrical performances, athletic contests, exotic journeys. But there was nothing quite like the private interior to represent the prying power of journalism, its invasion of forbidden spaces, regions not usually penetrated by mass readerships.

Decades earlier, tours through famous homes had been employed by publishers, authors, and editors to sell books and magazines. Often the subjects were literary types — poets, novelists, essayists — or clergymen. Occasionally the homes of politicians were included. Favored views included sketches of studies or dens where the thinking and literary creation took place.[17] This suggested that the interest in illustration had more to do with the fame of the home owner than the skill of the decorator. In much the same way that movie fan magazines would later probe intimate secrets of stars' lives, these more decorous intrusions into domesticity bore traces of celebrity culture.

The sensibility of the '80s and '90s had evolved into something different from the earlier model. There was now a double subject. On the one hand stood the home owner, the patron, the client, the collector, whose wealth and taste formed part of the equation. On the other was the artist decorator entrusted with the task of organizing and furnishing the presented spaces. Either personality might dominate; in several cases there was clear sharing. In any event, expanded coverage of wealthy homes was creating a new personality type: the celebrity room

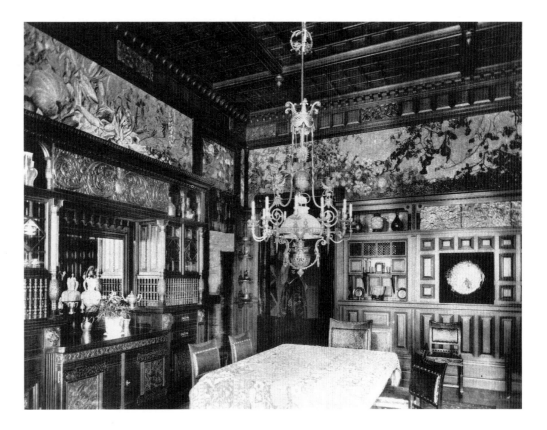

The dining room in George Kemp's residence on upper Fifth Avenue, New York City, in the 1880s. This was Tiffany's first important interior design commission. (Photo courtesy of the Art Institute of Chicago)

designer. Like the couturier he (or she, as the career of Elsie de Wolfe would demonstrate) shed fame on both himself and his client.

Oakey's article did not identify George Kemp as the owner of the illustrated rooms. But wealthy New Yorkers might have known whose house it was. And acquaintances must have savored the exposure given to the interiors they had enjoyed on social occasions. A Tiffany commission could bring media attention — such was one lesson of the *Harper's* piece. And within two years Kemp's house would be among the more than ninety home interiors featured in *Artistic Houses,* the opulent series of photographs published by D. Appleton in 1883-84 for a small number of subscribers.[18] Tiffany's firm had worked on part or all of seven interiors described by the text, including the apartment he had designed for himself and the East Room at the White House. None of them gained more space, however, than the Kemp House. Like the other interiors, it was clearly identified. Its owner could bask in the company of Morgan, Vanderbilt, Marquand, Villard, and the other great names that graced its pages.

The novelist Constance Cary Harrison, describing Associated Artists for *Harper's* in 1884, presented their work as "the first fruits of the American Renaissance," but added, somewhat misleadingly perhaps, that "very little was attempted by the association to secure the attention of the public that throngs and wonders. Their work, principally executed to beautify certain elaborate interiors, has been hurried by the owners from work-room or atelier into jealous seclusion as soon as it was finished."[19] *Artistic Houses* and magazine articles suggested otherwise.

One of the subscribers (and an unhappy one at that) to *Artistic Houses* was Mark Twain.[20] It was Twain's visit to the Veterans Room of the Seventh Regimental Armory, plus his own experience with Charles Tiffany's jewelry firm (and the recommendation of another decorator,

Herbert M. Lawrence), that persuaded him to entrust Tiffany's firm with redecorating his Hartford house.[21] In this tripartite posture — personal taste, professional recommendation, and knowledge of the New York store — Twain was probably typical of Tiffany's early clients. Twain had been buying in Tiffany's since the 1870s, trusting Charles Tiffany to "give honest measure." In one jocular episode he claimed to have attempted, in 1879, to buy cordwood there, but reported in his notebook Charles Tiffany's response that his license permitted him only to deal in jewelry. According to Twain, Tiffany noted that a great New York jeweler had once tried to defy the restriction and displayed a wood-pile in a showcase, but "the regular wood dealers mutinied in a body & began to sell diamonds in their woodyards at ruinous rates." Twain's happy conceit concluded by observing that "the two trades have never encroached upon each other's domains since."[22] The following year Twain was more successful in purchasing at Tiffany's membership badges for the young ladies of the Hartford Saturday Morning Club, who met once a year at his home.[23]

Mark Twain was not the young Tiffany's most famous client. President Chester A. Arthur occupied this position. But many of the same connections linked him to Tiffany. As a wealthy New Yorker and man about town, Arthur had been a patron of Tiffany's store for years before going to Washington. On his elevation to the Presidency he was faced with a White House in serious need of renovation. Congress had appropriated $30,000 for repairs in 1881, and Mrs. Garfield, the wife of Arthur's predecessor, had already invited Herter Brothers and Pottier & Stymus to submit proposals for redoing the state rooms. In the end Mrs. Garfield had decided on a somewhat old-fashioned Washington furniture store, W. B. Moses & Sons, whose services had the great advantage of convenience.

James Garfield's death ended these plans, but the White House still required attention. Arthur supposedly told an aide, "I will not live in a house like this." Modifying the recent plans, installing both an elevator and a French chef in the Presidential mansion, he expanded the decorating budget and, after expressing some dissatisfaction with the rooms done thus far, met with Tiffany to discuss fresh possibilities.

According to William Seale, the most recent historian of the White House, Arthur had seen in New York Tiffany's work in the Seventh Regimental Armory and in the new Union League Club.[24] He gave Tiffany the commission, and the Red Room, Blue Room, State Dining Room, and the transverse hall with its famous glass screen brought Tiffany still more publicity.

Most of it was good. E. V. Smalley declared in *Century* magazine that the redecorated White House had "none of the straining after striking effects" which he claimed was the bane of modern construction, and paid special tribute to Tiffany. In early days the hotel character of the Mansion had been reflected in the "formal, half-furnished appearance of the rooms," but "Louis C. Tiffany's decorative association has metamorphosed the place, and made the smaller rooms look like the abode of people of luxurious tastes." The corridor linking the East Room and the Conservatory, with its stained-glass mosaic screen, made for "a marvelously rich and gorgeous effect, falling upon the gilded niches where stand dwarf palmetto trees. . . ."[25]

Rich and gorgeous were natural words to emerge from descriptions of the Tiffany touch. The term "luxurious" no longer earned the almost unanimous reproach it had attracted in early republican America. Opinion was, at least, divided. On the one hand the *New York Times* could, in 1880, condemn unsparingly the enormous sums spent on dining, dress, drinking,

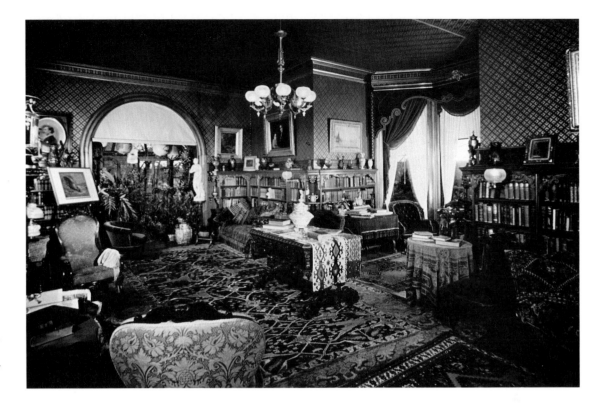

Interior view of Mark Twain's house in Hartford, Connecticut, around 1882. (Photo courtesy of The Mark Twain Memorial)

and partying. "Never in the history of this Republic has wealth been able to procure such an infinite variety of matter to please the eye, adorn the person, and tickle the palate. . . ." The "painted, gilded, art-decorated, and notoriety-seeking social extravagance" of the day had "nothing to commend it," the *Times* concluded.[26] But ten years later, after having proudly termed New York a "city of luxury" the *Times* observed wonderingly that "everybody seems rich here. . . . Every kingdom of the world is ransacked; every sea is traversed; every remote corner of the world is explored, to furnish us with new pleasures. . . ."[27] Luxury, in short, while bearing traditional suspicions in its train, served to validate national wealth and power. And a language of extravagance did not appear totally inappropriate applied to the public/private character of the President's home, simultaneously a family residence and the national symbol of executive office. Clients unafraid of such accusations or protected by public status from such a charge – like Mark Twain and President Arthur – could seek the New York decorator, in happy expectation of his special effects.

Twenty years later, during Theodore Roosevelt's administration, when the White House was extensively remodeled by McKim, Mead and White, such ornateness seemed inappropriate to many, including some reformers. When a number of Congressmen protested architect Charles F. McKim's program, the *New York Times* observed that they were probably objecting to "the simplicity and moderation, the chastity and good taste, which belong to the restoration of a Colonial Mansion," resenting the "absence of that 'palatial magnificence' which is to be found in so many hotels and so many steamboats and so many barrooms," but which was explicitly renounced in the newly redesigned President's House.[28] Tiffany, himself, was on to other things by this time.

Sometimes only personal idiosyncrasy could explain a commission. Historians are not certain why William S. Kimball, a Rochester industrialist, came to Tiffany to decorate his expensive new castle in the early 1880s. But Kimball had demonstrated his individualistic taste on a number of other occasions. He had commissioned a mammoth statue of Mercury to decorate the top of his tobacco factory; he was an inveterate orchid fancier; and he was an early enthusiast for Japanese design.[29] For him, Associated Artists created their special combination of tile, glass, wood, and textiles, a more sensuous setting than conventional millionaires might desire, and one that had clear links with the Kemp house, the Seventh Regimental Armory, and Tiffany's own apartments.

Another rather individualistic client who came looking for Tiffany appeared after Associated Artists had broken up. This was Louisine Elder Havemeyer who, with her husband Henry, got Tiffany and Samuel Colman to complete their new house in 1892. As Frances Weitzenhoffer has pointed out, Mrs. Havemeyer deliberately distanced herself from the decorating conventions established by members of her set, seeking escape from the plentiful plush and gilding.[30] Impressed by the Madison Avenue house built by Tiffany and Stanford White, taken particularly by Louis Tiffany's own apartment, the Havemeyers spent lavishly to create a distinctive setting for their art collection, and to highlight, among other things, the string quartets they subsidized. In her choice of interior designer, as well as her interests in painting and graphic art, Mrs. Havemeyer represented one type of Tiffany client: the self-confident problem solver who wanted simultaneously to meet specific display needs and to express a sense of personal taste. Turning a house over to a specialist could mean loss of control over details of appearance and layout. Professional architects had long since managed to dominate exterior building decisions. But clients could still work with decorators in shaping individual rooms.

The Havemeyer house also emphasized the use of these great homes as social arenas. Not given to the elaborate dinners and receptions that others preferred, the Havemeyers concentrated their entertainment efforts on music. But even so their home contained what might be called an "official residence," quarters that could be transformed within a few hours into something resembling civic apartments. The task of mediating between public and private seemed of particular interest to the young Tiffany, and certainly it also challenged contemporary designers. The White House, with its clear division into family and public sectors, simply exaggerated a trend apparent in hundreds of other great houses of the day.

Lavish entertainment, of course, was not new to this generation. Country houses and town dwellings alike had long contained reception areas, dining rooms, double parlors, which could accommodate large groups on special occasions. But the scale and polish of the rooms of the '80s and '90s were new — particularly when no court life or ceremonial season called for them. Describing "Idlehour," the Long Island home of W. K. Vanderbilt, the *Architectural Record* asserted that it was "difficult to deny to the public a legitimate curiosity respecting these private buildings. Indeed, in a sense, are they strictly private? Do they not overtop the individual?" The cost of such structures, the artistic resources they consumed, their scale and opulence invested them with significance "that very properly passed beyond the owner and his immediate personal circle of friends." Nominating the Vanderbilts as the "most significant patrons" of architecture since Louis XIV, the *Record* insisted proudly that nothing comparable "exists elsewhere in the world." American merchant princes — Goulds, Astors, Wetmores, Whitneys, Huntingtons — were creating homes that could be likened only to the Florentine palaces of the Medicean era. They were "the registers, and let us hope enduring chronicles of our very latest days. . . ."[31]

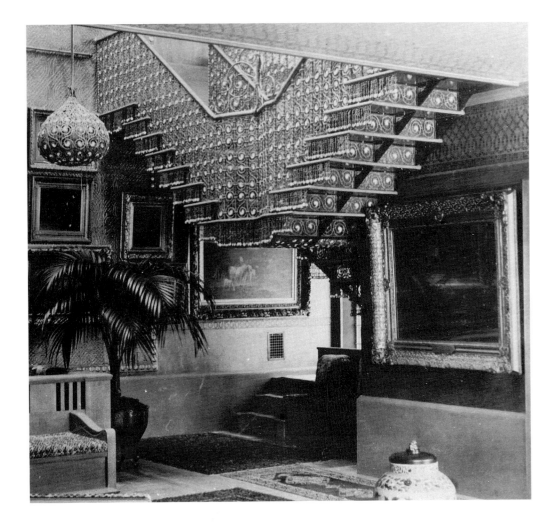

The salon in the New York residence of Henry O. Havemeyer, which Tiffany decorated in 1891-92. (Photo courtesy of the Metropolitan Museum of Art)

Thus flattered and reassured by decorators, architects, and professional journals alike, the wealthy home builders of the day identified their interest in display with public needs, and eagerly leapt over the frontiers hedging private retreats from a curious world. The very rich, argued the architectural critic Herbert Croly in 1902, are "mainly well-meaning and good-natured men, whose standards are too often deplorably low," but "as distinctly the victims of public opinion as are the great American majority." Their "faults are commonplace like their virtues." The American millionaire was no connoisseur as such, Croly continued. "Just as he hires an expert mining engineer to report on the value of the mine, so he hires the services of architects and decorators, who know the values of old tapestries or furniture." Indeed, this leasing of taste was the giveaway. No one with "a native love of beautiful things" could possibly "leave the furnishing and adornment of the rooms in which he lives and sleeps so completely in the hands of other people – no matter how competent."[32]

Croly's view of such patronage is the one that has survived. Aesthetic vulgarity, social banditry, economic irresponsibility, and unpatriotic historicism were among the labels applied to this generation by Progressives, and even in today's revisionist scholarship the patrons have fared much less well than the artists. But the recourse to expert decorators was only partly a confession of ignorance or a gesture of insensibility. For some it reflected a dim consciousness of public responsibility, a belief that disciplined display performed a social function. Frequently photographed, drawn, described, and visited, these great houses were, as the *Architectural Record* argued, more than the private property of their owners; they seemed a common cultural possession. Who wouldn't want expert help when the stakes were so high? The scale of these rooms, their capacities for crowds, the elaborate entertainments they housed, suggested an atmosphere of complex rituals.

American standards for social status and appropriate behavior were being formulated and defined with much greater precision than ever before during the 1880s and '90s. These added to the notion that house decorating, on some levels, was a semi-official act. Such a notion did require some work. Foreign examples revealed the play-acting. In contemporary London, for example, the town mansions of the nobility, including the hundreds of new peers created during the late Victorian and Edwardian regimes, reflected the lavish entertainment style demanded by a court. Nearby were ancient models, old palaces like Stafford House, Spencer House, Lansdowne House, and Londonderry House, their grand staircases, ballrooms, and great dining rooms prepared to receive members of the royal family, foreign ambassadors, dukes, earls, and barons of the realm. Coronations, openings of Parliament, Court receptions, royal birthdays all structured the annual season and provided some public resonance to these private residences.[33]

In New York, Chicago, Boston, and Philadelphia citizens received one another instead of representatives of the crown or the State. No hereditary dignities required ritual salutation. American millionaires "are not public officials, like the Italian potentates whose possessions they purchase," wrote Herbert Croly. "They are generally modest and retiring private citizens who do not relish the notoriety they obtain, and who should wish to make the paraphernalia and trappings of their lives as modest and homely as they themselves are."[34] Yet the size and splendor of their mansions suggested something fuller, more formal, more official. Reviewing "Some New York Palaces" in 1894, *Harper's Weekly* concentrated its attention on the Cornelius Vanderbilt complex created by George Post on Fifth Avenue, a group of edifices occupying a full block between 57th and 58th Streets, yet constituting a single dwelling. So grand a town house invited foreign comparisons. All over Europe stood houses that were "evidently less dwellings than they are scenes of social functions — dwellings the greater part of which the inhabiting family could not make use of. . . ." Now Americans could claim their own renditions. No official residence in America, not even the White House, "gives the spectator so much the sense of having been designed for the exercise of a ceremonious hospitality." Indeed, most foreigners would probably take Cornelius Vanderbilt's expanded home "for an 'institution' of some kind, preferably a museum, rather than for the private residence even of a well-to-do citizen."[35]

James Fullarton Muirhead, offering his mixed reactions to New York while preparing the first Baedecker guide to America in the early 1890s, had a similar response. New York's great homes, "some of the most sumptuous private residences in the world," were often adorned "with exquisite carvings in stone, such as Europeans have sometimes furnished for a cathedral or minster, but which it has been reserved for republican simplicity to apply to the residence of a private citizen."[36] And T. P. O'Connor, recording his "Impressions of New York" for *Munsey's Magazine* in 1907, turned to melodrama in describing the vast fronts and sculptured walls of the new houses, which he found to be an unprecedented mixture of Venetian palaces, German cathedrals and pasteboard towers. "I speak of melodrama because here was a curious sense of unreality and of the theatrical in this abounding luxury and display. I seemed to be living in a

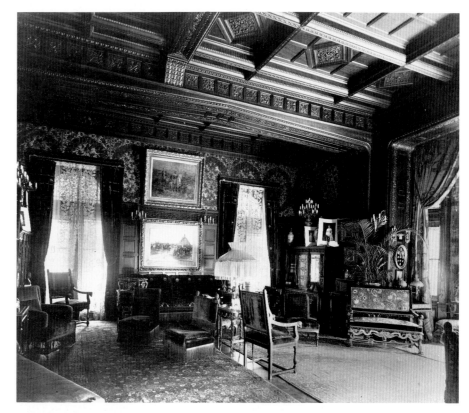

The sitting room on the first floor of Cornelius Vanderbilt II's residence at 57th Street and Fifth Avenue, New York, c. 1885. (Photo courtesy of the New-York Historical Society, New York City)

A view of the dining room in Henry Villard's mansion at 451 Madison Avenue, New York, c. 1885. The architects were McKim, Mead & White. (Photo courtesy of the Art Institute of Chicago)

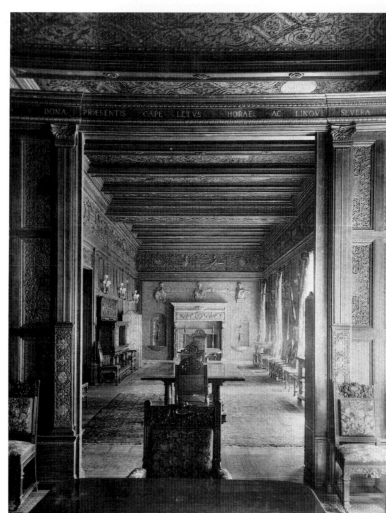

city where wealth, imperial power, unexampled conquests, desired to display and reveal themselves with the ostentation and pride we associate with cities like the Constantinople of the later Roman Empire. . . ."[37]

*Harper's* observation that private and public were easily confused by such grandeur was echoed in other ways. American towns and cities across the country presented their largest and most splendid homes as evidence of civic pride, along with libraries, churches, museums, and colleges. Since most Americans hoped for wealth, their fascination with the way the rich lived seems no odder than a later generation's infatuation with rock stars and their daily routines. Lifestyles of the rich and famous proved an inexhaustible theme, its subjects actively cooperating in the creation of wide publicity. "There is a certain beneficence in collecting beautiful things, and allowing other people the enjoyment of them," wrote "Jenny June" in *Cosmopolitan*. "Possession brings care, cost, and responsibility, and all the real satisfaction that a man or woman obtains from the ownership of a beautiful work of art, or even a much finer house than their neighbor, is the being able to look at it till they are tired, and hardly want to see it again." Such a point of view encouraged an image of dinner-giving as "the form of social life capable of the finest and most varied treatment. . . ."[38] The caterer, like the interior decorator, could easily become an indispensable means of setting a good example.

Tiffany's conviction, in the late 1870s and early '80s, that both money and influence could flow from a decorating career, reflected his awareness that competitive ambitions would spur clients on, and that public and private spheres were melting into one another. It wasn't only the domestic interiors that invited public interest. Non-domestic spaces were also changing in their variety and service functions at just the same time. Tiffany's string of such commissions and his eagerness to become involved with their planning, suggested his sensitivity to these

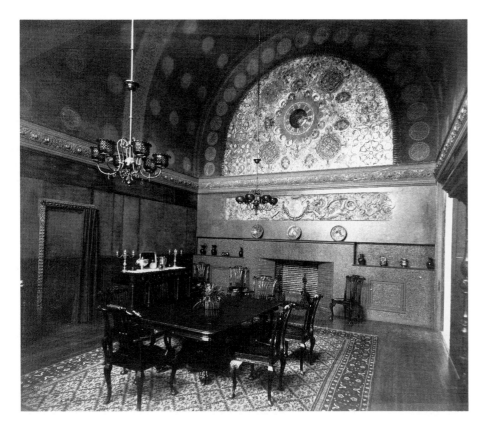

The dining room in Louis Comfort Tiffany's own house at 72nd Street and Madison Avenue, New York, in the late 1880s. (Photo courtesy of the Art Institute of Chicago)

special opportunities. And in a short while he would be exploiting them quite systematically with products as well as services.

The Seventh Regimental Armory remains the outstanding early example. This commission brought Associated Artists clients impressed by their memorable Veterans Room. But after all, construction of big urban armories was itself a new American enterprise, one born in the post-War years when labor violence succeeded in frightening the propertied. The Seventh Regiment, enjoying a distinguished and fashionable reputation, desired something more than space for maneuvers and storage of weapons, the kind of facility nervous legislators were beginning to promote in the interests of internal security. The regiment also craved a ceremonial setting to celebrate its glorious history, to impress upon newcomers the battles that had been won, and to evoke the heroism and energy of conflict. Instead of turning over the design of their Veterans Room to the architects, who might have been expected to extend the medievalism of the building's exterior, regimental officers applied to a decorating firm. Presumably they knew that the special expression of corporate personality they sought could not be achieved by manipulating architectural features alone.

The architect now became adviser to the decorator, for Associated Artists brought in Stanford White to help with the Veterans Room and the Library, the two rooms they were hired to design. In the Veterans Room, the more elaborate of the two, the firm employed a subtle color scheme and a lot of iron. Across the top ran the frieze interpreting the evolution of warfare, alternating with geometric shields and allegories. One signature of the Tiffany operation was clearly in evidence: a large brick fireplace surrounded by glass tiles and surmounted by an elaborately carved if somewhat obscurely inspired plaque. Candace Wheeler designed the portieres of Japanese brocade. The pale colors were unexpected and, to some, seemed in-

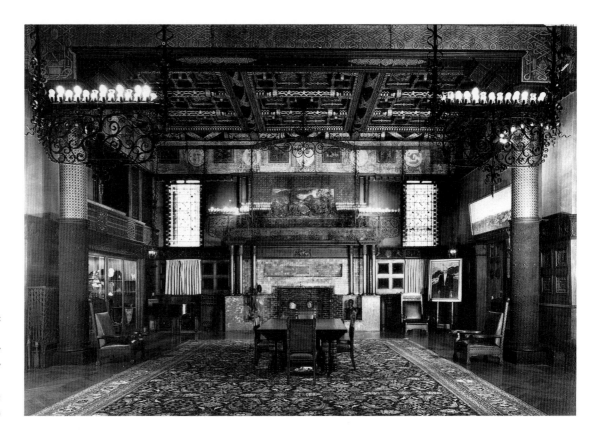

The Veterans Room in the Seventh Regimental Armory, New York City, designed by Tiffany, c. 1885. (Photo courtesy of The Historic Buildings Survey, National Parks Service; photographer Jack E. Boucher)

appropriate. But the room conveyed the unmistakable note of military triumph and evoked the clash of arms the regiment wanted. It was gaped at by visitors, and even critics acknowledged its special power. The promotional booklet produced for the opening spoke of the "chime" of its "side decorations, the clamp and clang of iron, the metallic lustres, the ponderous . . . beams," in a tone of contented affirmation.[39]

Forecasting Tiffany's later critical fate, some comments on his early work bore a highly qualified, occasionally even a hostile tone. A. F. Oakey, writing about the Veterans Room in *Harper's*, would have preferred "a revival of some fine old mediaeval guard-room," and objected to the "affectation of rudeness" in the room that "gave the whole a theatrical expression."[40] Yet Oakey admitted he found many details quite arresting. His journalistic colleague, William Crary Brownell in *Scribner's Monthly*, raised more fundamental questions. Calling the room a "decorative expression of the idea of the veteran," Brownell acknowledged that it clearly identified its purpose. But these were his kindest observations. He found the color scheme weak, the stained glass poor, and the symbolism far too mechanical. "A similar spirit would decorate the exterior of a post-office with letter-boxes, or cover the walls of a bathroom with pictures of towels and toothbrushes."[41] Mistrusting the capacity of any group or committee to plan an interior, because "the really organic unity" proceeds "only from the spontaneity and completeness" of a single mind, Brownell sympathized with professional architects and suspected "dilettanti" who broke with established conventions of form and color. He thought Associated Artists too tame and restrained in the end, unlikely to counteract the "mechanical tendency" of the average architect.

But Brownell's admiration for many of the room's touches, particularly when they were revealed by gaslight, his careful and attentive analysis, and his belief that decorators could effectively challenge or resist architects in planning interior space, showed that something was happening. In concerning themselves with corporate personality, seeking to convey a specific sense of interior purpose and associations, advancing a more ambitious and integrated set of goals, Associated Artists displayed a coherent and influential approach to professional goals. Rooms could be transformed into demonstrations of demeanor and disposition, expressions of intelligence and of idiosyncratic preference. Knowledgeable specialists were able to project collective aspiration as well as individual ambition. Potential clients, like Twain and President Arthur, sensed this in the Veterans Room. It was new, different, distinctive, and difficult to forget, qualities increasingly valued as waves of mass-produced objects and effects engulfed domestic and non-domestic settings alike.

In the 1880s and '90s other institutions with complex challenges of corporate display called on Associated Artists, and then Tiffany himself after the separation, to offer advice. One of them was the urban club. By the late nineteenth century most American cities were honeycombed by social organizations organizing men and women according to various ethnic, fraternal, professional, and athletic categories.[42] The clubs formed hierarchies of age, prestige, wealth, and distinction. Many of them at first inhabited rather modest quarters. Some rented rooms, taking over basements or converting town houses. But by the end of the century a number of the older or wealthier associations had begun to construct clubhouses of their own, incorporating, whenever possible, elegant dining rooms, lounges, billiard rooms, and libraries. Since many of these clubs contained prominent architects as members, they turned to them for help. The resulting buildings often became civic landmarks.[43]

Clubs served many purposes. As urban society grew more distended, as business and professional contacts became more heterogeneous, clubs emerged as places for self-selecting groups to celebrate ancestry, relish comfort, exchange views and information, and, for the wealthiest, to insulate themselves from the indiscriminate social contacts they suffered in other public places. Club memberships inevitably became significant elements of personal biography, indices to status and influence.

In purely physical terms there were many varieties. One of the newest versions, in New York at least, was the mid-air dining club. By 1901 Manhattan had an Arkwright Club for dry-goods merchants, a Drug Club, a Hardware Club, a Midday Club, a Transportation Club, a Fulton Club, and a Woman's Club, all located atop tall office buildings, offering members fine views and luxurious interiors. Cleveland Moffett told readers of the *Century* that there was "peace at a great height, hope and strength in a broad panorama," while he described the elegance and diversion the clubs contained.[44]

Another institutional variety flourishing simultaneously was the athletic club. Country clubs catered to the new passion for golf and tennis, but city clubhouses answered the need for more immediate recreational facilities. In the 1890s and thereafter elaborate clubhouses in New York, Chicago, Detroit, Boston, Denver, Providence, and elsewhere, mingled swimming pools and racquet courts with their billiard rooms and dining halls. Members enjoyed, throughout the year, boxing contests, smokers, concerts, athletic games, wrestling tournaments, water polo, sometimes in settings of great magnificence. The club parlor of the Chicago Athletic Club was likened, for example, to the House of Lords in Westminster. Carved oak in Gothic style, huge fireplaces, and high ceilings bespoke a lavishness that still seemed startling.[45]

Even more elaborate were the new clubhouses in New York of the upper classes, institutions like the Union League, the Metropolitan, the Union, the New York Yacht Club, the Harmonie Club, the Arion, the University, the Knickerbocker, the St. Nicholas, and the Calumet. Outside New York, other cities had their equivalents.[46] In some respects clubs were extended families and their clientage probably resembled the domestic customers who came to architects and interior designers for their own homes. But the clubhouse was also a civic facility, a venue for dinners, receptions, and meetings, many with great public significance. It offered special possibilities for demonstrating an attachment to higher values and also for displays of conspicuous magnificence.

The 1894 opening of Stanford White's Metropolitan Club, nicknamed the "Millionaire's Club" by locals, demonstrated just how far decorators could now go. The white marble exterior was imposing but simple, architectural critic Montgomery Schuyler conceded. But such plainness disappeared with a great entrance hall of polished marble boasting a gold encrusted coffered ceiling. This in turn led to an intimidating double staircase. The public rooms (appropriately enough Schuyler called them "state apartments") were of extraordinary dimensions, suggesting the atmosphere of a palace. It was not surprising that their dominating impression was of a sense of luxury "so overpowering as to make us forget or postpone the consideration of what of art may have gone to make it up. . . . These gorgeous interiors seem to indicate what those hardy pioneers, the decorators of the North River steamboats, would have done if they had had the advantage of a sojourn among the palaces of France and Italy and a course at the Beaux-Arts." The enormous dining room contradicted the law of Vespasian that cash was inodorous for "it exhales riches." A more modest private dining room, done up in colonial style, "produces much the same effect as a solo on the flageolet after the crash of a military band." Schuyler predicted that the average American would enjoy the sensuality of the new clubhouse greatly; a "more serious and strenuous art would not meet his views so well."[47]

Such special opportunities were tempting to architects and decorators. Tiffany had nothing to do with the Metropolitan Club, but he had become involved with the trend ten years earlier. The Union League Club, founded by fervent loyalists during the Civil War (including Tiffany's own father), determined upon a new clubhouse, to be built by the Boston firm of Peabody and Stearns.[48] This wealthy and conservative club pursued an ambitious set of goals. Instead of turning to a single interior artist it employed several specialists including Tiffany, the firm of Cottier, the sculptor Frank Hill, and Tiffany's great rival in stained glass art, the painter John La Farge, who designed its third-floor dining room.

Reviewing the building after the opening, the *Century* broke down its various features. With reference to La Farge's dining room, the magazine noted the chronic incompatibility between architect and artist-decorator, but expressed overall pleasure with the room's total effect. It seemed to unite "elegance and luxury" with "refinement and tact," rescuing the interior from any imputation of glitter. The color scheme, plaster scroll work, and light oak wainscoting made for an effective ensemble.

Tiffany's task was to decorate the main staircase and halls. Here the verdict, even if ultimately supportive, was mixed. Tiffany had sought splendor, said the *Century*, and splendor had one drawback: "If it fails to please, it offends." The green-and-silver scheme he employed demonstrated considerable originality, and disguised the obvious presence of a decorator. Still, it was Tiffany's windows that produced the most powerful impression on this critic; his stained glass had not yet established itself, so reactions to it were still fresh and excited.[49]

Other great clubhouses would be built in coming decades, many with elaborate allegorical painting and sculpture.[50] Clubs seemed determined to make claims for their civic and cultural significance, and to proclaim continuity with heroic virtues and great events. Shields, crests, coats of arms, classical legends, historic encounters were featured in stone, mosaic, mural work, and stained glass. The fifteen-story Gothic clubhouse for Chicago's University Club enjoyed a decorating scheme supervised by a local painter, Frederic C. Bartlett.[51] The Detroit Athletic Club, designed by Albert Kahn, was decorated by W. & J. Sloane of New York.[52] The Bankers Club, placed atop New York's Equitable Building, had its interior planned by a lawyer member, Henry J. Davison, who was also a lecturer on color and decoration.[53] Although Tiffany himself would not decorate any more clubs after the Union League experience, his early interventions helped popularize corporate interest in unifying interior spaces, and demonstrated the presence of specialists who could provide an appropriate look.

Armories, clubs, and official residences were joined in these years by other establishments poised between public and private spheres, and concerned with decorative expressiveness. One such was the apartment house. Freshly popular in New York during this period, the upper-class residences tried to distinguish themselves from tenements by ambitious names and elaborate appointments. These latter could be seen to best advantage in the lobbies, elevators, and entry halls through which residents and guests passed. More domestic than the hotel lobbies whose excesses had earned general condemnation, but still accessible to a whole variety of people, such areas cried out for more coherent presentation. Occasionally truly spectacular effects were achieved as in the Osborne, a luxury building on 57th Street

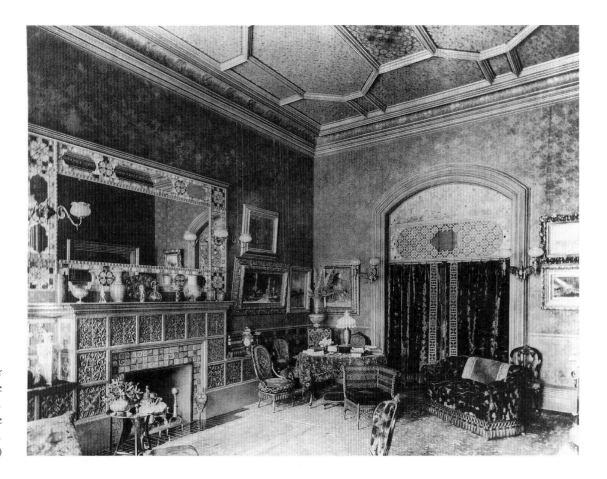

The parlor in J. Taylor Johnston's lower Fifth Avenue mansion, decorated by Tiffany, 1881-82. (Photo courtesy of the New-York Historical Society, New York City)

The dining room designed by Tiffany for the residence of Dr. William T. Lusk on East 37th Street, New York, 1882. (Photo courtesy of the New-York Historical Society, New York City)

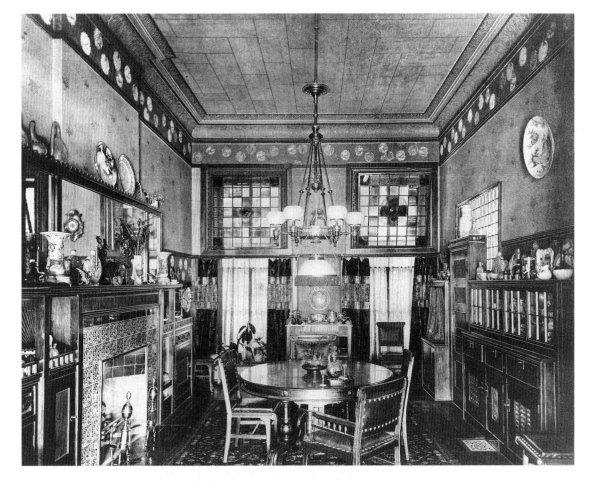

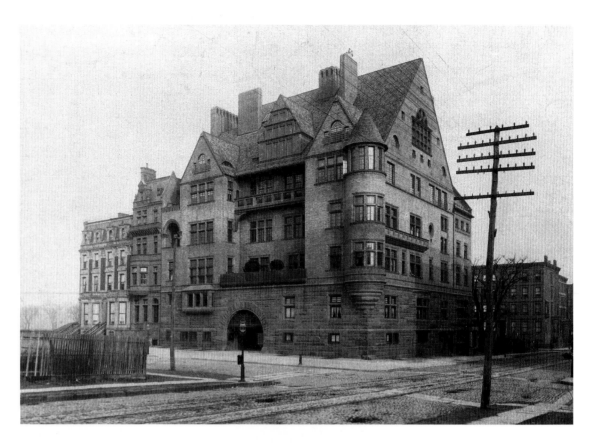

Tiffany's residence in New York City, c. 1885. (Photo courtesy of the Art Institute of Chicago)

The four-sided fireplace in the top-floor studio of Tiffany's home, 1890s.

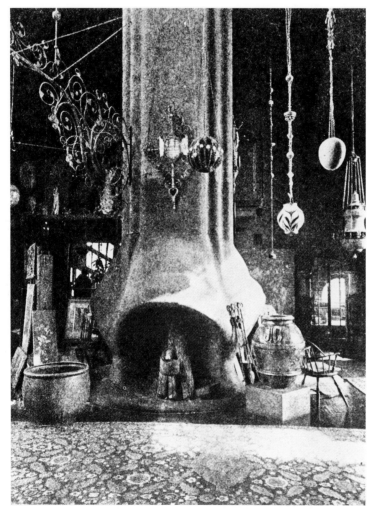

which opened in 1885, designed by James Ware, its lobby created by a Swiss-born decorator who worked for Tiffany, Jacob Adolphus Holzer, and who would later undertake several major Chicago commissions.[54] Tiffany probably supplied the lobby's stained glass, and the foil-backed mosaic was another Tiffany signature, used here by Holzer along with rare marbles and fresco work. Few other apartment houses could match the splendor of the Osborne's lobby, but Tiffany's ingenuity in apartment design — for both the Bella and the building Stanford White created on Madison Avenue and 72nd Street — indicated once again his involvement in a new building type.

Because of institutional growth and replication, planners and architects had become convinced that successful building projects required careful cooperation with interior designers. Plan standardization in the interests of traffic patterns, safety, and efficient operation meant that the principal differences between one hotel, theater, or club and another were signaled by the interior appointments and decorating schemes. These, along with commissioned murals and sculptured pieces, endowed their institutions with special character.

This at least was the view of architectural critics like Arthur David, when he reviewed the interior of David Belasco's new Stuyvesant Theatre in New York in 1908. Unhappy about recent auditorium decorations, insisting that theaters do more than simply shelter audiences in elaborately prettified settings, a traditional recourse, David objected to Belasco's rather novel attempt to suggest a private dwelling. Official descriptions called the Stuyvesant a "living room in a high sense of that sometimes commonplace phrase — a room wrapped in the atmospheric intimacy of which the spectator would feel not so much that he was in a public place, as in a private house to which he had been personally invited." David found the conceit unconvincing and vulgar, affected and melodramatic. Like Belasco's plays, this theater "was not to look like it was," but "to seem to be precisely what it was not." It was an "architectural hybrid," and David placed the "domesticated theatre" beside "the villas which look like palaces, the living rooms which look like banquet halls, and the libraries which look like mausoleums. . . ." Here was one critic unhappy about the ambitious new ambiguities he so effectively defined.[55]

As in other significant interior types of the period, Tiffany got involved with the theater in the 1880s, initially through creation of a special element rather than an overall effect. Tiffany produced a drop curtain for Steele MacKaye's innovative Madison Square Theater. Indeed this evocation of a Florida riverbank was the very first commission Associated Artists received. Realized by Candace Wheeler, it emphasized the illusionistic capacities of the auditorium itself, deploying its gorgeous exoticism as an aspect of the larger theatrical experience. But it was only a single part of somebody else's conception, in this case the illustrator, scene painter, and architectural delineator, Hughson Hawley.[56]

A few years later Steele MacKaye turned to Tiffany (now in his own firm) for the decorating scheme of the Lyceum Theater. Even more completely electrified (by Thomas Edison himself) than the Madison Square Theater, the Lyceum, however financially disastrous it may have been for Tiffany and MacKaye, demonstrated Tiffany's skill in exploiting the new lighting systems, and his ambitious capacity to create an entirely novel setting.

The Lyceum, like most of Steele MacKaye's enterprises, touched off lively debate. Originally planned as a simple extension of the Lyceum School, a small auditorium without much pretension, Tiffany turned it into an exotic extravaganza, crammed with "newfangled notions and decorations," complained a New York Times reviewer who spoke of an "orgy of Oriental decoration." He (or she) was reminded variously of the Alhambra, cashmere shawls, Buddhist priests, an Arabian "burnous," and the Mosque of el Teefhanneh al Afrasiab. "You hardly know," intoned the reviewer, staring at the big brass wheels which controlled the perforated doors of the boxes, "whether you are in Ceylon or Connecticut." The light bulbs hung "like the suspended ostrich eggs in the Tomb of the Prophet." Who "but Mr. Louis C. Tiffany could have dribble melted lead so frantically over pieces of parti-colored glass like those blue bull's-eyes with electric lights behind them . . .? Let us confess — it is a jumble. It is a trifle confusing."[57] While W. J. Henderson argued that it was "the least showy but most costly theatrical interior in New York," another *Times* commentator likened the central chandelier to "a lot of great inflated beef bladders."[58] If nothing else, the Lyceum evoked colorful prose.

The imagery, the (sometimes) good-natured flippancy, the bewilderment indicate again how startling and radical were Tiffany's methods in the 1880s. Twenty years before theater architects like Henry Herts and Hugh Tallant would create such atmospheric masterpieces as the New Amsterdam, extending "the atmosphere of the drama into the auditorium itself, enveloping the audience within a single, sensual experience," Tiffany had set an analogous goal.[59] Even the *Times* reviewer admitted that a visit to MacKaye's Lyceum became, through Tiffany's work, "something more than a carnal pleasure of the eye or a sensuous luxury; it rises to the level of instruction; it forms a sort of 'object lecture' on the decorative art of all nations, with special attention given to that of the extreme orient."[60]

It was specialization, however, which characterized Tiffany's involvement with another representative building type: the resort hotel. During the '80s and '90s large urban hotels had begun to attain new levels of elaborate display. In Europe the hotel was a means to an end, as Paul Blouet observed in 1889. In America, it *was* the end. "Hotels are for them what cathedrals, monuments, and the beauties of nature are for us."[61] Chicago's Grand Pacific and Palmer House and Auditorium, New York's New Netherlands, Holland House, and Waldorf-Astoria, its Plaza and Belmont and Manhattan Hotels, Cleveland's Hollenden, the West in Minneapolis, Detroit's Pontchartrain, Philadelphia's Bellevue-Stratford, were symbols of the new era. "The city hotel has grown to be a combined art gallery, music hall and club casino," observed the *New York World*.[62] These huge structures were filled with atmospheric rooms done up in Moorish, Egyptian, Louis XIV, Elizabethan, Renaissance, Art Nouveau, and Georgian styles.[63] A hotel is by design a "building of a distinctly public nature," David Tarn observed some years later, and "it is safe to say that the public, generally considered, is pleased if it is given what it expects. Consequently, if a hotel has no marble, no gilt, no mirrors, the public is apt to feel itself grievously slighted. . . ."[64] Muralists like William de Leftwich Dodge, George Maynard, Maxfield Parrish, Charles Y. Turner, Edwin Austin Abbey, Thomas Dewing, and colorists like Tiffany, James Finn, and Frank Millet, soon rushed in to fill the vacuum.

Such luxury was not confined to the city. In the '70s and '80s resorts began to multiply, usually tied to railroad expansion. In Florida, California, and Colorado, these hotels now drew on national constituencies eager to follow their physicians' orders and enjoy the appropriately milder or more bracing climates. One of the most popular of these institutions appeared in the 1880s with the building of Henry Flagler's lavish and influential Ponce de Leon Hotel in St. Augustine, Florida, an extravaganza bringing together the young firm of Carrere & Hastings, the Californian Bernard Maybeck, Pottier & Stymus of New York, George Maynard the mural painter, and Louis Tiffany.[65] In this enormous Moorish palace it was Maybeck, an architect

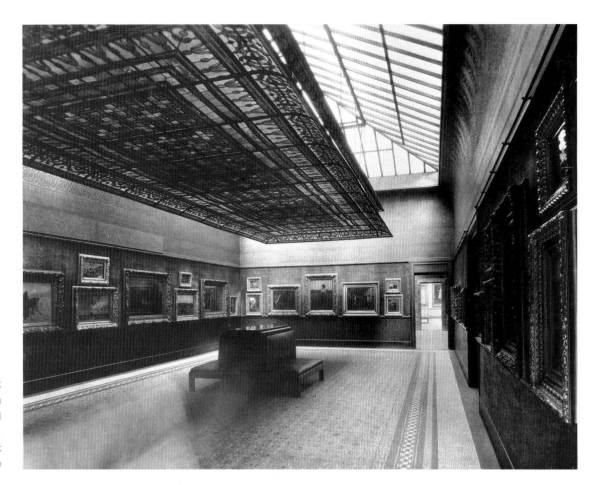

An interior view of the Art Institute of Chicago, showing a hanging stained glass panel designed by Tiffany in 1899. (Photo courtesy of the Art Institute of Chicago)

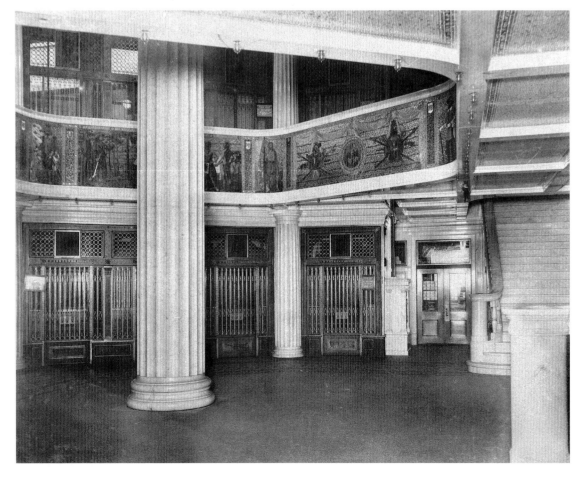

The lobby of the Marquette Building, Chicago, with a Tiffany mosaic depicting the explorer P. Marquette, c. 1900. (Photo courtesy of the Art Institute of Chicago)

working at the time for Carrere & Hastings, who provided the central decorating scheme. But Tiffany created some of the hotel's most memorable details, including a number of windows and chandeliers. Once more, Tiffany contributed only an element of the larger scheme. But his impact was again powerful enough for him to rival in celebrity the designer for the entire commission.[66]

The Tiffany signature was unmistakable, at least when glass and metal were involved. Decorators of theaters, hotels, and railroad stations, designers like the painter Frank Millet, who worked for Tiffany at certain times, James Finn, Elmer E. Garnsey, who specialized in library decorations, Bernard Maybeck, and others, often had a more difficult time securing public recognition.[67] But they did provide overall guidance, a change from the days when architects relied almost entirely on catalogues and supply houses for their ornaments and furniture. A painter might be brought in to provide a mural, a sculptor for some busts or allegories, but the decorating task had been, in general, filling in left-over spaces and turning to the appropriate stocks of institutional furniture. Tiffany's successes and those of the artists who worked for him introduced a new dimension, and the presence of his work — expensive, elaborate, popular, spectacular in effect — humanized and dignified what were sometimes forbidding and intimidating settings.

Indeed, the glass and metal contributions of Tiffany's companies became among the most sentimentalized parts of the new public landscape, popular favorites by reason of color, light, and intricacy of design. They were variously confirmatory (in cultural institutions) or redemptive (in places of business). Chicago's great mosaic and glass spectacles — in the Public Library and the Art Institute, on the one hand, and the Marquette Building and Marshall Field's on the other — exemplified the duality. "Lovers of beauty," wrote University of Chicago professor Edmund Buckley of the Marshall Field mosaic, "may see in this masterly mosaic over a mart of trade" a step toward William Morris's goal of winning back art to the people. The "greedy graspers that want to own everything in sight, can only be chagrined at meeting with an object they can never even hope to acquire." And reformers bemoaning the mosaic's high cost "may take comfort in the thought that under the current competitive and individualistic social system, the poor will always be with us . . . meanwhile humanity desperately needs the uplift of beauty. . . ."[68] The Chicago Public Library, with its Tiffany decorations, was, said *Harper's Weekly*, a "delightful relief" to those who habitually found the city's architecture "a rather crude embodiment of brute force, asserting itself by Brobdingnagian height and ponderousness. . . ."[69]

Tiffany's Chicago projects were not unique. In the '80s and '90s, and into the next century, Tiffany lamps, light fixtures, windows, glass domes, and mosaic tiles were placed in public libraries, office building lobbies, banks, hospitals, university gymnasia, art museums, restaurants, reading rooms, department stores, hotels, lecture rooms, and terminal waiting rooms all across the North American continent, as well as into the even more numerous ecclesiastical and mortuary settings which sought their presence. The Tiffany Studios, and the other producing organizations that Tiffany had a hand in, eventually grew less concerned with any overall design logic (although there were some exceptions) and more with supplying the accent marks, the particularities, the special effects that would render a lounge, a café, a dining room, or an atrium memorable.[70] This was really the second Tiffany career, as creator and marketer of a somewhat more accessible splendor that could be incorporated, through lamps, vases, mosaics, and stained glass, into any kind of interior from a home to a mausoleum. Major clients now came to Tiffany Studios not for a broader scheme (although Tiffany Studios did offer decorating advice along with the furniture, rugs, lamps, and vases it marketed), but for a token of Louis Tiffany's easily recognizable ornamental genius, allying themselves with his commitment to visual opulence. Sporting a stable of powerful artists — Frederick Wilson, Edward Peck Sperry, J. A. Holzer, Agnes Northrop, and Will H. Low among them — Tiffany Studios became in effect a collection of industrial painters, producing under supervision a clearly ordered and well tested series of formulas for special settings.

Printed surveys showed prospective purchasers what they might expect. Stained glass windows were custom designs, commissioned by individual clients, but occasionally they copied one another and most of the time they were fitted into spaces whose character was already defined. The lamps, the desk sets, many of the bowls and vases were not unique, even though hand-made. Their variations moved for the most part within recognizable limits. Such recognizability was part of their appeal. Like the hand-made books put out by contemporary private presses, these pieces appeared in multiple editions that could be large or small.

The essence of this, the most popular phase of Tiffany's career, was personalized industrial production, an aggressively marketed workshop output achieved by designer and worker collaboration. Some product lines could be sold over a counter as well as on special order, in specially licensed stores. The Tiffany stamp was singular enough to provide the cachet of the artist without losing the advantages of a brand name. Tiffany, after all, was competing in a world of producers newly sensitive to the possibilities of national recognition. This period gave birth to a flood of trademarks, slogans, and well advertised corporate personifications: Kodak Cameras, Kellogg's Original Corn Flakes, Sapolio, Aunt Jemima's Pancakes, Ivory Soap, Postum, Uneeda Biscuits, all arrayed in their liveried packages. Louis Tiffany products did not require slogans or special wrapping. But their mark was unmistakable. Having begun his decorating career as a special adviser to individual projects, obtaining influence through distinguished example, Tiffany now proved to be a master of influence through distribution, his objects reiterating, by their multiplication and use of certain materials, the stylistic and technological contributions which had absorbed so much of his energy.

This point was made, among many others, in the sumptuously produced text that Tiffany helped design (and write), Charles De Kay's *Art Work of Louis C. Tiffany*, published (in a limited edition) by Doubleday in 1914. Louis Tiffany's real fame came not from his stained glass windows, De Kay (and Tiffany) argued, but from the Favrile glass he had begun to produce in the 1890s, for "the appeal made to the people's love of color was not misunderstood when it came to small objects." With such products Tiffany could construct an image of consumer democracy, and present his career as a campaign to legitimize and dignify the often vilified but powerfully influential decorative arts. The fact that "things of daily use like lamps, flower-vases, and toilet articles reached a wider public than do paintings and sculpture," wrote De Kay, "make the 'decorative' arts more important to a nation than the 'fine' arts. Hence the value to a community of artists who devote their talent to making things of use beautiful. They are educators of the people in the truest sense. . . ."[71]

This was true even of indulgencies like personal jewelry. "Articles of personal adornment are wont to be rated low throughout the wide field of art," De Kay admitted, but "they appeal to the very widest imaginable circle of buyers . . . . It is well, therefore, that objects of the sort should be beautiful." Indeed, he continued, the quality of a people's jewelry measured its level in art. "Each piece acts as a little missionary . . . and tries in its own dumb way to convert the Philistine."[72] Tiffany himself, at a birthday masque in 1916, claimed his interest in portable adornment was part of his larger quest for beauty. "When the savage searches for the gems from the earth or the pearls from the sea to decorate his person, or when he decorates the utensils of war or peace . . . he becomes an artist in embryo."[73]

Closing his text, focusing now on Tiffany's gardening interests at Cold Spring Harbor on Long Island, De Kay exploited Tiffany's color sense one more time in the interests of a popular cause. "Mr. Tiffany has been one of the most efficient among modern combatants on the side of those who have been trying to restore the balance in art and permit poor color-starved humanity to enjoy its birthright of splendid color."[74] The purveyor of luxury, the designer who for decades had worked for the merely wealthy and the fabulously wealthy, was actually wrestling back for the deprived majority a threatened heritage of delight. Such a notion, before World War I, obviously involved something of a conceit. But at a later day, when Tiffany objects have become popular symbols of a pre-modernist nostalgia, the words assume a deeper meaning.

In these years, when he was involved simultaneously with a whole range of business enterprises, Louis Tiffany's tightrope walk between serving market demand and fulfilling artistic visions teetered most precariously. The Tiffany firm "conforms to the wishes of customers," wrote Cecilia Waern in the *International Studio*, "and adapts itself to any problem presented as adroitly as a clever milliner — yet it has given us that classically beautiful product, the 'Favrile' blown glass." The workplace combined handiwork and large-scale production so skillfully "it allows for worker's personal interest and obedience to the inspiration of the fountain head." Such an operation resisted the thrust of standardization, varying wage rates with worker skill. It did not allow for trade unions which, Cecilia Waern argued pointedly, "are powerless against the intelligent planning of the whole." When the presence of too many boy apprentices produced a strike, the only one Tiffany had experienced, he simply replaced them by young women from the art schools, retraining them for mosaic work or ornamental windows, reserving the larger memorial windows for men in other workshops.[75]

Writing for Europeans, Miss Waern confessed that Tiffany's was an assimilating eclecticism, pulling together Japanese, Moorish, Byzantine, and many other stylistic elements. Its tendency was "to grace and worldliness, rather than dignity and austerity; but that is the big American note." It did indeed exhibit the "commercialism" that reformers worried about. Unlike Morris and Co. in England, Tiffany Studios did not aspire primarily to educate the public taste; "their aim is to sell, to persuade, not to elevate or instruct," and they showed a tendency always to simplify labor processes as far as possible to reduce the production cost.[76] S. Bing, the French entrepreneur and popularizer of Art Nouveau, was also impressed by Tiffany's business-like operations, his frank embrace of industrial discipline, his capacity to merge the most up-to-date processes with the most refined and personalized of designs, and to marry the national genius for mass production to an artistic obsession with form and color.[77]

Because he was so emphatically a colorist, Tiffany was able to move easily from the decorative adviser status he assumed in the '80s to the manufacturer, marketer, and promoter he became so quickly thereafter. In paint, pottery, enamels, jewelry, glass, mosaic tiles, textiles, and metalwork the struggle to interact with the customer was aggressively sustained.

Although colored glass reflected rituals and traditions that were much older than the American republic, and even bore ideological overtones that were overtly alien to national ideals, Tiffany continued to identify himself, and the glass as well, with a spirit of improvement and experiment. Acknowledging that before his day stained glass was one of the things visitors could not find in America, Tiffany in 1893 boasted that American glassmakers were "untrammeled by tradition, and were moved solely by a desire to produce a thing of beauty," irrespective of any doctrine or theory. True art, he continued, "is ever progressive and impatient of fixed rules. Because a thing has always been done in a certain way is no reason why it should never be done in any other."[78] With all the luxuriousness of color and even occasional voluptuousness of theme Tiffany happily exploited for selling purposes, he also cultivated the image of the ingenious Yankee innovator, striking out boldly on paths that seemed too risky for the conservative. Reviving an ancient art through modern technology brought the best of two worlds together. If "the decorators of the 18th century had possessed a glass similar to Tiffany favrile," the New York Mail and Express argued, describing a conservatory with a Louis XVI Tiffany glass window, "they would have used it in the very manner" of the Tiffany Studios.[79]

His materials, moreover, proved well suited for certain modern challenges. When the First National Bank of Pittsburgh opened its new banking rooms in 1898, its interior finish in marble and glass mosaic supervised by Tiffany, the Pittsburgh Post argued that the treatment was perfect for its city. Local smoke and grime could not dim the Vermont marble and mother-of-pearl glass mosaic pilasters. A "wet sponge" or even "a hose" could clean the whole with ease.[80] The rainbow glass Tiffany was placing in dining rooms, churches, parlors, and public buildings displayed a spirit of bold experimentation. Its iridescence, said the New York Sun, demonstrated that "a Yankee brain can outdo nature."[81]

By the 1890s, of course, Tiffany Studios was only one of many manufacturers of glass, art metal, and mosaic ornament. Most major cities – Chicago, Detroit, Philadelphia – had their own purveyors of stained glass and wrought iron, their own producers of terra cotta ornament and marble flooring. At the Columbian Exposition of 1893, where Tiffany Glass & Decorating won fifty-four medals, there were eleven American stained glass makers exhibiting, seven of whom came from Chicago. Largely forgotten today, companies like Flanagan & Biedenweg, Healy & Millet, McCully & Miles, J. and R. Lamb of New York, The Detroit Stained Glass Works, and Willet Stained Glass Studios of Pittsburgh (later of Philadelphia) were competing energetically for customers in the 1890s. These were followed, in the early twentieth century, by still others like Charles J. Connick Associates of Boston, the Henry Keck Stained Glass Studio of Syracuse, Giannini & Hilgert, The Munich Studio of Chicago, and a series of smaller firms who worked for architects and furniture designers associated with the Prairie School.[82] The taste that La Farge and Tiffany helped popularize in the 1880s now had spread into structures of every size and description, and was often satisfied by standardized, machine-produced ornamental glass.

Such rapid multiplication of glass ornament led naturally enough to a sense of vulgarization and meaningless proliferation. The reputation of the Tiffany name in the early twentieth century, the prestigious special commissions won by the firm, the exposition prizes and extensive displays, the handsome catalogues and the artistry of the craftsmen Tiffany attracted to his employment, all put some distance between the company and its rivals. In city after city, as major memorial windows were dedicated in churches and colleges and courthouses, newspaper publicity added further lustre.[83] Each Tiffany window enjoyed its own moment of communal attention, indeed usually several such moments: announcement of the gift or decision to purchase; details of installation; and ceremonies of dedication. Like premier producers of other luxury goods – Steinway, Rolls Royce, Dior – Tiffany's claims to quality standards of design and production were intended to keep it in a class to itself.

But the intense commoditization that resulted from an expanding industry, along with the explosion of ornament that accompanied the rise of the movie palace, must only have confirmed Louis Tiffany's sense of preaching to the unconverted. Having helped pioneer the interior design profession and transform tastes in glass and tile, Louis Tiffany seemed, in his later years, to withdraw from active supervision over the products bearing his name and to move on to a level of greater ideality. Like many another artist and architect, he sought, in his various residences, to bring together an exemplary selection of his best work, to create for himself and his entourages settings of perfect beauty. His personal quarters had been exemplifying his taste since the Bella Apartments in the 1870s, but Laurelton Hall in Cold Spring Harbor emphatically climaxed this self-absorption. It was his Taliesen, his Menlo Park, and his Giverny rolled into one. The obsession with Laurelton Hall reflected Tiffany's third career – that of teacher, pedagogue, master, and host, the presiding genius of a group of acolytes who could spread the gospel in years to come.[84]

Again it is possible to find many analogues, particularly in the America of the Progressive Era, figures absorbed by architecture or printing or painting or sculpture or the arts in general, who founded atelier-like settings for the pursuit of truth and beauty: Elbert Hubbard, Frank Lloyd Wright, Gustave Stickley, Charles Booth. At Roycroft, Taliesen, Cranbrook, Pasadena, Carmel-by-the-Sea, groups of missionary artists and craftsmen gathered, often under tutelary spirits, to promulgate their doctrines. Tiffany had always considered his own industrial enterprises as breeding places of beauty, but the building of Laurelton Hall in 1902 opened new possibilities. Devising strategies of use and application, which were ultimately expressed in creation of the Tiffany Foundation, took up the next several decades.

These activities were highlighted by three distinct but revealing events, suggesting where Tiffany's interests had finally led him. These were the great fetes that began in 1913 with a Shrove Tuesday Egyptian pageant-masque at the Tiffany Studios, continued with an elaborate dinner and musical entertainment at Laurelton Hall the following year, and climaxed in 1916 with an expansive birthday spectacle, again in Tiffany Studios, built around a Delmonico-catered Roman supper and still another masque entitled *The Quest of Beauty*.[85] Elaborately costumed, carefully lit, accompanied by specially commissioned music, attended by artists, socialites, publishers, former patrons, musicians, important members of New York's cultural establishment, covered enthusiastically by the local press, these last flings indicated (along with the commission of Charles De Kay's book) Tiffany's lingering desire for higher recognition, a concern that the message of his art, his technological interventions, his marketing and self-promotion, might still be insufficiently esteemed and comprehended. The desire for control, for the total shaping of reality that architects and decorative artists so often seek, found expression in the maze of details that Tiffany supervised, everything from the printing of invitations to the choice of costumes. For the Egyptian masque, actually the reception of Mark Antony by Cleopatra, Tiffany guests played the parts of Romans, Syrians, Ethiopians, Greeks, Egyptians, and Arabs. John D. Rockefeller, Jr., appeared as a Persian nobleman; his wife, who would little more than a decade later help to found the Museum of Modern Art, came dressed as Minerva. Louisine Havemeyer was there and another notable Tiffany patron, Captain Joseph DeLamar; so were Edward Harkness, Robert W. De Forest, and George Seligman.

The pageants were opportunities for statements, moments of consolidation for New York's most prominent artists and architects — Daniel Chester French, Childe Hassam, Edwin H. Blashfield, Arnold Brunner, Donn Barber, Albert Herter, Guy Lowell, Lloyd Warren, Carroll Beckwith, George Breck — keepers of the Beaux-Arts tradition and true believers in the religion of ideality, to show the flag one more time. At the 1916 breakfast Tiffany denounced the modernists passionately as narrow specialists bemused by technical discoveries. Most of his guests could only have agreed.

When not arrayed in the robes of splendor he donned for such occasions, Tiffany was photographed in elegant attire, often fastidiously dressed in white, the kind of garb Mark Twain had chosen for his old age a generation earlier. The young artist who had presented himself as a rebel designer was now a patriarch, a prophet messenger whose vision required an invited audience.

The last years, as Tiffany's biographers describe them, were touched by a sense of public indifference and dampened by financial stringency. The extravagant hopes Tiffany entertained for his Foundation and Laurelton Hall had to be drawn in. The 1920s and '30s hosted a new generation of celebrity designers, no less flamboyant, theatrical, and self-celebrating than Tiffany but employing very different vocabularies. Figures like Joseph Urban, Winold Reiss, Donald Deskey, Paul Frankl, Addison Mizner, Harold Rambusch, Raymond Loewy, Lee Simonson, Walter Dorwin Teague, and Norman Bel Geddes would bring to interiors, public and private, to furniture, product lines, theater sets, and commercial art, insights shaped by modernist ideologies, marketing strategies, and new synthetic materials.[86] Architects, illustrators, craftsmen, they would, like Tiffany, provide signatures for an entire era.

But for all their proclamations of newness and boldness, for all their repudiation of the mannerism, idealism, and sentimental rhetoric associated with their predecessors, it is clear they had been anticipated. And, to some extent, also outdistanced. In many ways Louis Tiffany remains our first great industrial designer, absorbed by the task of communicating his vision to a broad audience. It was, however, a vision dominated by dreams of beauty rather than visions of efficiency. His salesmanship was exercised in the interests of transforming standards of taste and reasserting ancient powers through modern formulas. First through direct decoration, then through quantity production and distribution, and finally through training and instruction Tiffany advanced his case. In the process he promoted a new joy in decorative splendor for a society whose art conventions had been shaped by academic eclecticism.

Some recent analysts have argued that Tiffany's free-flowing, original, incessantly dynamic mixture of shapes and colors in glass and mosaic forecast the artistic experiments we label abstract expressionism. Thus the resurgence of interest that came in the 1950s and '60s reflected the new art's pervasive presence. Without our denying any linkage between the two, or the influence of contemporary abstraction on his new legitimacy, it is possible to point to something else as well. And that is the rediscovery of decorative art as an instrument of transcendence. Tiffany's clients and customers responded to the power of natural imagery in realistic or conventionalized form. The rich colors of the stained glass and the mosaics, the iridescence of the vases, the light contrasts of the lamps and the tiles were emblematic. S. Bing called some of them "glowing fantasies."[87] Decorative exuberance has the power to lift onlookers beyond the limits of place and time to aspirations and associations of boundless scope. Tiffany transformed both sacred and profane spaces, offering the religious intimations of immortality, and presenting to the secular the exhilaration of ornamental variety. His rediscovery has coincided with a new defense of the decorative arts as humanizing agents in a fast-paced, rationalized, mechanically driven world. The gates have reopened to admit embellishment and subjective fantasy.

The political implications of this taste remain cloudy. The love for adornment coincided, after all, with indifference to the social sources of patronage. Tiffany's art was popular, but its consumption — outside religious and cultural settings — was open to only a few. Its glitter could be seen as distracting and its idealism serviced establishments of every type.

But the influence Tiffany sought, in the end, was a personally liberating one. Suspicious of dogmatism, pragmatic and experimental, he was frustrated by intellectual currents he never quite understood, and by the inevitable changes in taste and marketing that make one generation's delight its successor's aversion. His reemergence reenacts what the first clients of Associated Artists found so exciting: unapologetic virtuosity in the interest of sensory pleasure. Many of his artistic contemporaries remain in the shadows. Tiffany's present celebrity reflects his personal judgment and technical mastery, as well as the persisting alternations of human taste. Even if it does, in time, ebb into a decent obscurity, it seems clear that such will be, once more, only a temporary fate. And that the influence Tiffany saw swell and then decline, has a permanent role in our larger design traditions.

# NOTES

1. I have relied heavily on several Tiffany specialists for biographical data and interpretive assistance. The starting point remains, of course, Robert Koch, *Louis C. Tiffany, Rebel in Glass* (New York 1964). Hugh F. McKean, *The "Lost" Treasures of Louis Comfort Tiffany* (Garden City 1980) is encyclopedic in its coverage of Tiffany's varied career, and contains an excellent bibliography. Alastair Duncan, *Tiffany Windows* (New York 1980), covers in detail this aspect of Tiffany's work, while Diane Chalmers Johnson, "Louis Comfort Tiffany and Art Nouveau Applied Arts in America," chapter 2 of *American Art Nouveau* (New York 1979), places Tiffany within the art world of late 19th-century America. The larger story of the family and the jewelry firm is covered by Joseph Purtell, *The Tiffany Touch* (New York 1971).

2. "The Furniture Craze," *New York Times* (June 10, 1877), 6.

3. Scholarship on this domestic literature has been extensive. Among other guides are Clifford E. Clark, Jr., "Domestic Architecture and the Cult of Domesticity in America, 1840-1879," *Journal of Interdisciplinary History*, 7 (Summer 1976), 33-56; David F. Handlin, *The American Home: Architecture and Society, 1815-1915* (Boston 1979); Dolores Hayden, *The Grand Domestic Revolution: A History of Feminist Designs for American Homes, Neighborhoods, and Cities* (Cambridge, Mass. 1981); Kirk Jeffrey, "The Family as Utopian Retreat from the City: The Nineteenth-Century Contribution," *Soundings*, 55 (1972), 21-41; Kathryn K. Sklar, *Catharine Beecher: A Study in American Domesticity* (New Haven 1973); Dell Upton, "Pattern Books and Professionalism: Aspects of the Transformation of Domestic Architecture in America, 1800-1860," *Winterthur Portfolio*, 19 (Summer/Autumn 1984), 107-50; and Gwendolyn Wright, *Building the Dream: A Social History of Housing in America* (New York 1981).

4. Roger B. Stein, *John Ruskin and Aesthetic Thought in America, 1849-1900* (Cambridge, Mass., 1967), is particularly incisive on this general issue.

5. For some background see Dianne H. Pilgrim, "Decorative Art: The Domestic Environment," Brooklyn Museum, *The American Renaissance, 1876-1917* (New York 1979), 111-51; and Mary Jean Smith Madigan, "The Influence of Charles Locke Eastlake on American Furniture Manufacture, 1870-1890," *Winterthur Portfolio*, 10 (1975), 1-22. And for some caustic comments on the Eastlake art furniture vogue see two papers by M. G. Van Rensselaer, "Decorative Art and Its Dogmas," *Lippincott's*, 25 (February 1880), 213-20; and (March 1880), 342-50.

6. Charles Wyllys Elliott, *The Book of American Interiors* (Boston 1876), 94.

7. "Interior Arrangement of Dwellings," *Architectural Review and American Builders' Journal*, 1 (July 1869), 43-4. Forty years later another writer on home decoration could write, "One does not have to be very old to remember a time when the very idea of a room obviously arranged for the reception of visitors was preached against and ridiculed, the real compliment to the guest being then declared to be a welcome to the more intimate side of family life . . . ." Lillie Hamilton French, *The House Dignified* (New York and London 1908), 52.

8. See Martha Crabill McClaughtery, "Household Art: Creating the Artistic Home, 1868-1893," *Winterthur Portfolio*, 18 (Spring 1983), 1-26; and Jean Gordon and Jan McArthur, "Interior Decorating Advice as Popular Culture: Women's Views Concerning Wall and Window Treatments, 1870-1920," *Journal of American Culture*, 9 (Fall 1986), 15-23.

9. For a comment on the fact that the wealthy home builders required no guidebooks see Rhoda and Agnes Garrett, *Suggestions for House Decoration in Painting, Woodwork, and Furniture* (Philadelphia: n.d.), 7.

10. Marilynn Johnson, "The Artful Interior," Doreen Bolger Burke *et al. In Pursuit of Beauty. Americans and the Aesthetic Movement* (New York 1987), 110-41, and in the same volume her "Art Furniture: Wedding the Beautiful to the Useful," 143-75, provides an immensely useful overview of high style decorating and furnishing in this period.

11. For more on Associated Artists and their commissions see Wilson H. Faude, "Associated Artists and the American Renaissance in the Decorative Arts," *Winterthur Portfolio*, 10 (1975), 101-30, as well as the larger studies by Koch and McKean.

12. John Sweetman, *The Oriental Obsession. Islamic Inspiration in British and American Art and Architecture, 1500-1920* (Cambridge 1988), is one of the more recent surveys of the origin and character of Western taste for Eastern motifs.

13. The social connections enjoyed by Tiffany were many and complex. Consider as an example his relationship to the De Forest family. William F. De Forest had been an attorney for the Tiffany firm. One of his sons, Lockwood, a collector of Indian objects and an artist himself, became a partner of Louis Tiffany in Associated Artists. Another son, Henry, an attorney, became a director of Tiffany Glass. And still another son, Robert W. De Forest, not only commissioned work from Associated Artists for his own house, he married Emily Johnston, daughter of John Taylor Johnston, president of the Metropolitan Museum of Art, who also commissioned work from Tiffany in the 1880s. Like his father-in-law, De

Forest became President of the Metropolitan himself and with his wife founded the American Wing in 1922. He also served as the personal counsel for Mrs. Russell Sage, who herself commissioned a major Tiffany window in memory of her husband for the First Presbyterian Church in Far Rockaway, Long Island. De Forest helped to set up the Russell Sage Foundation, whose scientific director would be the physiologist, Graham Lusk, Louis Tiffany's son-in-law. Louis Tiffany named one of his daughters Julia de Forest, presumably in honor of one of the brothers.

14. Mitchell's 1850 novel provoked the praise of Emily Dickinson, and what one critic calls his "preexistentialist philosophy that dispensed with religious doctrines altogether and placed total faith in an imaginative engagement with the Eternal Now," may have prepared him to enjoy the exotic beauty of Tiffany's decorative achievements. See David S. Reynolds, *Beneath the American Renaissance. The Subversive Imagination in the Age of Emerson and Melville* (New York 1988), 34-5. For Tiffany's early relationship with Mitchell see Koch, *Rebel in Glass*, 8.

15. Donald G. Mitchell, "From Lobby to Peak," *Our Continent*, 1 (1882), 5, 21, 37, 69, 85, 101, 132, 138, 185, 217. See also "House Interiors," *The Works of Donald G. Mitchell*, (New York 1907), V, 262-83, in which Mitchell argued for eclecticism and charm in a text published originally in 1884. "The extreme of propriety, and of artistic keeping in the furnishing of a home, is rather chilling than otherwise . . . . Absolute and unshaken adjustment of every detail, is as fearful a thing to encounter in a house, as a man who never pronounces a word wrongly, and is always on the lookout for a bad pronunciation of yours," 274-5.

16. A. F. Oakey, "A Trial Balance of Decoration," *Harper's Monthly*, 64 (April 1882), 734-40. Oakey also evaluated the work of John La Farge, and considered the decorations by both in the new Union League Club (which he did not particularly like). Here and there he found brilliant effects "but these do not save the whole from the imputation of experimentalism," (736). Oakey's ambivalent response to the rising tide of orientalism is interesting. He found something "encouraging in the instinctive adoption of Oriental conventionality," particularly in juxtaposition to traditions of Greco-Italian realism in portraiture, but he wondered, after describing the opulence of the Kemp interiors, whether "an assemblage of black coats and trousers seems consistent with this Oriental magnificence," and hoped for the day when the "floundering on with spasmodic devotion now to the Persian style, again to the East Indian or the European mediaeval" ended, replaced by a "sense of style" which "shall be as much ours as the Renaissance was the feeling of cinque-cento artists."

17. Among others might be mentioned *Homes of American Authors* (New York 1853), a series of biographical sketches and descriptions of homes, accompanied by more than thirty steel engravings and woodcuts; R. H. Stoddard, *Poets' Homes* (Boston 1879); and Mrs. Martha J. Lamb, *The Homes of America* (New York 1879). Texts like these contained only the most general descriptions of house interiors, however, and would be outdistanced by the material to be published in the 1880s and '90s.

18. *Artistic Houses*, published by D. Appleton in 1883-4, appeared in two volumes, each in two parts, containing 203 photographs. It was actually distributed in ten sections. Increasingly rare, a version of the book, with all the photographs correctly printed, introduction, annotations, and new text (incorporating most of the George Sheldon commentary), has recently appeared: Arnold Lewis, James Turner and Steven McQuillin, *The Opulent Interiors of the Gilded Age* (New York 1987). The introduction and annotations are invaluable, both in themselves and for making sense of this most important book.

19. Constance Cary Harrison, "Some Work of the 'Associated Artists,'" *Harper's Monthly*, 69 (August 1884), 343.

20. In a letter to Charles Webster from Indianapolis, Feb. 8, 1885, Twain complained about the "humiliating swindle" played on him by Appleton with *Artistic Homes*. Receiving a bill for $300, the balance due on his contract, he got the idea of writing "a neat & readable" account of the episode, and offering Appleton the chance to buy the manuscript for $300. See Samuel Charles Webster, ed., *Mark Twain, Business Man* (Boston 1946), 299-300.

21. Kenneth R. Andrews, *Nook Farm. Mark Twain's Hartford Circle* (Cambridge, Mass., 1950), 81-2, gives some background for Twain's purchase of the house. Faude, "Associated Artists," 119-123, provides further details concerning Twain's reaction to the decorating job. Details of the negotiations with Tiffany can be found in Frederick Anderson, Lin Salamo, and Bernard L. Stein, eds., *Mark Twain's Notebooks & Journals* (Berkeley, Los Angeles, London, 1975), II, 399-401.

22. *Mark Twain's Notebooks . . .*, 317-318.

23. *Ibid.*, 371.

24. The entire story has been told most recently and completely by William Seale, *The President's House. A History* (Washington: White House Historical Association, 1986), I, 529-51.

25. E. V. Smalley, "The White House," *Century* 28 (April 1884), 803-15.

26. "Social Extravagance," *New York Times* (April 4, 1880), 6.

27. "The Modern Sybaris," *New York Times* (February 13, 1891), 6.

28. "The New White House," *New York Times* (February 17, 1903), 8. See also the comments of architect Charles Moore, that the colored glass "which represented the high-water mark of the decorator's art when Chester A. Arthur was President has disappeared; original and ingenious designs, as ephemeral as fashion-plates, have

been replaced with forms and materials that, belonging to all times, have been used by all great builders to express ideas of permanence and dignity." Charles Moore, "The Restoration of the White House," *Century*, 65 (April 1903), 829.

29. Kimball is described in Arnold Lewis *et al.*, *Opulent Interiors*, 80.

30. Frances Weitzenhoffer, *The Havemeyers. Impressionism Comes to America* (New York 1986), 48-52, 70-9, describes the relationship with Tiffany and the decoration of the Havemeyer home, estimated to have cost more than $250,000. The Havemeyers collected porcelains, bronzes, pottery, and glass besides their pictures, and Louisine Havemeyer was tired of the "murky red velvet which was in vogue with our dealers," (77). The house and the collection were both extravagantly admired by visiting Europeans like S. Bing, and the Berlin Museum director, Wilhelm Bode.

31. "Idlehour," *Architectural Record*, 13 (May 1903), 457-92.

32. Herbert Croly, "Rich Men and Their Houses," *Architectural Record*, 12 (May 1902), 27-32. A string of contemporary publications focused on New York's wealthy classes and their houses. See, for example, Paul R. Cleveland, "The Millionaires of New York," *Cosmopolitan*, 5 (September 1888), 385-98; and "Two Miles of Millionaires," *Munsey's*, 19 (June 1898), 345-61.

33. Alastair Service, *Edwardian Interiors. Inside the Homes of the Poor, the Average and the Wealthy* (London 1982), chap. 8, is one of a number of texts describing the scale and ceremonial uses of these great town mansions.

34. Croly, "Rich Men and Their Houses," 32. See also Herbert Croly, "The Contemporary New York Residence," *Architectural Record*, 12 (December 1902), 705-22.

35. "Some New York Palaces," *Harper's Weekly*, 38 (April 7, 1894), 317-18. Note also the comments on the residence of Mrs. R. H. Townsend by Carrere and Hastings, Percy C. Stuart, "Recent Domestic Architecture in Washington, D.C.," *Architectural Record* 10 (April 1910), 425-37, concerning the social demands of Washingtonians on their houses. The Stuart house contained main floor rooms that opened into one another for 120 feet in length, as well as a dining room that was 45 by 52 feet.

36. James Fullarton Muirhead, *The Land of Contrasts. A Briton's View of his American Kin* (Boston, New York and London 1898), 194-5. Muirhead also termed the Tiffany house on Madison Avenue "one of the most daring and withal most captivating experiments known to me in city residences," (196).

37. T. P. O'Connor, "Impressions of New York," *Munsey's*, 37 (June 1907), 387-91.

38. Jenny June, "The Art of Dinner-Giving," *Cosmopolitan*, 3 (March 1887), 63-66.

39. The Armory is described and illustrated in Koch, *Rebel in Glass*, 14-16, 36-7; McKean, *"Lost" Treasures*, 103-6; and in most detail by W. C. Brownell, "Decoration in the Seventh Regiment Armory," *Scribner's*, 22 (July 1881), 370-80.

40. Oakey, "A Trial Balance of Decoration," 736.

41. Brownell, "Decoration in the Seventh Regiment Armory," 375.

42. Francis Gerry Fairfield, *The Clubs of New York* (New York 1873), describes the clubs of an earlier era. For social life and clubs in New York during this period see Robert Stewart, "Clubs and Club Life in New York," *Munsey's*, 22 (October 1899), 105-22; Frederick Cople Jaher, "Style and Status: High Society in Late-Nineteenth Century New York," Frederic Cople Jaher, ed., *The Rich, the Well-Born, and the Powerful: Elites and Upper Classes in History* (Urbana 1973), 258-84. For elite clubs in Boston and Philadelphia see E. Digby Baltzell, *Puritan Boston and Quaker Philadelphia* (Boston 1979), 238-40; and Alexander W. Williams, *A Social History of The Greater Boston Clubs* (Barre Publishers, 1970.)

43. For a contemporary description of one of those new clubhouses, see A. R. Macdonough, "The Century Club," *Century*, 41 (March 1891), 672-89. "An air of severe simplicity reigns in these marble-lined halls and oak-wainscoted apartments, relieved by color of onyx panels, by graceful curves of classic chimneypieces, by columns of dark wood and veined marble, and by the gilding of capital and balustrade," (689). The building by McKim, Mead and White, would become a New York landmark.

44. Cleveland Moffett, "Mid-Air Dining Clubs," *Century*, 62 (September 1901), 644.

45. Duncan Edwards, "Life at the Athletic Clubs," *Scribner's*, 18 (July 1895), 204.

46. For Chicago see George D. Bushnell, "Chicago's Leading Men's Clubs," *Chicago History*, 11 (Summer 1982), 79-88.

47. Montgomery Schuyler, "The Metropolitan Club," *Harper's Weekly*, 38 (March 10, 1894), 226. See also Paul Porzelt, *The Metropolitan Club of New York* (New York 1982), chaps. 3-8.

48. For the history of the building project see Will Irwin, Earl Chapin May, and Joseph Hotchkiss, *A History of The Union League Club of New York City* (New York 1952), 101-09.

49. "Some of the Union League Decorations," *Century*, 22 (March 1882), 745-52. Drawings of the clubhouse accompanying the article were by Hughson Hawley, who would be involved with some of the Tiffany theatrical decorations in the 1880s.

50. Among them, besides those already mentioned, would be the University Club, whose McKim, Mead and

White clubhouse would open in 1899, covered and filled with all sorts of emblematic ornament. The color systems of portions of the interior were supervised by Elmer E. Garnsey and H. Siddons Mowbray. See James W. Alexander, *A History of the University Club of New York, 1865-1915* (New York 1915), chap. xiii.

51. "The New University Club in Chicago," *Architectural Record*, 26 (July 1909), 1-23. "One misses entirely that hodge-podge of effects, those unrelated essays in decoration, that museum of color schemes and assorted designs which irritate the senses in so many of our modern attempts to achieve splendor . . . . There are absolutely no irrelevancies in the work," (23). Frederic Clay Bartlett would go on to present a major group of French paintings to the Art Institute of Chicago, some years later, including Seurat's fabled *La Grande Jatte*.

52. Albert Kahn, "Detroit Athletic Club Building," *Architecture*, 32 (July 1915), 174-6.

53. Henry J. Davison, "The Bankers' Club of America — An Art Achievement," *Architecture*, 32 (September 1915), 221-4.

54. See Davida Tenenbaum Deutsch, "The Osborne, New York City," *Antiques*, 130 (July 1986), 152-8.

55. Arthur David, "An Intimate Auditorium," *Architectural Record*, 23 (January 1908), 223-7.

56. For the Madison Square Garden Theater see Koch, *Rebel in Glass*, 12, 30; *New York Times* (February 1, 1880), 5; (May 11, 1880), 5. The architects were Kimball & Wisedell, and according to the *Times*, some of the lobby decorations were the work of L. V. Stiepevitch. Doreen Bolger Burke, "Louis Comfort Tiffany and His Early Training at Eagleswood, 1862-1865," *American Art Journal*, 19 (1987), 29-39, points out that Tiffany first met Steele Mackaye when he was a student at Eagleswood Military Academy in Perth Amboy, New Jersey; like Tiffany, Mackaye was a student of the American painter George Inness. Burke also discusses the Madison Square Theater curtain, which, she suggests, was adapted by Tiffany from a design by Mrs. Oliver Wendell Holmes. For more on the Madison Square Theater and its varied innovations, including an elevator stage, a new system of ventilation, and other items see Percy MacKaye, *Epoch, The Life of Steele Mackaye Genius of the Theatre* (New York 1927), I, 352-3.

57. "The Lyceum Theatre," *New York Times* (March 29, 1885), 8. The architect, P. J. Hobart, in a *Times* interview, refused to accept responsibility for some of the theater's problems, arguing that it was not originally meant to be a public theater. See *New York Times* (April 2, 1885), 3. For more on the Lyceum see MacKaye, *Epoch*, I, 480-2; and Craig Timberlake, *The Bishop of Broadway. The Life & Work of David Belasco* (New York 1954), 123-5.

58. W. J. Henderson, "Some New York Theatres," *Magazine of Art*, 9 (1886), 402; and *New York Times* (March 22, 1885), 14. Henderson's piece concerned three of the most exotic of the theatrical houses in New York in the 1880s: the Madison Square, the Casino, and the Lyceum.

59. The New Amsterdam description is taken from Robert A. M. Stern, Gregory Gilmartin and John Massengale, *New York 1900. Metropolitan Architecture and Urbanism 1890-1915* (New York 1983), 211. The discussion of the transformation of New York theaters, 203-20, suggests some directions which Tiffany anticipated.

60. *New York Times* (March 29, 1885), 8.

61. Max O'Rell and Jack Alleyn, *Jonathan and His Continent (Rambles through American Society)* (New York 1889), 295. For other travel comments on American hotels see Paul Bourget, *Outre-Mer. Impressions of America* (New York 1895), 30-4, 405-6; and John Kendall, *American Memories: Recollections of a Hurried Run through the United States during the Late Spring of 1896* (Nottingham [1896]), 19. See also Henry Collins Brown, *In the Golden Nineties* (Hastings-on-Hudson: Valentine's Manual, 1928), 311-23.

62. As quoted in *Chicago Record-Herald* (October 8, 1908), 8.

63. The splendor of the American hotel had long been proverbial, but the structures of the 1880s and '90s had an amplitude and luxury that set new standards. For the hotel as such see Jefferson Williamson, *The American Hotel* (New York 1930). The new era was best symbolized by the Waldorf-Astoria. See Edward Hungerford, *The Story of the Waldorf-Astoria* (New York and London 1925); Montgomery Schuyler, "Henry Janeway Hardenbergh," *Architectural Record*, 6 (January-March 1897), 335-75. Stern, Gilmartin, and Massengale, *New York 1900*, 253-79, discusses the hotel revolution of the era in New York. For Chicago see "Hotel Decoration," *Architectural Record*, 23 (February 1908), 151-4. Wherever "the trail of the tourist leads, chateau or palace has arisen," (153).

64. David E. Tarn, "New York's Newest Hotel. Notes on the Hotel McAlpin," *Architectural Record*, 23 (March 1913), 233.

65. The St. Augustine Hotels are described by Thomas Graham, "Flagler's Magnificent Hotel Ponce De Leon," *Florida Historical Quarterly*, 54 (July 1975), 1-17 (he calls Tiffany the hotel's decorator); David L. Chandler, *Henry Flagler. The Astonishing Life and Times of the Visionary Robber Baron Who Founded Florida* (New York 1986), chap. 8 (he argues the stained glass windows provided the basis for Tiffany's future reputation); Jeffrey Limerick, Nancy Ferguson, and Richard Oliver, *America's Grand Resort Hotels* (New York 1979), 81-9; Bourget, *Outre-Mer*, 405-6; and most memorably by Henry James, *The American Scene* (Bloomington, Ind., and London 1968), 456-60.

66. Other hotels Tiffany would be involved with included the St. George in Brooklyn, designed by Montrose Morris and sporting a cathedral glass arched roof, see *Brooklyn*

*Citizen*, May 9, 1898; and the King Edward Hotel in Toronto.

67. Many of these artists were mural painters who were simply given specific commissions, but they also began to assume the task of coordinating overall color and decorating schemes. Thus Elmer E. Garnsey, for example, fourteen years younger than Tiffany assisted Frank Millet who coordinated the decorating at the Columbian Exposition, and went on to supervise decoration at the Boston Public Library; Carnegie Institution in Pittsburgh; New York Stock Exchange; Columbian University Library; Library of Congress; the Yale and Union Clubs; the State Capitols of Rhode Island, Minnesota, Iowa, and Wisconsin; the St. Louis Public Library; the Ryerson Library of the Art Institute of Chicago, among others. Other active decorators and colorists, most of whom were also muralists, mosaicists, or enamelists, included Albert Adolphe, Hugo Ballin, Albert Herter, Carroll Bill, Edwin Blashfield, Frederick Dielman, F. V. Du Mond, Violet Oakley, Jules Guerin, Gustav Ketterer, Hildreth Meiere, Ernest Peixotto, Herman T. Schladermundt, Andrew Schwartz, and John H. Wareham. Tiffany was the oldest among these decorators of court houses, banks, stores, libraries, clubs, hotels, schools, churches, synagogues, theaters, and his career undoubtedly made it easier for others to follow.

68. Edmund Buckley, "Artistic Aspects of America's Greatest Store," *Fine Arts Journal* (April 1908). The custom of enhancing the lobbies of important office and headquarter buildings with mosaics, marbles, and glass, also grew popular at this time. For a description of one of the most elaborate such structures of the 1890s, the Metropolitan Life Insurance Company Madison Square complex, see Barnet Phillips, "A Mercantile Palace," *Harper's Weekly*, 38 (May 12, 1894), 453. Newspaper and magazine articles delighted in careful depictions of the onyx, the bronze, the many kinds of marble, the mosaic tiles, the grand staircases and woodwork, all of which appeared to testify to the humanizing impact of art on American business. Grand lobbies were features of even the more "austere" Chicago School skyscrapers of the 1880s and '90s.

69. "Chicago Public Library," *Harper's Weekly*, 41 (September 18, 1897), 934. The popularity of the Tiffany mosaics was one of the most potent forces in the campaign to save the building of the Chicago Public Library, and their restoration was a central part of its conversion to the Chicago Cultural Center.

70. To publicize its work among the public, Tiffany Studios held occasional exhibitions of both the stained glass windows and the special mosaic commissions. Thus the *New York Times* (February 27, 1897), Saturday Supplement 5, described a display at 333 Fourth Avenue of Favrile glass being used for lamps, bowls, and vases, as well as several stained glass windows under way for Philadelphia, a mosaic Last Supper design for a Baltimore church, the Chicago Public Library project, and the mosaics designed for the Alexander Commencement Hall at Pittsburgh. Visitors could also see cartoons and studies by Tiffany, Frederick Wilson, Edward L. Sperry,

Howard Pyle, Will H. Low, Joseph Lauber, Agnes Northrop, Lydia Emmett, Elihu Vedder, F. S. Church, and J. A. Holzer, most of the active artists working for Tiffany Studios.

71. [Charles De Kay] *The Art Work of Louis C. Tiffany* (Garden City, 1914), 26-8. Hugh McKean, *"Lost" Treasures*, 149, suggests the volume was part of Tiffany's active promotional activities, and the book clearly offered Tiffany a chance to present something of a philosophical and artistic apologia.

72. *McKean*, 35.

73. As quoted in *International Studio*, 58 (April 1916), lxiii.

74. [De Kay] *The Art Work of Louis C. Tiffany*, 71.

75. Cecilia Waern, "The Industrial Arts of America: The Tiffany Glass and Decorative Company," *International Studio*, 2 (September 1897), 156-7.

76. *Ibid.*, 162.

77. Bing's comments are scattered within a book and an essay he wrote in the 1890s: *Artistic America* and "Louis C. Tiffany's Coloured Glass Work." Both are translated and reprinted in Samuel Bing, *Artistic America, Tiffany Glass, and Art Nouveau* (Cambridge, Mass. and London 1970), 12-223. For further discussion of Bing and his relationship to Tiffany (and a correction of the name to Siegfried) see Gabriel P. Weisberg, *Art Nouveau Bing. Paris Style 1900* (Washington and New York 1986), *passim.*

78. Louis C. Tiffany, "American Art Supreme in Colored Glass," *Forum* 15 (July 1893), 623, 625.

79. *New York Mail and Express*, November 19, 1868, n.p. The conservatory window was meant for Louis Stern.

80. *Pittsburgh Post*, June 19, 1898, n.p.

81. *New York Sun*, January 16, 1898, n.p.

82. For more on the stained glass makers of this era see Sharon S. Darling, *Chicago Ceramics & Glass. An Illustrated History from 1871 to 1933* (Chicago 1979); Cleota Reed, ed., *Henry Keck Stained Glass Studio 1913-1974* (Syracuse 1985); and Nola Huse Tutag with Lucy Hamilton, *Discovering Stained Glass in Detroit* (Detroit 1987).

83. Typically, Tiffany Studios exhibited important mosaic and stained glass commissions to the New York public just before shipping them off for installation. They did this also with important World's Fair installations like the Columbian Exposition Chapel, later installed in the Cathedral of St. John the Divine. Company scrapbooks are filled with invited or planted news stories about such events, as well as a long series of journalistic visits. Thus the *Commercial Advertiser*, February 13, 1899: "From the rush and the glare of Fourth avenue, just above 23rd

street, with its aggressive modernity, one may step into a bit of the middle ages, an oasis of quiet and restfulness, where the sound of the trolley cars still comes to the ears . . . but faintly, chastened, as the light, which streams through the stained glass . . . ."

84. Laurelton Hall is described in some detail by Koch, *Rebel in Glass*; and McKean, *"Lost" Treasures*, but it was particularly well covered in the first ten or fifteen years of its existence by New York newspapers and national magazines, several of which also interested themselves in the various lawsuits involving the landowners of Oyster Bay. Samuel Howe, journalist and for a time a supervisor at Tiffany Glass & Decorating, wrote half a dozen descriptions of the house for *Town and Country, House Beautiful, Arts and Decoration*, etc. All are listed in the Koch and McKean bibliographies.

85. All these pageants were extensively covered by the local press, complete with photographs and guest lists. The Egyptian Fete took place February 4, 1913; the feast at Laurelton Hall, May 15, 1914; and the Quest of Beauty birthday party February 19, 1916. McKean *"Lost" Trea-sures*, 255-63, describes the events and reproduces some extraordinary photographs of the Egyptian fete.

86. Information on these artists can be found in a series of books on the architecture and design of the period, among them Karen Davies, *At Home in Manhattan: Modern Decorative Arts, 1925 to the Depression* (New Haven 1983); Bevis Hillier, *The World of Art Deco* (New York 1971); Jeffrey L. Meikle, *Twentieth Century Limited, Industrial Design America, 1925-1939* (Philadelphia 1979); Rudolph Rosenthal and Helena L. Ratzka, *The Story of Modern Applied Art* (New York 1948); Robert A. M. Stern, Gregory Gilmartin, and Thomas Mellins, *New York 1930. Architecture and Urbanism between the Two World Wars* (New York 1987); and Richard Guy Wilson, Dianne H. Pilgrim, and Dickran Tashjian, *The Machine Age in America 1918-1941* (New York 1986). It is interesting to note that in the indices to the two most recent and massive surveys, *Machine Age in America*, and *New York 1930*, Louis Tiffany makes no appearance whatsoever, not even as analogue or despised predecessor.

87. S. Bing, *Artistic America*, 138.

1. Helen Gould Landscape Window, leaded Favrile glass, 130" x 70", Tiffany Studios, New York, 1910

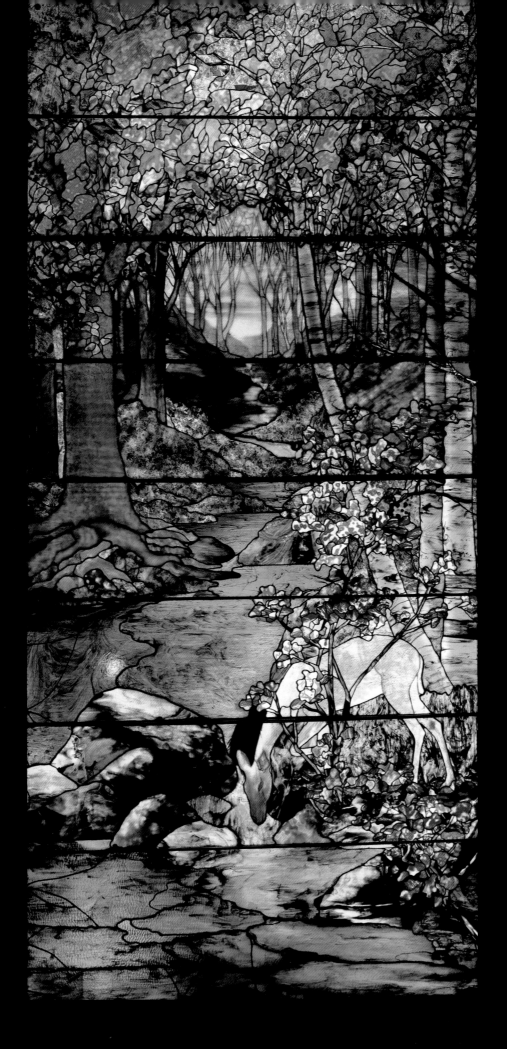

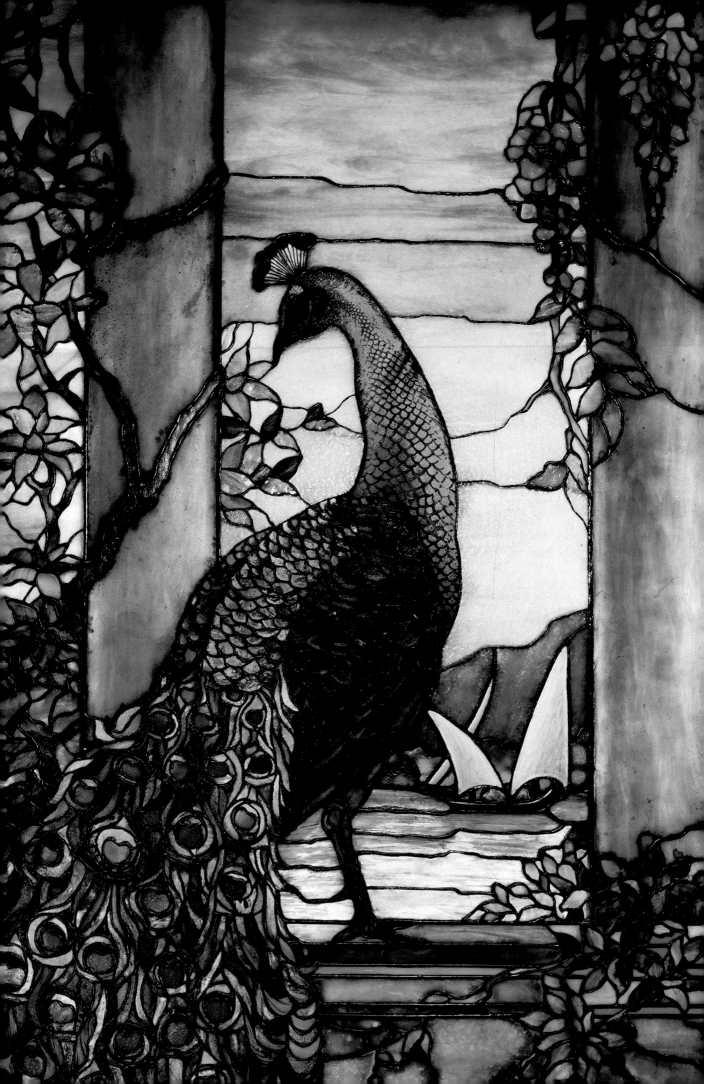

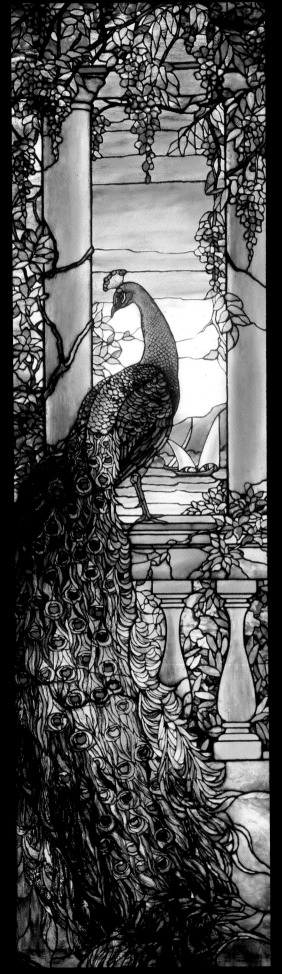

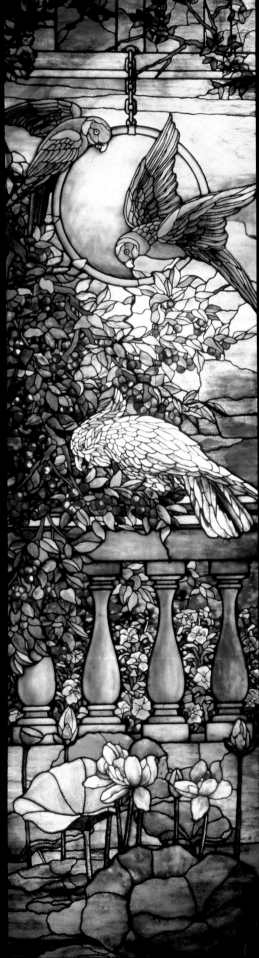

2, 3. Peacock Window, leaded glass, 111½″ x 29¾″, Tiffany Studios, New York, c. 1912

4. Cockatoo and Parakeet Window, leaded Favrile glass, 109½″ x 29¾″, Tiffany Studios, New York, c. 1912

5.  Punch Bowl with three ladles, Favrile glass and gilded silver, bowl 14½″ high, 24″ diameter, ladles ½″ x 3½″, Tiffany Studios, New York, 1900

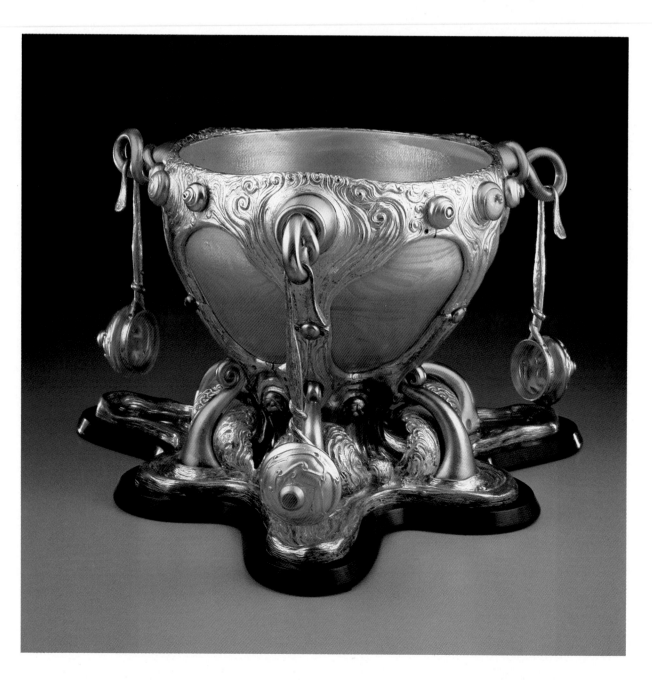

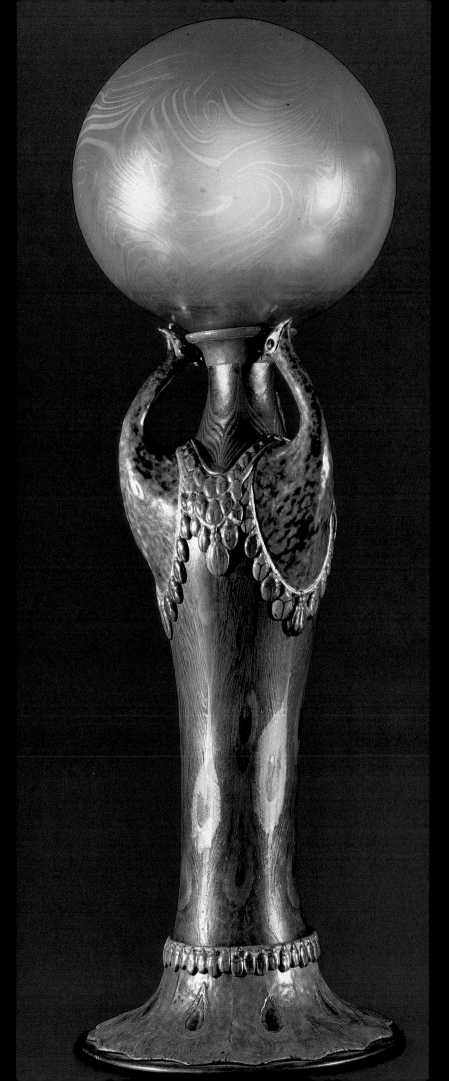

6. Gould Peacock Lamp, Favrile glass
and enamel on copper, 40½″ high,
13″ diameter, Tiffany Studios, New York,
1908-13

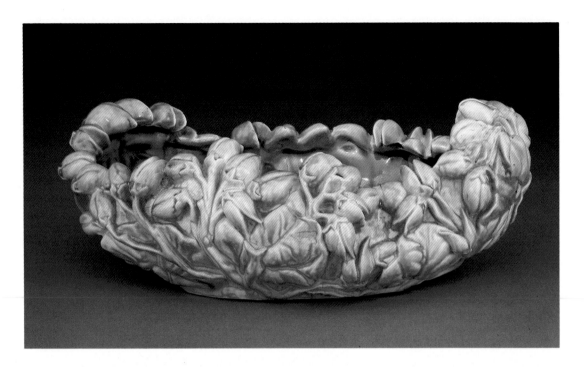

7. Lotus Bowl, Favrile pottery, 4¾" high, 12½" long, 7 ³⁄₁₆" wide, Tiffany Studios, New York, c. 1905

8. "Fern" Ceramic Vase, Favrile pottery, 12" high, Tiffany Studios, New York, c. 1905

9. "Salamander" Vase, Favrile pottery, 9½" high, 6½" wide, Tiffany Studios, New York, 1905-10

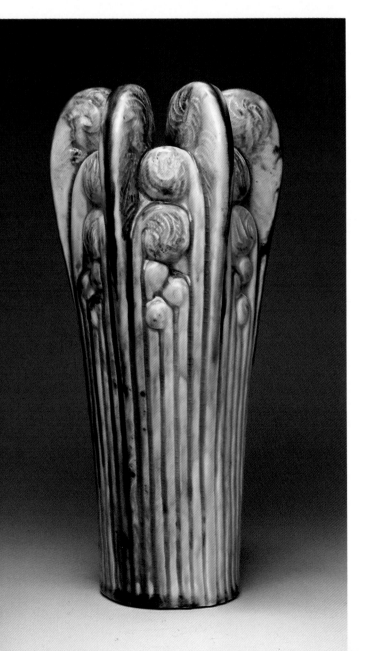

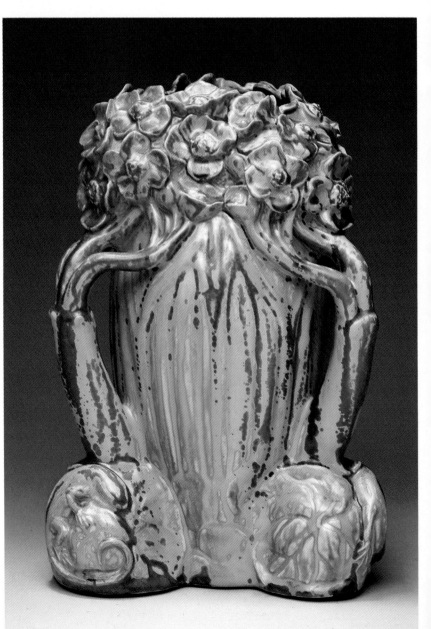

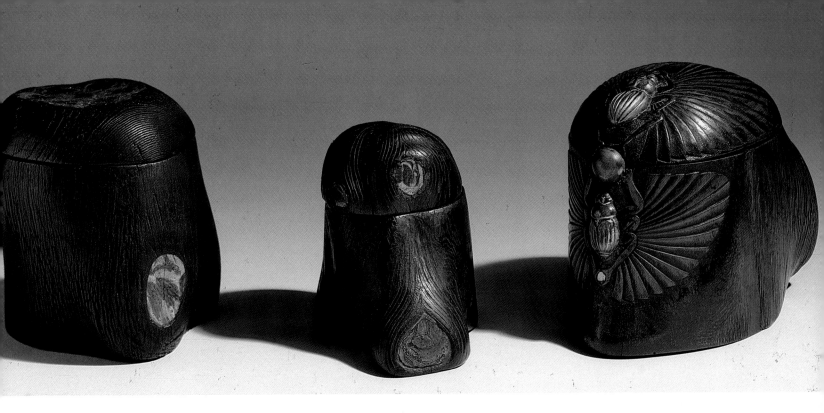

10. Double Card Case, wood and Favrile glass with mother-of-pearl, abalone, and enamel insets on the cover, 5½″ high, 5½″ long, Tiffany Studios, New York, 1905-10

Humidor, wood and Cypriote Favrile glass, 4⁹⁄₁₆″ high, 4½″ long, Tiffany Studios, New York, 1905-10

Humidor with mounted scarab decoration, wood and Favrile glass scarabs, 5½″ high, 6¾″ long, Tiffany Studios, New York, 1905-10

11. Bronze-mounted Cypriote Glass Covered Box with salamander decoration, Favrile glass and bronze, 9¼″ long, Tiffany Studios, New York, 1895-1905

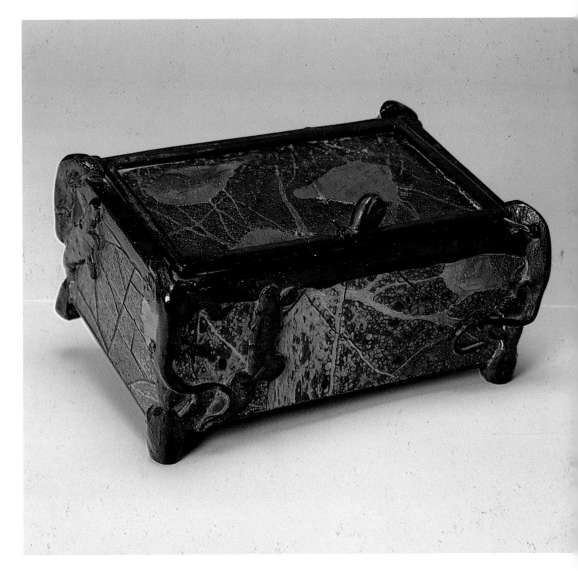

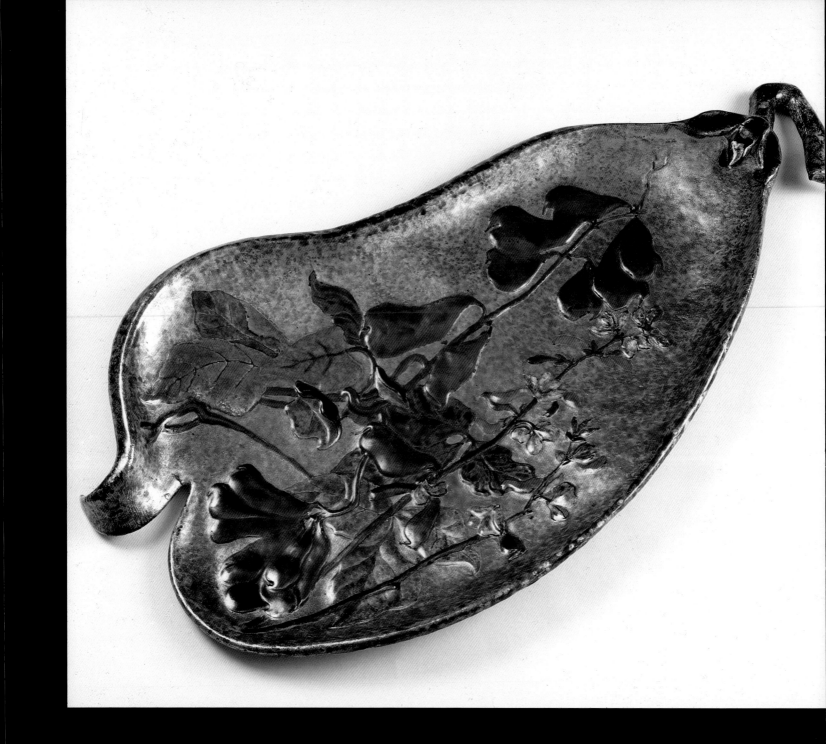

12.  Enameled "Gourd" Tray, enamel on copper, 25½" x 14", Tiffany Studios, New York, c. 1900

13.  "Morning Glories" sketch, watercolor on paper, 22⅝" x 21⅜", Louis Comfort Tiffany, 1913

14, 15.  Enameled Frog Paperweight, 5" diameter, Tiffany Studios, New York, 1900-10

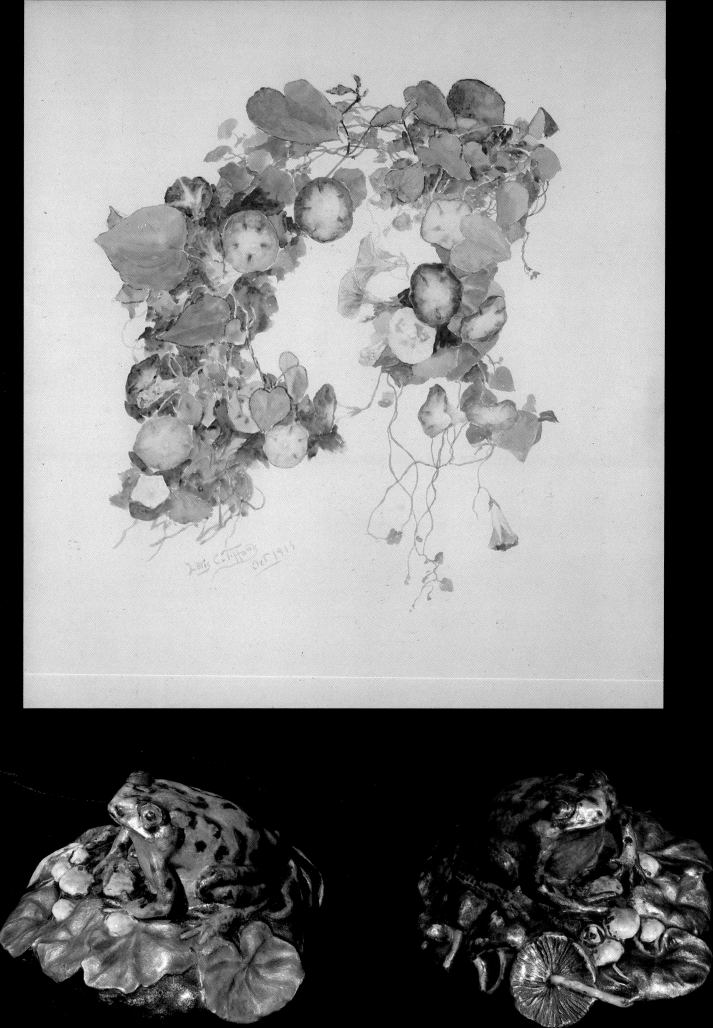

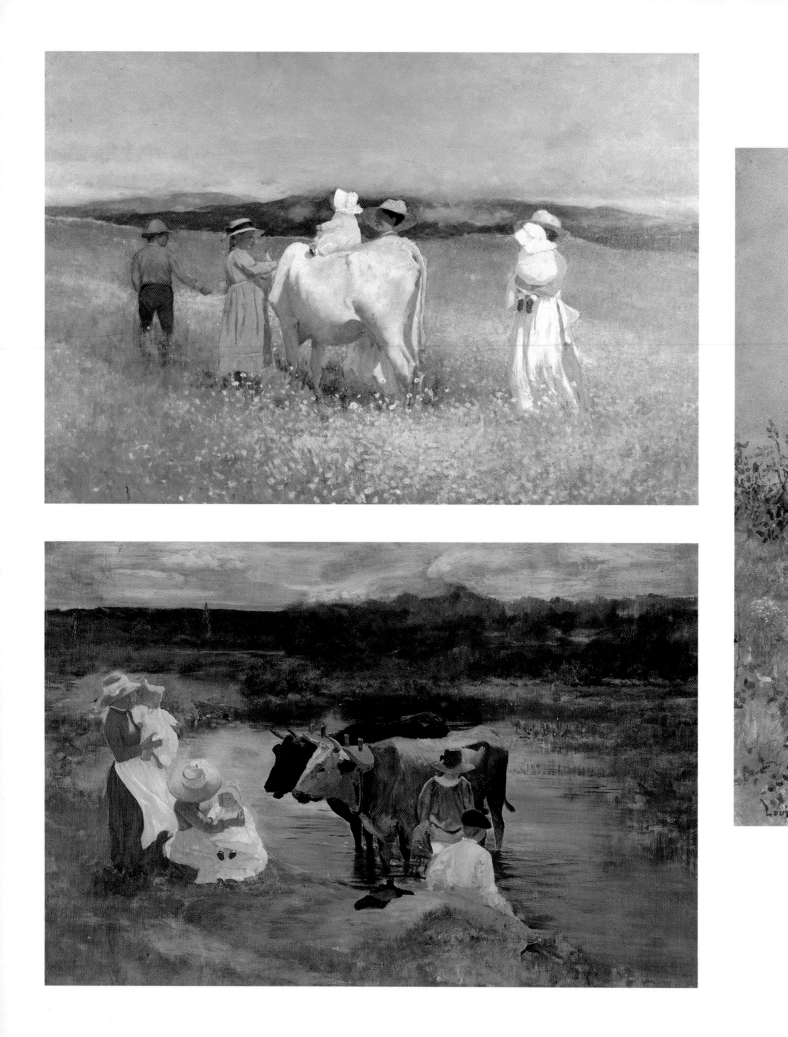

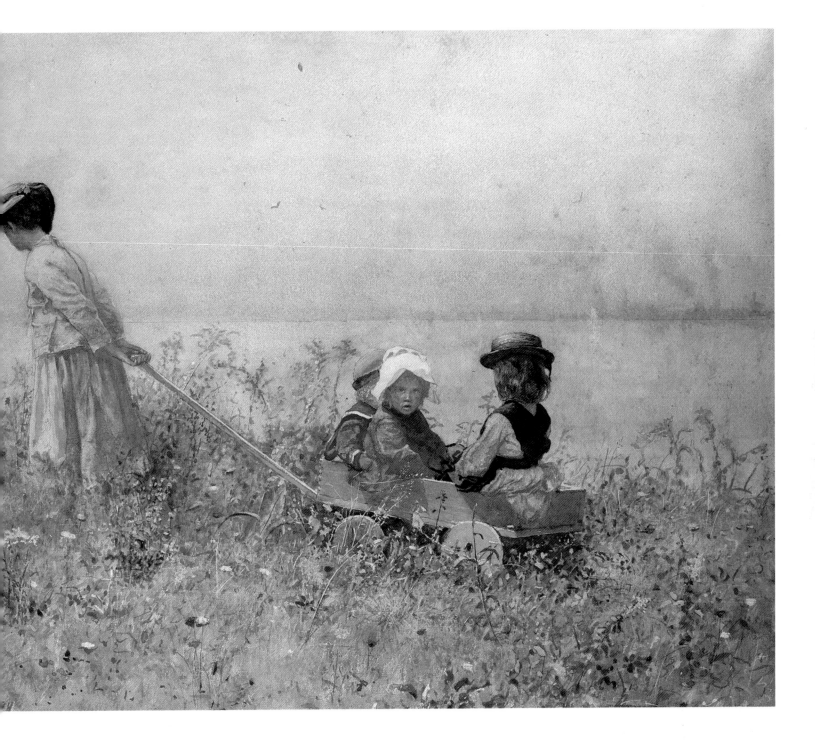

16. "My Family at Somesville", oil on
canvas, 24" x 36", Louis Comfort Tiffany,
c. 1888

17. "Family Group with Oxen", oil on
canvas, 22¾" x 35⅛", Louis Comfort
Tiffany, c. 1888

18. "Fields of Irvington", watercolor,
19" x 26", Louis Comfort Tiffany,
1879

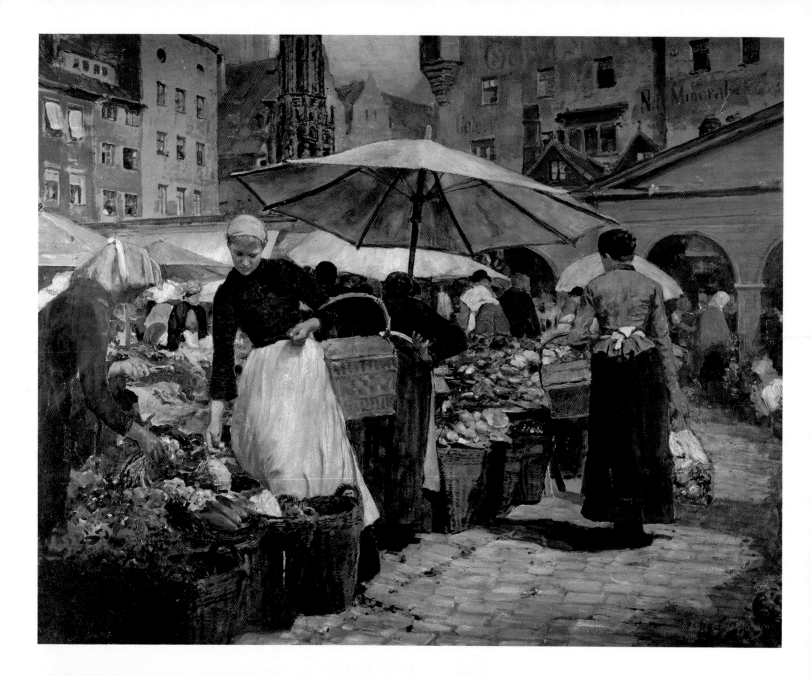

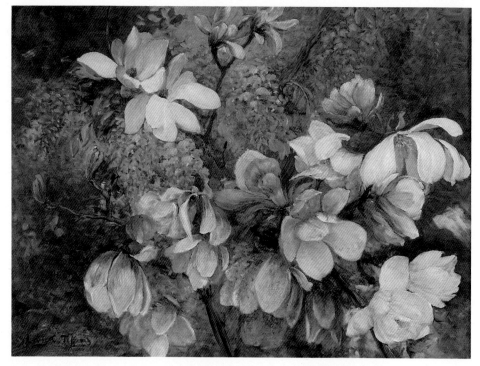

19. "Marketplace at Nuremberg", oil on canvas, 30½" x 39", Louis Comfort Tiffany, c. 1893

20. "Magnolias", oil on canvas, 21" x 30", Louis Comfort Tiffany, 1885-95

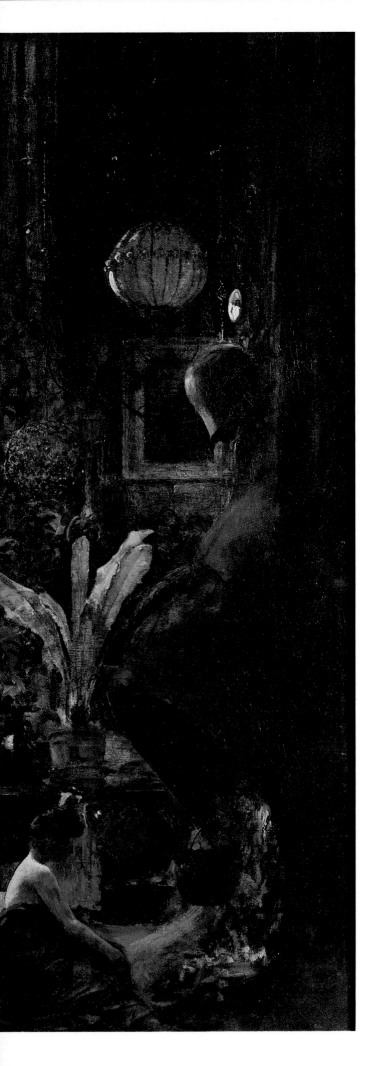

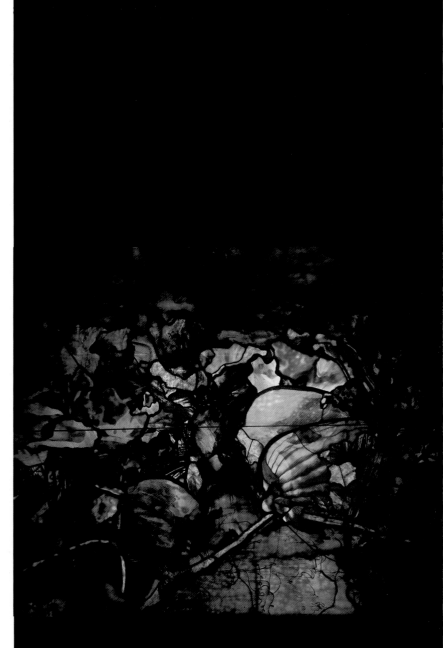

21. "A Corner of My Studio", oil on canvas, 30⅛" x 12¼", Louis Comfort Tiffany, 1890

22. "Pumpkin and Beets" Window, leaded glass, 46⅜" x 58", Tiffany Studios, New York, c. 1900

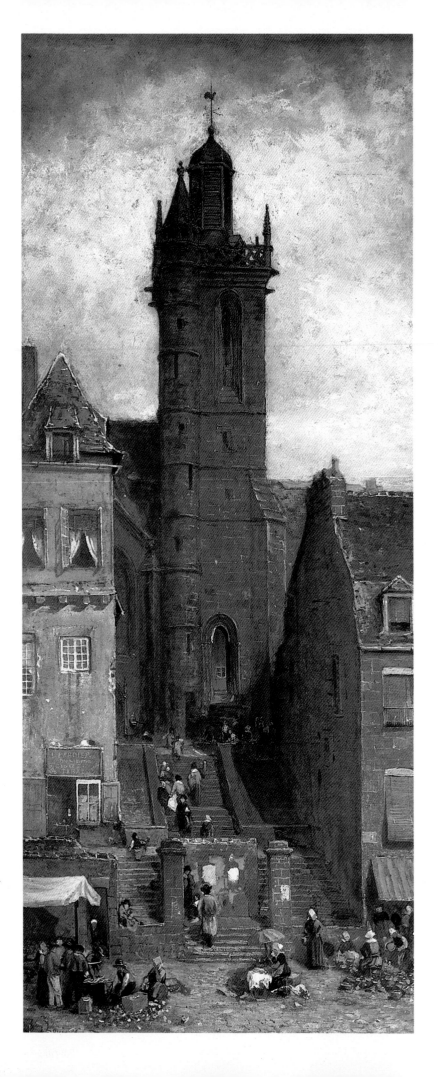

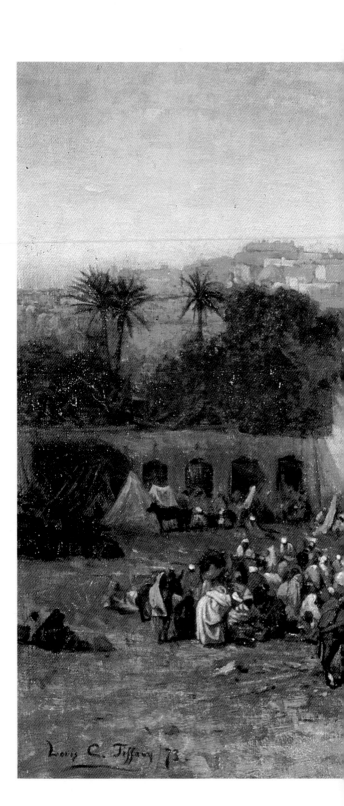

23. "Cathedral Steps, Morlaix, Brittany",
watercolor, 40" x 17", Louis Comfort
Tiffany, 1890

24. "Market Day outside the Walls of
Tangier, Morocco", oil on canvas,
35" x 56", Louis Comfort Tiffany, 1873

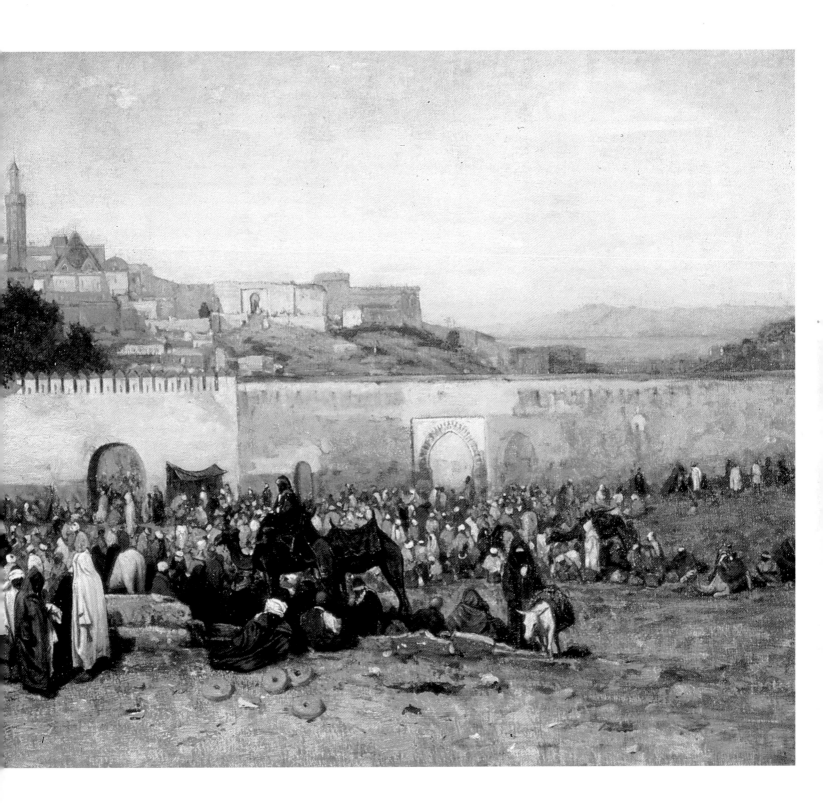

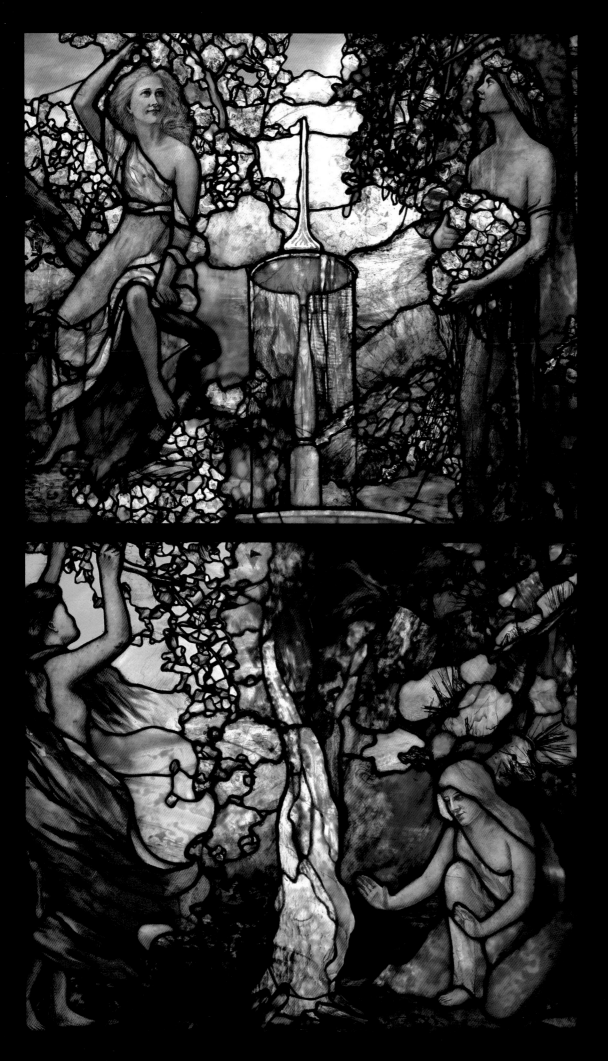

25, 26. "Four Seasons" Window, leaded
Favrile glass, 78" x 45", Tiffany Glass &
Decorating Co., New York, 1897

# TIFFANY AND THE CULT OF NATURE

## Martin Eidelberg

he decorative arts of Louis C. Tiffany are as internationally famous today as they were almost a century ago, when they were first created. Whether glass or bronze, ceramic or enamel, his brilliantly polychromed *objets d'art* proclaim the work of an artist who rightly saw himself as a colorist. There is even a vocabulary of familiar motifs: wisteria, jack-in-the-pulpit, Queen Anne's lace, apple blossom, spider's web, mushroom, peacock feather, etc. Yet, despite the unmistakable appearance of his work, we are still to come to grips with defining Tiffany's style.[1]

In many minds, Tiffany's decorative arts are inextricably linked with the concept of Art Nouveau. The names of the artist and the style, as well as the year 1900, are forever bonded into a triad. Indeed, for many, Tiffany is the outstanding exponent of the American Art Nouveau style.

There might seem to be historical justification for this opinion. Tiffany's glassware and windows were featured in the inaugural exhibition of L'Art Nouveau, Siegfried Bing's shop in Paris which gave the style its very name. Tiffany's creations were included in Bing's subsequent exhibitions, including his celebrated Art Nouveau pavilion at the Paris World's Fair of 1900. Articles about Tiffany's work appeared with regularity in all the major European periodicals which featured the new style — a style which, despite the various and often pejorative names it bore, was generally known as Art Nouveau. In the United States the situation was no different. In addition to Tiffany's substantial self-promotion, the critics were quick to report on him and his international achievements. Yet Tiffany's name rarely, if ever, was directly associated with the term "Art Nouveau" nor did Tiffany himself use it for his creations.[2]

The situation changed after World War I. Although Art Nouveau had fallen from grace and remained in a nadir until well after World War II, nevertheless a period of reevaluation began in the 1930s. In those first tentative reappraisals one can discern both Tiffany's return to favor (at least among American critics) and the association of his work with Art Nouveau. Philip Johnson, for example, though a major champion of the International Style, was one of those who sought a more careful and positive assessment of Art Nouveau; among his examples, he mentions a Tiffany lampshade.[3] Just a decade later, Tiffany was being called one of "the high priests of Art Nouveau in the United States."[4]

After World War II, when the Art Nouveau revival became a more sustained and ultimately successful movement, Tiffany's works were an integral part. In the first major European exhibition, staged in Zurich in 1952, a substantial number of Tiffany's glass vases were included.[5] At the 1958 retrospective exhibition of Tiffany's work which was held at the Museum of Contemporary Crafts in New York, it was declared that "Tiffany's span of creative work embraced the Art Nouveau movement. . . ."[6] In the Museum of Modern Art's groundbreaking Art Nouveau exhibition of 1960, Tiffany was proclaimed "the American master of the style" and, in fact, he was the only American decorative artist whose works were represented.[7]

Almost three decades have passed since then, and Tiffany's work has become increasingly and unquestionably associated with the Art Nouveau style. An ever-growing chorus has praised Tiffany and has linked his works with Art Nouveau. Mario Amaya described him as "the most monumental" of "the several masters of Art Nouveau," and claimed that Tiffany glass "became synonymous with the style throughout America up to the outbreak of World War I."[8] Thomas S. Buechner, then director of the Corning Museum of Glass, called Tiffany "the American giant of the *Art Nouveau* style."[9] In her study of American Art Nouveau, Diane Chalmers

Johnson claimed that "Louis Comfort Tiffany was and perhaps still is the most widely recognized American Art Nouveau artist."[10] All books on Art Nouveau – European or American – have included examples of Tiffany's glass vases or lamps. Likewise, all studies of Tiffany have included at least some allusion to Art Nouveau. The consensus is clear and unchallenged: Tiffany's mature work is Art Nouveau.

Central to this discussion, though, is the issue of what is meant by the term "Art Nouveau." Over the last three decades it has become increasingly clear that the turn of the century enjoyed a multiplicity of styles. Most agree that "High Art Nouveau" in its purest form is the dynamic, linear and abstract idiom practiced by Henry Van de Velde, Victor Horta and Hector Guimard. At the same time there was another abstract style, but one which depended upon rectilinear rather than curvilinear forms, one which sought architectonic stability and simplicity rather than biological vitality and complexity. This mode is well represented by the sober work of C.F.A. Voysey, as well as the elegant, spare creations of Charles Rennie Mackintosh in Glasgow and Josef Hoffmann in Vienna. Another mode was literal rather than abstract, and turned to Nature for inspiration. Emile Gallé and the School of Nancy are, of course, the chief representatives of this form of expression, but one could easily turn to other European centers. In fact, as we shall see, this emphasis on Nature was perhaps the dominant mode at the turn of the century. Symbolism also had an impact on the decorative arts, from the sexually charged furniture of Rupert Carabin to the poetic images in René Lalique's jewelry. Although we are primarily concerned with avant-garde idioms, there was still a great deal of historicism as well. Japonisme and Gothic Revival, Neo-Rococo and Beaux-Arts all had their attractions.

Moreover, while it is useful for us to isolate each stylistic current, designers at the turn of the century frequently combined two or more modes to create interesting hybrids. Botanically specific plants were incorporated into patterns dominated by whiplash curves. Languid symbolist maidens had their hair coiffed into patterns worthy of Van de Velde, or their bodies were encased in vertical, architectural forms. Poetic, brooding faces mysteriously emerged from flowers, just as whiplash lines merged with Gothic architectural forms. One need only consider Mucha's posters, Mackintosh's frieze from the Buchanan Street Tea Room, or the patterns in Eugène Grasset's *La plante et ses applications ornamentales* to realize how pervasive these hybrids were.

The issue of defining Art Nouveau is an old polemic. Is Art Nouveau a specific style or does it denote the general renewal of the arts at the turn of the century? This polemic goes back to the time of Bing himself.[11] Bing declared that the name "Art Nouveau" represented only the search for a style. But the history of his own gallery shows that while there was no uniformity of vision when he began in 1895, the situation changed, and before 1900 Bing had fixed upon an atelier style which was cohesive: its basic elements were taken from the dynamics of Van de Velde's abstract, linear style.[12]

Indeed, it is the whiplash style which is invariably cited when critics want to define "High Art Nouveau." Then, almost as though not to offend, recognition is given to the other modes as well. As a result, the issues remain confused. Yet the aesthetics of Guimard and Gallé cannot be contained by a single term, unless that term is meant to denote just a chronological period rather than a cohesive style.[13] If it were decided that Art Nouveau should refer only to a chronological period, that still leaves the problem of naming and understanding the styles which came into being.

Semantics need not be pedantic; indeed, clarity of terminology and clarity of thought are often linked. We might think of the state of scholarship when Mannerism and Baroque were not distinct art historical categories; "Renaissance" and "Late Renaissance" were the only operative terms, but they clouded the issues and inhibited an understanding of each period's aesthetics and the artists' real intentions. The same sorts of problems arise when one reads the literature on Tiffany, for the critics seem confused by and vacillate between the opposite poles of abstract rhythmic dynamics and naturalism when they discuss Tiffany's work. I am reminded of the problem which arose in the Metropolitan Museum's 1970 exhibition, *19th Century America*.[14] Apropos of Tiffany glass vases with naturalistic motifs, Art Nouveau was defined in an inclusionist manner as being "characterized by elongation, flowing lines, and the frequent use of certain natural forms – flowers, human hair and waves." On the other hand, an abstract Tiffany Studios lamp base was considered to reflect European Art Nouveau, with the implication that sophisticated, Continental Art Nouveau is abstract. Complicating matters still further, a goblet in the form of a thistle plant by Tiffany and Company was linked to mid-nineteenth-century naturalism rather than the naturalistic art which flourished at the turn of the century.

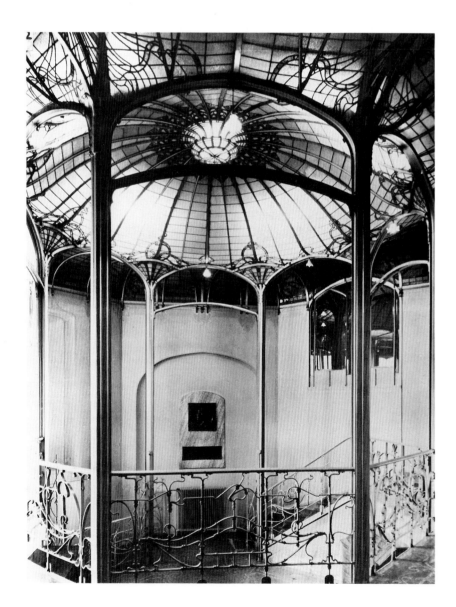

The central hall of the Hôtel Van Eetvelde, Brussels, designed by Victor Horta in 1897.

68

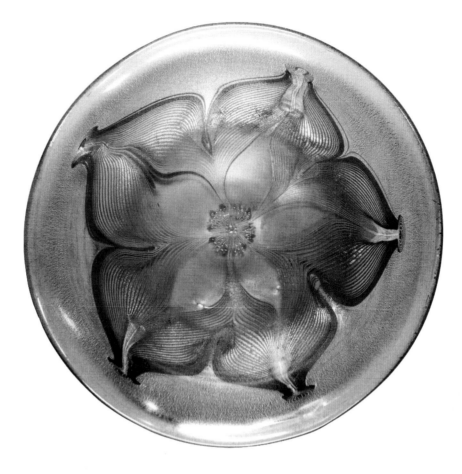

A glass plaque executed by the Tiffany Glass & Decorating Co., 1894-95. (The Metropolitan Museum of Art, New York; Gift of Henry O. Havemeyer, 1896)

This sort of bewildering relationship and/or dichotomy between Art Nouveau and naturalism is found in many instances. Robert Koch seems to have intended us to compare Tiffany's glass with illustrations of some of the most famous examples of High Art Nouveau architecture — Gaudí's Casa Mila and Horta's Hôtel Van Eetvelde — but he does not explain his visual analogies. Indeed, for the most part, when Koch discusses Tiffany as an Art Nouveau designer, it is generally because the works evoke "the growth forms found in nature."[15]

In the recent exhibition sponsored by the Boston Museum of Fine Arts, we read, "Of the several American potteries that interpreted the energetic lines of the Belgian and French Art Nouveau styles, Tiffany's is the most naturalistic and least derivative from European models."[16] This conclusion is deduced from a ceramic vase with jack-in-the-pulpit plants. But where in this instance is there an interpretation of Belgian energetic lines? And why, by implication, is Europe again excluded from naturalism?

Robert Schmutzler is one of the few critics who specifically tried to explain Tiffany's style in terms of abstract, High Art Nouveau style. He did so by analyzing the threaded design on a Tiffany plaque:

An example of the alternation between positive and negative forms and the subtle shift from rigid symmetry to forms of organic life is given by the star-like flower at the bottom of a Tiffany bowl [sic]. . . . Individual radiating lines and paths of design illustrate here the typical behavior of the so-called "Belgian line." Its characteristic is that . . . it becomes thicker in the narrow curves where the change of direction is most stressed, and thinner again in those curves that swing more widely.

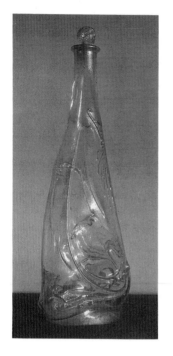

A cologne bottle designed
c. 1899 by Hector Guimard.
(Photo courtesy of The Museum
of Modern Art, New York)

. . . Ambiguous as the form and structure of the whole design may be, so is also its "meaning": an organic flower design has grown out of the inorganic glass, . . . the flower-like design of its interior becomes something like the pulsating organism in the gelatinous and transparent wrapping that sheaths the body of a Medusa jellyfish.[17]

Schmutzler's argument is seductive, but it is not sufficient to win the case. In the first place, Tiffany's design is not as consciously constructed as a design by Van de Velde, Horta or Guimard; these masters of the Belgian line show a more taut precision of rhythmic movement. Keeping even within the same medium of glass, one to which they turned only infrequently, we can see some revealing differences. Just before the turn of the century, Van de Velde designed some vases for the Val St. Lambert factory with engraved patterns, and Guimard designed some molded flacons for the Revilon-Millot perfume firm. The linear dynamics of these objects are far more consistent with the structured rhythms of High Art Nouveau. By comparison, the ornament of the Tiffany plaque seems more natural and organic. It is telling that Schmutzler repeatedly refers to the design as "flower-like;" in fact, the center of the plaque was engraved with pistils, showing that Tiffany intended us to see this as an opened flower. In many ways, the curvaceous lines that Tiffany introduced here are closer in spirit to a type of Japanese-inspired, rhythmical ornament than to High Art Nouveau.[18]

It could be argued that other Tiffany designs come closer to the Belgian line. We might consider his vases with the so-called "rat tail" decoration, where pulls of glass emerge from the fabric of the glass, somewhat like Guimard's molded decorations, or we might turn to Tiffany's tour-de-force of a punchbowl which was commissioned by Henry O. Havemeyer and which was exhibited at the Paris World's Fair of 1900. But even in such works, where undulant curves and whiplash lines abound, there still is a feeling of the organic. More telling than any single example, though, is the totality of Tiffany's mature oeuvre. When we look at the wisteria and maple leaf lamps, the lava vases and the fern frond ceramics, we must inevitably recognize that the greater part of Tiffany's energy was far removed from an abstract, dynamic, linear vocabulary, whereas, in strong contrast, Van de Velde and Guimard were wholeheartedly committed to such a program.

These differences should not be surprising. Horta, Van de Velde, and Guimard were of one generation (born in 1861, 1863 and 1867 respectively) while Tiffany was somewhat older (having been born in 1848). The three European Art Nouveau masters made their first significant contributions in the early to mid-1890s whereas Tiffany had been active since the 1870s. Although they all enjoyed great international fame at the turn of the century, Horta, Van de Velde and Guimard were exponents of a new idiom, while Tiffany's work was centered in an older generation's vision.

To understand Tiffany's particular achievements, I think it is far more useful and appropriate to compare his work and career with that of his French contemporary, Emile Gallé. Gallé was born in 1846, just two years before Tiffany. Not only were they contemporaries, but their careers are strikingly parallel. Since they are the two great glassmakers of the turn of the century, their works have often been brought into conjunction, but comparisons have inevitably stressed the differences between the two. Emphasis has always been placed on the supposedly opposite ways the two men approached the glass: it has been traditionally said that Gallé carved the decoration onto the surface and showed specific flowers, whereas Tiffany's decoration of colored filaments was integrated into the glass and his designs were abstract or, at least, more veiled. Although this sort of distinction is basically true, since Tiffany also carved floral designs throughout his career it is not as accurate as it purports to be. However, all differences pale when we consider the overwhelming similarities between these two men's careers and their general attitude toward their art.

Both men were born into families of substance and both their fathers' businesses were concerned with the decorative arts. Gallé's father, Charles Gallé-Reinemer, headed a firm which specialized in fine glassware and ceramics. The young Emile Gallé had a broad artistic training, but also pursued natural sciences (mineralogy and botany) at Weimar, studied briefly in London and, quite naturally, worked in the workshops associated with his father's business.

Tiffany's father, Charles Lewis, headed the famous silver and jewelry concern. The young Louis, forsaking a traditional college education, studied painting, first in the United States with George Inness and then with Leon Bailly in Paris. We can presume that he had been stimulated by his father's business in the decorative arts and his importation of the finest European goods. It is significant that Tiffany & Company was already an old client of Gallé by the late 1870s.[19] Also, we can imagine that Louis would have frequently come into contact with Edward C. Moore, the chief designer for Tiffany, whose taste was cosmopolitan and who had an avid interest in the arts of the Near and Far East.[20]

In the late 1870s both Gallé and Tiffany had embarked on their careers as decorative artists. By 1874 Gallé had taken over the artistic direction of his father's business and by 1879 Tiffany had entered into partnership with Samuel Colman, Lockwood De Forest and Candace Wheeler to form Louis C. Tiffany and Associated Artists. (At this point we might remember that Van de Velde, Horta and Guimard had still another decade before their careers were to begin.) Both Gallé's and Tiffany's artistic visions were rooted in the historic revivalism which dominated much of mid-nineteenth-century design. With the firm belief that inspiration could be drawn from the experience of past European styles and from foreign cultures, both artists turned unabashedly toward such sources. Much of Gallé's work, for example, was based upon the Rococo, as befitted an artist whose natal city of Nancy still remembered its heyday during the reign of Louis XV, and whose family firm owned the eighteenth-century St. Clement faience factory. While there also were traces of Medievalism and Renaissance revival as well, the most important element for Galle's future artistic development was his strong admiration for the newly found charms of Japanese art. Gallé discovered exotic new Oriental shapes for his vessels and novel motifs of bright-eyed insects and smiling fish taken from Japanese prints.

Tiffany's early interiors register similar artistic attitudes. The projects of Tiffany and the Associated Artists reveal the same wealth of ornamentation and potpourri of styles. Alongside traditional Louis XV and XVI furniture and *objets d'art*, there was Islamic furniture and star-patterned ceilings, Oriental vases and silk-lined walls, Indian panels of intricately carved patterns — all combined with equal delight. The Veterans Room in the Seventh Regiment Armory of New York (1879-80) shows that typical blend of elements: the great table suggested the Romanesque in its short but sturdy, clustered columns, the stenciled frieze bore Celtic interlaced patterns and scenes of chivalric knights, the balcony and its intricately carved grill were based on one in a Turkish harem, the portière was made of Japanese brocade and overlaid with steel rings to resemble a medieval coat of mail. Everyone wrote in praise of the richness of color and material and of the inventiveness of design, but clearly it was an inventiveness which looked backward as well as forward.

While it might be tempting to dismiss this opening phase of the two men's work as merely a preliminary stage, this is not the case. Throughout their careers, their choices of forms and decorative motifs were tempered by this early experience. It perhaps contributed to the slightly conservative elements in their work, elements which separate them from the next generation of Van de Velde, Horta and Guimard, men who sought with greater consistency a more modern, non-historical language of form and decoration. Although, as we shall see, both Gallé and Tiffany would soon change their artistic aims and emphasize natural forms, explicit historicizing elements remained visible throughout their careers. Since the fame of Gallé and Tiffany rests on their later works, works of the 1890s and 1900 which are renowned for their rich coloration and floral imagery, we need to consider how these artists came to modify (but not really change) their artistic visions as they matured.

In the case of Gallé we can trace an explicit development, not only because there were a series of specific events but also because the French artists articulately explained them. The 1878 World's Fair in Paris, one in which Gallé participated and which brought him his first significant accolades, was also an exposition at which the pervasive nature of historicism in the decorative arts was both manifest and criticized. As A.R. de Liesville bemoaned:

> In short, ceramics which are very brilliant, very varied, but above all imitative — that is what French ceramics are. Japan, Persia and Muslim art give it its most beautiful accents. In the details of the dinnerware we have come to the point of almost not having anything to envy Asia for. But as for decoration, we have found nothing French, nothing European, nothing decisive, since the eighteenth century. [21]

Liesville then reviewed the glass and found exactly the same situation:

> Following these visits to the sections for modern industrial art in manufacture, the definite impression is one of constant progress, continual improvement of the general appearance, since Ancient art, Oriental art, that of the Renaissance, are copied and recopied without stop. . . . But won't we be then only the age of copyists? [22]

Equally critical was Adrien Dubouché, who wrote in his official, government-sponsored report:

> Japonisme! Attraction of the age, disordinate rage, which has invaded everything, taken command of everything, disorganized everything in our art, our customs, our taste, even our reason. [23]

Such criticism *per se* did not put an end to historicism. But it was indicative of a new mood shared by Gallé and some of his avant-garde colleagues. One of them, the jeweler Lucien Falize, wrote a telling account (an account which Gallé could have written) of how he had been among the first to be attracted by Japanese art, how he had been enthralled by Japanese bronzes, porcelains and ivories, and how he had traced the images on Japanese prints. But then Falize turned away from this literal copying of Japanese art:

Now my love is not extinguished but it is calmer, like what happens when the fever of possession is calmed and you see your mistress of the previous night in broad daylight; she is still beautiful, smiling and full of grace but you hesitate to take her for a wife.

The comparison seems strange or brutal to you but have not all we artists more or less cohabited with the Japanese fairy? Have we not each had children born of this love?

Do you know what made the artisan of Kyoto give his vase the shape of a gourd or a bulbous root? Have you penetrated the symbol of the white deer? To what end do you copy these peach flowers or these quince branches? You write this language drawn by the Japanese as you have copied the religious symbols of all peoples – without understanding them.

Falize also gave a positive solution to the issue:

And us, what are we to do? To copy still? No, but to be inspired by this art and likewise return to a healthy doctrine, to simple means, to the study of Nature.[24]

As we shall see, the idea of a return to Nature became the crux of the matter. Writing about the Japanese artist Hokusai, Ary Renan suggested similar thoughts:

The *Man-gwa* is addressed beyond all to the handworking artists who maintain our industries. Why do they leave the country, the streams, the fields, the sea? Why do they not surround themselves with models from nature, brightly colored and lively? Why do they not add seaweed, butterflies, a branch of clematis to their limited designs? If they loved their models as the author of the *Man-gwa* loved his, they would pass from the ranks of artisans to that of artists.[25]

By 1900 this bonding of Japanese art and Nature became a major principle of French decorative arts.[26]

Gallé's writings and work show that he too believed in the idea of returning to Nature as well as remembering the lessons learnt from Japanese art. This transition must have been an easy one for Gallé, since his interest in Nature had been longstanding. His early studies in Weimar had emphasized botany and mineralogy, and the natural sciences remained a major aspect of his mature career. Nancy itself had an important school of horticulture and Gallé retained an active interest in botany.[27] Flora and fauna became the major aspect of his artistic work. While many of the motifs were studied directly from Nature, the humble forest and meadow flowers, insects and small birds, seaweeds and crustacea all suggest an iconography based upon what he had seen on Japanese objects and in Japanese prints.

This harmonious dualism of Nature and Japanese art was further reinforced for Gallé by a fortuitous event in 1885. In that year several Japanese students arrived in Nancy to study at the horticultural school and Gallé became friendly with one of them, a certain Tokouso Takasima. Supposedly they painted together in the countryside of Lorraine, and one can well imagine their rich interchanges, as Gallé learnt to explore the humorous movements of the insects, the graceful bending of the flowered branches, the poetry imbedded in the smallest of natural phenomena.

A word should also be said about the changes in Gallé's sensibilities toward color and materials, for here too we can see a similar duality of mineralogy and Japonisme. At the outset of his career Gallé employed a clear, limpid glass, but as he matured the glass became a more color-laden and ultimately opaque substance. After his initial triumph with a slightly opalescent clear-to-blue glass known as *clair-de-lune,* he began, like Eugène Rousseau before him, to add irregular streaks and flecks of mineral coloring, creating effects which were likened to agate, opal, jade and other natural minerals.[28] Also Gallé expanded the palette of enamels which he used. While many of his experiments were those of a chemical engineer, it was his poetic mind and eye which bade him seek the fleeting effects of "vaporous clouds" and "undulating smoke" as well as tints delicate as "the green of sleeping waters" and the "cream white of nacreous flesh." This listing of effects and delights may cause us to think of that consummate aesthete Des Esseintes, the hero of Huysmans' *Au rebours* who reveled in such exquisite pleasures, but on a more practical level, we would do well to remember how the French were impressed by the Japanese love for semi-precious and veined stones and the way Japanese workmen took advantage of the accidents of nature to create beautiful *objets d'art.*

The importance of Nature in French aesthetic doctrine might have registered more clearly if the Union Centrale des Arts Décoratifs — the most important organization for the decorative arts in France — had held an exhibition in the early 1890s, as they planned, to be devoted to the theme of the plant.[29] It was conceived by none other than Lucien Falize, and it was to have included a display of plants and flowers intended to inspire French decorative artists. Also, the major portion of the exhibition was to have included objects, both old and new, from Europe and from exotic cultures, which had been inspired by plant forms. For various reasons, the exhibition was first postponed and then canceled. But even though it did not take place, it drew a great deal of attention in the *Revue des arts décoratifs,* the publication of the Union Centrale which was the leading French journal of decorative arts at this time. There were articles not only by Falize in support of this program, but also by Gallé.

It was at this time that Gallé published his by now famous drawing of glass vessels whose shapes were derived from leaf forms. And it was at this time that he created a dining table based around the concept of garden vegetables.[30] It bore the poetic inscription, "Our roots are in the depth of the woods, among the mosses, alongside the streams."[31] The same inscription, the central maxim of Gallé's philosophy of design, was also inscribed on the doors of his furniture factory. Gallé believed personally in this religion of Nature and created designs in this mode; moreover, he was an eloquent proselytizer and wrote at great length to champion the cause of Nature.[32] The table, for example, was the subject of an article he published in the *Revue des arts décoratifs* and which, not coincidentally, he dedicated to Falize.

Perhaps the most significant of all of Gallé's exquisitely conceived essays is the one he devoted to his sideboard, *The Roads of Autumn.*[33] Gallé's sideboard had a very explicit program which the artist explained in minute detail. In that it was intended for a Rheims vintner, its thematic program, on the simplest level, revolved around viniculture and autumn — the season of the grape harvest. The principal structural elements of the cabinet represented gnarled vines, terminating at the top in leafy excrescences. The autumnal roadside plants and insects are depicted in the marquetry panels below, and in the darkened upper portions of the cabinet are autumnal asters and gourds seen against a starred sky. Throughout the cabinet are short poetic phrases, inlaid in marquetry, to solicit the spirit and awaken the intellect. An inscription

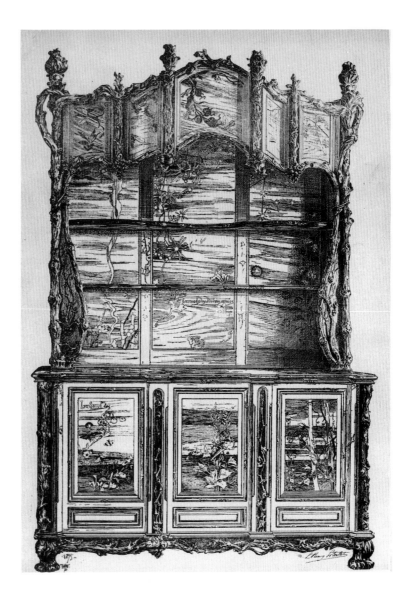

Gallé's sideboard, *The Roads of Autumn, c.* 1892.

from Victor Hugo: "The globes, gilt fruits on heavenly branches," alludes to the gourds on the branches and to the stars on the lines that fix the constellations. The flowering asters are likened both in name and form to the stars ("astres" in French) in the heavens above. At the top of the cabinet is a spider, symbol of the poetic laborer, who weaves its web like a constellation of stars. The autumnal plants, birds and insects bear associations of time, climate, smells, and sounds. Gallé summons up an orchestration of visual, aural and olfactory senses in a program of synesthesia, which paralleled and probably was derived from Baudelaire's idea of correspondences.[34] The all-enveloping but mysteriously shrouded program linked the terrestrial and celestial, and emphasized the opposition between tangible reality and visions of distant things.

Not all the French were so intellectually or poetically gifted as Gallé. Indeed, he was an extraordinary exception. But many French artists, each at his own level, took inspiration from Nature and in his own way translated it into something concrete. As Falize wrote, "Nature is the eternal creator where each art comes to be renewed, where the eye of every thinker and artist reads a different poem."[35] The designs which were submitted for the Union Centrale's pending

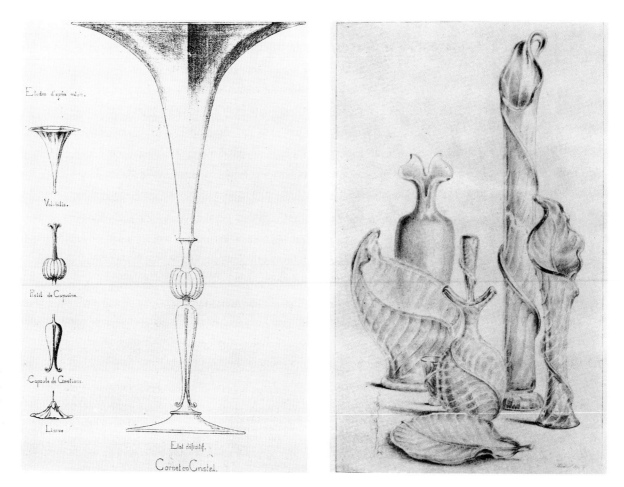

Edme Couty's design for a crystal goblet, *c.* 1890, which appeared in the *Revue des arts décoratifs.*

Designs by Gallé for glass vases based on natural forms.

exhibition show quite different approaches to the use of plant forms. Edme Couty's proposal for a crystal goblet, for example, is far less poetic and organic than Gallé's. It has a decidedly Beaux-Arts character and, were it not for the fact that each of the parts was explicitly analyzed in terms of the particular plant which had inspired it, one might never have recognized the "natural" origins of the object.[36]

Luckily, however, by the turn of the century the more organic type of designs of Gallé and Falize triumphed. Indeed, when one looks at the works exhibited by the French in the 1900 World's Fair – the jewelry, ceramics, *pâte de verre* and metalware exhibited by Lalique, Dammouse, Decorchemont, Husson – we realize that this emphasis on Nature was at least as strong – if not stronger – than the dynamic rhythms of the High Art Nouveau style. And, moreover, it was a view of Nature that had been tempered by experience of Japanese art.

In the early 1890s, Tiffany's art was just beginning to mature. As in the case of Gallé, there were the two polarities of Nature and historicism, but in Tiffany's case historicism was still the dominant mode. Its impact is clearly registered in his two most important undertakings of this time, the chapel he exhibited at the Chicago World's Fair of 1893 and the Havemeyer House of 1890-91. Although one was ecclesiastical and the other domestic, although one was meant more for display and the other for daily habitation, both show a free blending of historical styles. The chapel was essentially Romanesque in its overall architectural scheme, but this was offset by Byzantine-looking mosaics and basket-weave capitals, Flamboyant Gothic candlesticks, and a great many accessories which looked as though they had come from a Merovingian treasury. The accent in the Havemeyer House was perhaps more on the Oriental and

Byzantine, as could be seen in the silk-lined drawing room, the fabulous hanging staircase (reputedly based on one in the Doge's Palace in Venice) and glass-jeweled lamps, but here too there were medieval elements, as in the Cosmatesque entrance hall and the Celtic interlace on some of the furniture. More important than the derivation of the individual motifs, though, was the overall impression of color and richness of materials, as stone, glass and bronze were intricately interwoven. The lamp which hung over Mr. Havemeyer's desk and the candlesticks which graced the chapel's altars are of a single artistic vision.

Tiffany's leaded glass windows from this period register a similar development. A number of them were as conservative in design as the individual details of his decorative schemes. A great many were ecclesiastical and were banal exercises in late-nineteenth-century religious art, redeemed only by the color and beauty of the glass material itself. Some of the windows were transcriptions of other artists' easel paintings; these ranged from Old Masters such as Botticelli (a window based on his Berlin *Madonna of the Candelabra* was featured at Chicago in 1893) to popular French salon painters such as Jules Lefebvre and Americans such as Will H. Low.

While it is true that Tiffany created some daring abstract windows, such as the one that was in his Bella Apartments, these were not displayed publicly.[37] Not surprisingly, the one area in which Tiffany's windows struck a new note was that in which the theme was taken from Nature. Tiffany had occasionally used such windows in domestic interiors in the late 1870s, as in the squash and eggplant windows for the Kemp house. Sometimes, as in the chapel for the Chicago Fair, windows with symbolic Easter lilies provided a background for the ecclesiastical setting, but Nature was not yet a dominant aspect.

Yet, indicative of the future, one of the windows exhibited at Chicago showed parakeets perched on the branches of a blossom-laden fruit tree, and a goldfish bowl hanging from one of the boughs. Over the next few years Nature would become a more significant feature of Tiffany's artistic endeavors. At his 1899 display at the Grafton Galleries in London, for example, Tiffany included two windows with fish as their subject, two with floral motifs, and one landscape – these five constituting almost half of the windows on display and suggesting the significance that Nature was beginning to assume in his oeuvre.[38]

In the 1890s Tiffany and his artisans began to expand their repertoire of media. Starting about 1893 and continuing for another decade or so, they explored one new area after another: blown glass, metals, enamels, ceramics, jewelry. It was perhaps the most fertile portion of Tiffany's career and the period in which Tiffany gained his international fame.

The first glass vessels were made in 1893 and were advertised for sale the following year. It is relatively easy to identify the style of these earliest efforts and, unlike his later works, they are unsigned or bear distinctive early paper labels.[39] In a brochure issued by the company in 1898, the forms were described as "largely derived from natural motives . . . [and] Parting-eaux, Cantharus, Lecythus, Amphora, Pelike, Buire, Ewer, Tazza, etc."[40] Once again we see this dichotomy of Nature and historicism. The latter group of shapes are, for the greater part, Greco-Roman, and, indeed, this can be seen in some of the early covered jars and vessels resting on bronze stands. Even the pinched vase form, which so many think of as one of Tiffany's inventions (some would perhaps claim "Art Nouveau" invention) was based on a Roman shape, just as the iridescence which sparkles on the surface of many of these early pieces was an attempt to recapture the effect of corroded Ancient glass.[41] Lastly, we need to consider the impact of Oriental art on Tiffany's works, especially the gourd- and pear-shaped vessels and those with undulant forms. This is not to say that each vessel had a specific historical prototype; rather, as in the case of the Havemeyer House interior, Tiffany began with certain conceptions derived from the past and then gradually transformed them, at times transcending the original impetus.

The decoration of the vases was generally achieved through the application of threads of colored glass while the vessel was still a molten sphere; sometimes they were arranged in arabesques or allowed to expand in freer patterns.[42] Often the effects simulated veined marble or agate, a concept which had been popular since the early nineteenth-century innovations of Friederich Egermann but which, after all, also suggests certain ideas that Gallé explored. Tiffany had certainly been well aware of Gallé's growing success in the areas of ceramics, glass and furniture (some of which continued to be bought and sold by Tiffany & Company). More to

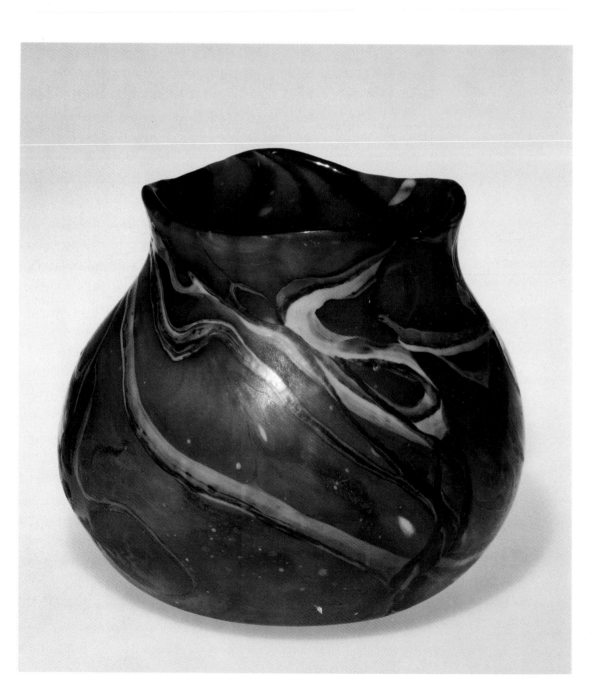

A glass vase executed by the Tiffany Glass & Decorating Co., c. 1894. (Photo courtesy of the Metropolitan Museum of Art, New York; Bequest of James H. Stubblebine, 1987)

the point, on Tiffany's trip to Europe in 1889 – probably in conjunction with the Paris World's Fair where Gallé had triumphed – Tiffany traveled to Nancy and visited Gallé's factory.[43]

Some of Tiffany's early glass vessels have a decoration of applied threads and pads that suggest vegetal forms. A few of the early vases have abstracted leaves and stems floating on the surface, evoking a watery and iridescent marine life. In certain instances, these suggested forms have been made more specific by engraving the glass. One such vase is in the Smithsonian and another in the Victoria and Albert Museum. Both have carved designs of swimming fish, which recall not only Japanese art but Gallé as well. Another early vase suggestive of Nancy is the one with carved flowers in the Cincinnati Art Museum. Others perhaps recall English cameo glass by Thomas Webb, but even here the sense of movement in the flowers and the openness of the design show how Tiffany, inspired by Japanese art, had gotten away from the stiff quality of Webb glass.[44] A word must also be said of his flower-form vessels, for

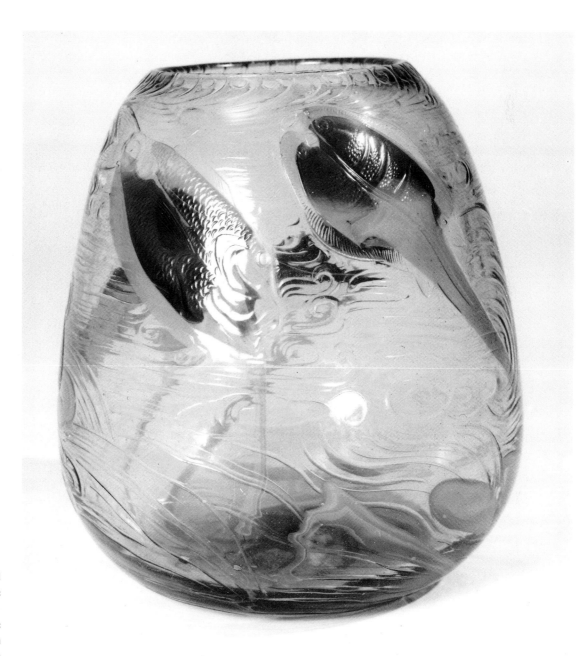

Cameo glass vase with internal fish decoration, executed by the Tiffany Glass & Decorating Co., 1893-96. (Photo courtesy of the National Museum of American History, Washington, D.C.)

from the very start Tiffany tried his hand at these delicate fancies. Some were even set in sculpted bronze bases, replete with leaves, that Gallé could have admired.[45]

In short, then, Tiffany's blown glass – the medium which made his international reputation – was marked by the strong influences of historicism and Nature, as well as his concern for color, and these are the very same factors that we have seen in his interior decoration and his leaded windows.

Although Tiffany had used a great deal of bronze and iron accessories in his work as an interior decorator, especially for candelabra and hanging lamps, and had used metal supports for some of his first blown glass vessels, only in 1897 did he establish a foundry and metal shop as part of his expanded factory at Corona. This resulted in (or, more probably, was prompted by) a greatly expanded production of lamps in which glass and metal work were elaborately combined.

The first lamps that Tiffany showed in the years between 1896 and 1898 prove to be quite different from the popular image we have today. There were no wisteria or peony or magnolia lamps on elegant bronze standards. Rather, the lamps were heavy, cumbersome creations, generally with blown glass spheres and elaborate wire frames.[46] The overall feeling is of a hybrid of the Oriental and the medieval – understandably not far removed from the lighting fixtures used just a few years earlier at the Havemeyer House.

Then, over the course of the next few years, Tiffany gradually introduced themes from Nature. By 1899 a number of familiar motifs had entered his vocabulary. One lamp, though it was still probably with a blown glass shade, had a base with fully modeled crabs which suggest

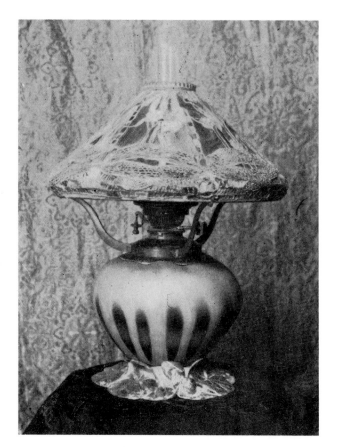 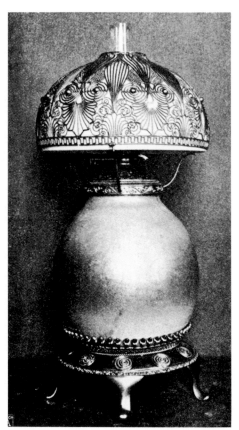

Five examples of the lamps the Tiffany Glass & Decorating Co. were producing prior to 1900.

analogies with certain types of Japanese bronze vessels that were favored in those days.[47] A second lamp was supported by three-dimensionally sculpted frogs. A third, whose design is attributed to Clara Driscoll, had a design of dragonflies worked in the leaded glass shade, and the oil container below rested on fully sculpted bronze water lily leaves.[48] The choice of motifs — insects and other charming denizens of a watery habitat — reminds us of the Japanese-inspired view of Nature which Gallé and Falize had been propounding for a decade.

Another and spectacular example of the theme of Nature emerging in Tiffany's lamps is the butterfly lamp which was introduced in 1898-99.[49] Here too we are reminded that this insect is one which had been popularized by Japonistes (consider, for instance, the butterfly signature of that arch Japoniste, James McNeill Whistler) and which Tiffany had himself used a decade earlier in a window, where they swarmed against a Japanese paper lantern. The narcissi in the mosaic base are so beautifully fresh and their iridescent colors so vibrant that we may not stop to consider how Tiffany had transformed the medium. In his earlier interiors, mosaics were intentionally used to summon up the spiritual glory of Early Christian and Byzantine monuments, and their patterns corresponded to those specific historical styles. But in this lamp the mosaic has been freed from that historicizing context. This lamp and others which are from the same creative moment — such as the one with spider webs and apple blossoms in the shade — reveal the same choice of Japanese-inspired motifs and constitute Tiffany's growing paean to Nature.

Tiffany's metal department began to produce inkstands, candlesticks, boxes, paperweights and other small accessories as well. Inkstands that he exhibited in 1899 included one with a

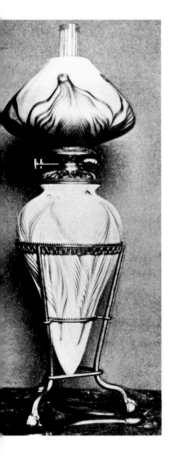
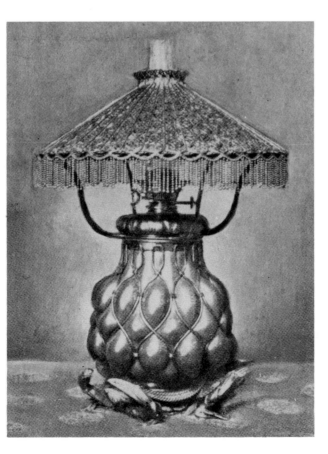
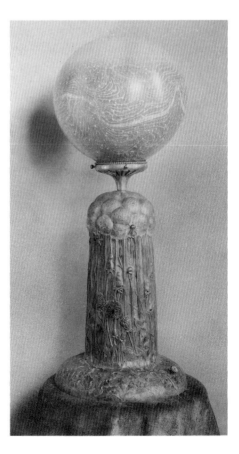

crab design, one with a wild carrot flower (Queen Anne's lace), and one with a dahlia design.[50] He also maintained a small metal workshop in his home at 72nd Street where trays, tea services and other handwrought items in metal were being made, perhaps on an experimental basis. Julia Munson Sherman recalled that when she began working there shortly before 1900, her first pieces were copper trays, one based on the mullein leaf, the other based on kale.[51]

Working in metals seems to have sparked experimentation with enameling. One of the primary reasons for using enamels was to introduce a coloristic harmony between metal and glass. Those in Tiffany's circle were quick to point out that the physical properties of enamel were close to those of glass.[52] It is also useful to recall that at that time there was a renaissance in artistic enameling in Europe, especially in England and France, and at that very moment, Tiffany's European representative, S. Bing, was setting Tiffany glass in delicately enameled and jeweled silver mounts. But whereas Bing's mountings, designed by Edward Colonna, were in a High Art Nouveau style, Tiffany's were – predictably – based on naturalistic themes.

Among the first such enamels were covered jars whose surfaces were repoussé-ed and enameled with wild Indian pipes and other flowers, lamp bases with dandelions and peacock feathers, and a small paperweight in the form of a fully modeled frog.[53] The intense, saturated tones of the enamels represent Tiffany's never-ending concerns as a colorist. Samuel Howe reported an anecdote of how Tiffany compared one of his enameled vases against sapphires, topaz, opal, aquamarine, and other stones, and concluded that the enamels "showed much more depth and perspective than were found in the stones."[54] But despite the high coloration, the drawing and modeling of the decorative motifs was, inevitably, naturalistic.

In 1900, after seeing the success of French ceramics at the Paris World's Fair, Tiffany turned his attention toward this medium.[55] But there was also a certain logic to this expansion. Not only is there a relation between the chemistry of enamels and ceramic glazes but, in fact, most of the first ceramic shapes were taken directly from those which had been created in copper by the enameling department. Thus, a great many had the type of floral design that we have already discussed. At the same time, though, the ever-conservative Tiffany produced some restrained Oriental forms, undecorated save for their beautiful glazes. There were even a few models which were explicitly historicizing, with Near Eastern and Romanesque motifs.

One of the last areas which Tiffany explored was that of jewelry, this not until about 1904.[56] Enamels, metals and brilliantly colored stones were combined to create artistic jewelry and, in a sense, repeated that earlier experiment in which Tiffany tested the color of his enamel against natural stones.[57] His jewelry was of two major types. In one the effect centered on the combination of many colored stones – a refined form of medievalizing encrustations to which he was accustomed. The other type was of jewels fashioned in the form of flowers – Queen Anne's lace, bunches of grapes, nightshade, dandelions – and even the occasional dragonfly or octopus. Certainly Tiffany remained true to his iconography.

If we look back now at the course of Tiffany's development over these years from 1893 to 1904, we can see not only this incredible creativity of design and richness of materials, but also, and central to this study, the gradual triumph of Nature. His selection of motifs is indicative: wildflowers such as Queen Anne's lace, Indian pipes and narcissi, flowering apple and magnolia trees, forest ferns and mushrooms, insects such as dragonflies and spiders. The peacock aside, one finds little of Romantic exotica. The choice is insistently in favor of native and unassuming flora and fauna – choices that Gallé had made as well. Indeed, when

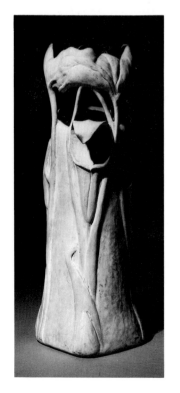

Ceramic vase with jack-in-the-pulpit plants produced by Tiffany Studios, c. 1906.

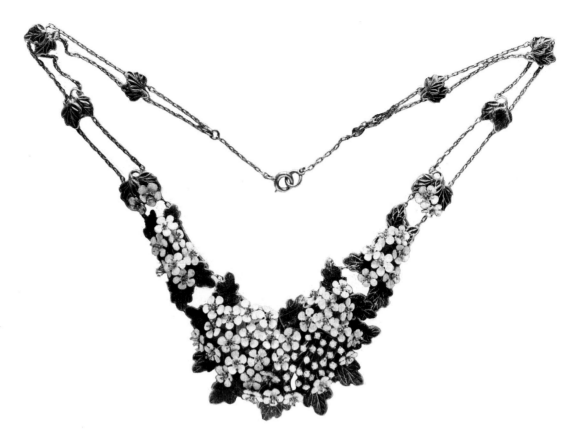

A floral necklace in enameled gold designed by Louis Comfort Tiffany and produced by Tiffany & Co., c. 1910. (Photo courtesy of Tiffany & Co. Archives)

one thinks how both artists favored certain motifs such as dragonflies and frogs and umbelliferous flowers (for Gallé the cowparsley, for Tiffany the Queen Anne's lace), one cannot deny the community of impulse.

As Tiffany's work matured in the years just before and after the turn of the century, these natural motifs were often developed into bold, three-dimensional schemes. Unlike Gallé, Tiffany generally did not attempt to create glass forms based upon natural motifs; the flower-form goblets, onion-bulb and jack-in-the-pulpit vases are the exceptions. However, Tiffany did experiment with organic shapes for many of his lamps, bronzes, enamels and ceramics. Lamps took on the forms of mushrooms, miniature maple trees, clusters of water lilies, branches of wisteria. Inkwells and paperweights were treated like naturalistic, fully modeled sculpture and many of the jewels were like sprays of real flowers.

One of the interesting questions that arises in relation to Tiffany's interest in Nature is what pictorial sources were used, especially since biological accuracy was apparently an important criterion. Julia Munson Sherman recalled the importance of Tiffany's large library of scientific books about plants and animals.[58] Also, photographs played a significant role. Tiffany was an avid photographer, and just as he relied on his early photographs for his early genre paintings, so his later photographs of natural motifs — such as studies of Queen Anne's lace and daffodils — were apparently a vital resource for his artisans.[59] Among the possessions left behind by Agnes Northrop were photographs of branches of flowering magnolias that reportedly looked

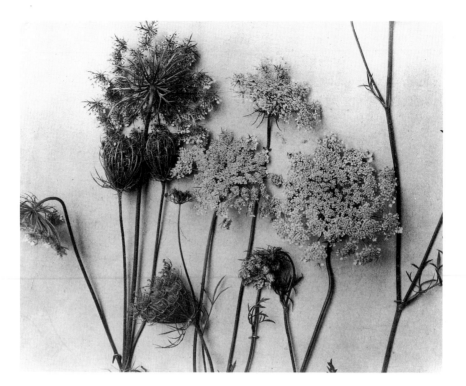

Queen Anne's lace plants photographed by Louis C. Tiffany. (Photo courtesy of The Morse Gallery of Art, Winter Park, Florida)

very much like the windows she designed for Tiffany.[60] A curious oddity, recently discovered, is a photograph of a stuffed peacock that was in Tiffany's workshop and which, according to the notation on the back of the photo, was the model used for the Gould lamp. According to Mrs. Sherman, the artists did not work directly from live specimens. There may have been some experimentation in electroplating live plants, such as the jack-in-the-pulpit used on the enameled copper vase; but I believe that such instances were exceptional, if they occurred at all.[61]

Whereas Tiffany was undoubtedly inspired in good measure by the biological shapes themselves, we should not discount the stimulus that European decorative arts may have offered.[62] Unlike other American designers of the period, though, Tiffany does not seem to have been directly influenced by European design manuals nor did he generally copy specific European prototypes. Nature freed him from that type of servitude.

It would be wonderfully convenient if we could now turn to Tiffany's writings and discover that he had laid out a program like Falize's or Gallé's which enunciated how his art was based on a study of Nature. While he did write a number of articles in the 1910s, these deal primarily with his concern with color. Occasionally there are pertinent remarks, as when Tiffany wrote, "'Nature is always right' — that is a saying we often hear from the past; and here is another: 'Nature is always beautiful' . . ."[63]

Alastair Duncan shows in his essay how Tiffany's staff justified the presence of floral motifs in ecclesiastical windows through various restatements of the favorite nineteenth-century aphorism, "God is Nature." But all too often the saccharine utterances and banal allegories seem like carefully calculated public justifications rather than true inner visions.

It is only here and there, in Tiffany's writings and in the reports of his contemporaries, that we can find snippets which give us some sense of Tiffany's thoughts. One of the most revealing

A bittersweet "girdle" and a blackberry hair ornament in garnets, carnelians, Mexican opals, gold, silver and enamel, designed by Louis C. Tiffany; executed and exhibited by Tiffany & Co. at the St. Louis Exposition of 1904. (Photo courtesy of Tiffany & Co. Archives)

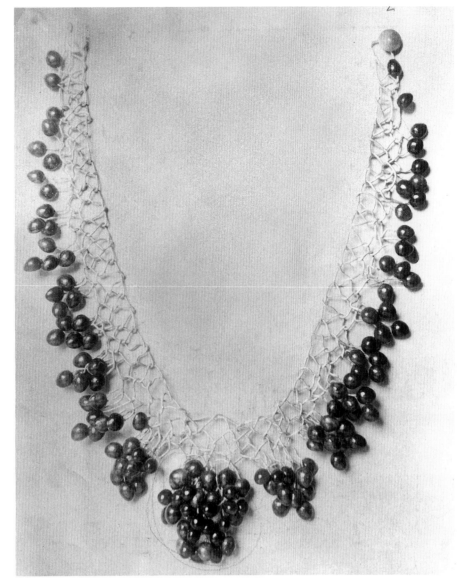

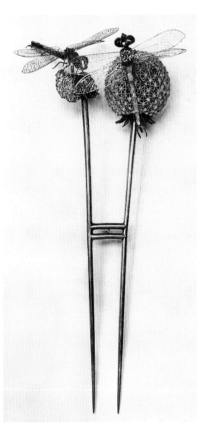

A dragonfly and clover hair ornament designed by Louis C. Tiffany and executed by Tiffany & Co. around 1904.

A selection of scarab pendants in Favrile glass with gold mounts, executed by Tiffany & Co. and offered in their Blue Books for many years under the heading of "Beetle" jewelery. (Photo courtesy of Tiffany & Co. Archives)

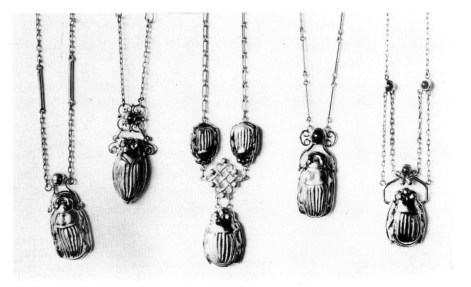

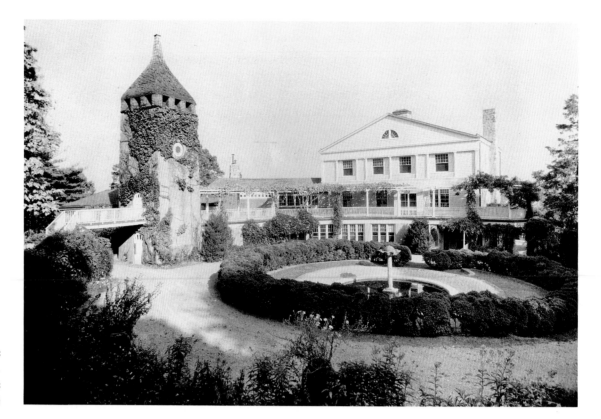

The Briars, a summer residence of Louis C. Tiffany, *c.* 1900. (Photo courtesy of private collection)

documents is an article written by his colleague, Samuel Howe, and it was not about the products of Tiffany's atelier but, rather, about the gardens around The Briars, his country property adjacent to and preceding Laurelton Hall.[64] Tiffany evidently had a large hand in this essay, since it was written by a close associate, contained several quotations attributed to the artist, and the photographs were taken by Tiffany himself. Its principal theme was that Nature — especially flowers — were the source of Tiffany's strength as a colorist. Writing in the belletristic prose of the early century, Howe described Tiffany:

> For years a Painter has given himself up to the peculiar study of transmitting beauties of nature to elements of decoration. Here has he lived for twenty years, working and resting and working again. The garden his school, the flower his companion, his friend and his inspirer.

Howe's article emphasized a view of Nature which was consistent with that of Gallé's. Just as Gallé's roots were "in the forest, along the streams . . . ," so too Tiffany's preference was for relatively simple and indigenous plants:

> Love of these native woods has led to their preservation. They are not simply tolerated, but preferred. [Then, in the voice of Tiffany:] "This is the natural home of the birch, both black and yellow; of the chestnut and of the oak. Occasionally an evergreen pine or hemlock darkens or a dogwood brightens things. We have also maple and silver beech. When the old chestnuts get disturbed, — blown over and uprooted, or die out, we plant others of the same kind, and so restore the woods." . . . The same catholicity of taste rejects double flowers

where single ones are to be had. . . . The circular rose garden is . . . a crown of glory filled with the roses of yesterday. Not the highly cultivated darlings of fashionable society — prisoners of the greenhouse; but naturalized emigrants. . . .

The same "natural" program was maintained when Tiffany bought and transformed the adjoining property of Laurelton Hall.[65] Seemingly unsupervised mantles of daffodils, phlox and daylilies bloomed in their due seasons. Wisteria, myrtle, and golden creepers were encouraged to meander. One portion of the property, the so-called "Grandmother's Garden," contained jack-in-the-pulpits, bird's-eye violets, ferns and other wild plants which Tiffany, his children, and his thirty-five gardeners transplanted from their natural habitat.

Apropos of the creeping vines which covered The Briars and the walls of its garden, harmonizing the disparate parts of the rambling architecture, Howe expressed sentiments which were presumably Tiffany's own and which are very much akin to those which Gallé expressed about the grape vines on *The Roads of Autumn* transforming the cabinet from something man-made into something which seemed to have risen from the ground:

The creepers frame the openings, giving a charm and graceful unity to everything. They are great travellers, verily — tramps. They go underground, across door-heads, over cornices, stopping up gutters, filling odd corners, doing no end of mischief. . . . Yet who would check them, the truants. What harmonizers! What decorative artists! . . . Can architectural embellishment, pediment or cornice surpass the fringe of living glory presented by the creepers? Always in style; exempt from even the dictation of Dame Fashion! Always mellowing, softening, harmonizing withersoever they go.[66]

The correspondences between Tiffany's activities as artist and horticulturist are striking. On one level we could note the direct, one-to-one relationship between the plants in his art and those which grew on his Long Island properties. The apple blossoms of his lamps, the ferns of his ceramic vase, the jack-in-the-pulpit on his enamel, the saxifrage of his candlestick, these and almost all his motifs found their parallel if not their very inspiration in the plants on his estate. But if the artist was a horticulturist, the horticulturist was also an artist, an artist who planned for color harmonies, who planned a cooler palette of flowers in one area to blend with the fog which rose from the harbor, and who set "the intense russet brown and green of the red cedar" against the "emerald copper of the roof."[67] For Tiffany, art and Nature were inseparably bound.

This is not to say that Tiffany and his employees remained totally unmoved by the appearance of the High Art Nouveau style in Europe. The butterfly lamp, with its movement-filled metal and glass structure comes remarkably close to some of Horta's cage-like glazed domes. Also, I wonder if the fabulous Havemeyer punch bowl was not designed, at least in part, as Tiffany's response to Europe's new style. These were unusually forceful expressions for Tiffany, but they were exceptional and from a seemingly short-lived moment.

Rarely does one find a Tiffany design in which floral elements have even been stylized into rhythmic patterns. Only occasionally, in a few lampshades or objects, are floral motifs presented with a rhythmic flourish. Tiffany was not as bold as Grasset in stylizing natural forms. For Tiffany the natural motif itself was the chief element of his art. Confirmation of this point of view can again be found in the writings of Samuel Howe:

by their refreshment at the fountain of Nature, the architects, sculptors and decorators of France have been able to give a new impetus of growth to certain forms and branches of the Fine Arts. But the new graft has dangerous tendencies which must be cut off in their budding stage. Otherwise, degeneracy will ensue. The 'art nouveau' ornament in the hands of a master who knows how to stay his touch, is beautiful and soothing to the eye. . . . But the same system of ornament given over to the power of an insincere draughtsman is only to be avoided and censured. The obscured plant-form becomes in this case a non-structural wavy line, which is repeated and echoed in some dragon or reptile type, or in the tortured anatomy and drapery of a female figure. . . . In ornament we need, we must have, life. But we must purify it of that destructive, restless line which seems to set it in motion without measure or rhythm . . .[68]

It is understandable that Tiffany railed against the most avant-garde developments, as in 1913 when he returned from Paris and was quoted as saying, "the cubists are hammering away, but I think they will peter out."[69] (A few years later he explained that it is called "modern because it can't be called art.")[70] But Tiffany eschewed most of the bold ideas of High Art Nouveau, especially those of abstraction and linear dynamics. In fact, he never even accepted the stylistic innovations of the Post-Impressionists of the 1890s.

Much has been made of the fact that in 1895 Bing commissioned Tiffany to translate designs by Toulouse Lautrec, Bonnard, Ranson, Vuillard, and other Nabis into leaded windows. But, as celebrated and well-received as these windows were at the time of their creation, they seem to have offered little inspiration to Tiffany and his staff. The windows and mosaics they made thereafter utilized little of the flatness and abstract pattern-making that the works of the French artists should have inspired. Tiffany's figurative windows after 1900 still bore the dulling effects of nineteenth-century academic propriety, and certainly shunned all the modernistic elements of design that he could have learnt from Bonnard and Ranson. Major figurative windows, such as The Bathers of 1914, which Tiffany praised highly because of the realism of the flesh tones, seem to me like hopeless anachronisms by contrast.

Tiffany's aesthetics ran in a different direction. Realism was the quality he vaunted when describing the window exhibited in 1893 at Chicago: "there is portrayed a number of paroquets resting upon a branch of a fruit-tree in blossom, from which is hanging a globe of gold fishes; the effect produced is most realistic . . ."[71] Another window, the Woman Feeding Flamingoes, was described as "far more realistic. . . ."[72] Twenty years later, two such windows, one with a peacock and the other with parakeets, both amid blossom-laden branches, were still being praised for the same qualities of verisimilitude: "The stately and majestic air of the bird is naturally depicted . . . The opalescence, iridescence and beauty of finish of the Favrile glass have made possible accuracy of perspective and reality in atmospheric effect."[73] And is it not this same drive toward realism which explains why he introduced the paperweight vases and, still later, the aquamarine vases — in which naturalistic morning glories, gladioli, and water lilies are imbedded within the walls of the vessel? Far from accepting the stylistic innovations of abstraction and of two-dimensionality, Tiffany in fact remained true to an older idea of beauty.[74]

The absence of modernism of design is perhaps less distressful in his landscapes and floral compositions. In major late commissions, such as the Dream Garden of 1915 designed by

Maxfield Parrish (in itself a significant barometer of taste) or the 1911 theater curtain for the National Theater of Mexico, the works are redeemed by their abundance of extraordinary color and their profusion of flowering plants – the strengths on which Tiffany always drew, but not by avant-garde qualities of design.

Tiffany did not become more adventurous in the years after 1900. On the contrary, there was an undercurrent of conservatism, an element which seems to have grown as the artist aged. The small *objets d'art* of glass, enamels, ceramic and jewelry often exhibit a restraint of form and decoration. Unlike the sculptural boldness of the earliest floral lamps, such as the butterfly, spider web, lily cluster and wisteria lamps which speak the organic language that Gallé had espoused, most of the later floral lamps such as the poppy and magnolia (and these are the ones to which we have become accustomed), have formal, domed shades and bronze standards that recall the type of academic exercise that Edme Couty proposed. Although interior decoration did not form an important part of his career as it had before, and he was further estranged from this area than from others, still, whereas the pre-1890 rooms were noted for their eccentric blending of exotic styles as well as their richness of colors and odd materials, those after 1900 were more formal in character and were executed in "proper" period styles.

One might wish that Tiffany in his late years – like Michelangelo, Titian, Rembrandt and Monet – would have broken old boundaries and extended his vision even further. His rich sense of color and his poetic view of Nature might have led to an *ultima maniera* like those of so many great masters and which Gallé himself had. But in the case of Tiffany, this seems not to have occurred.

Tiffany's age and conservatism (he was fifty-two years old when the twentieth century began) also help to explain why historicism remained such a strong part of his later career. Modern writers are relatively at ease in noting this aspect in his early career, but his work in this mode after 1900 seems to have become a troublesome matter. For the greater part, it has been de-emphasized or, more generally, entirely neglected. In the attempt to minimize these elements in Tiffany's late work – a contradiction to the popular belief that "modernism" implies a break with the past – there has been a lot of fancy footwork. But it remains clear that there were specific references to such modes of thought in Tiffany's work.

It was in the years after 1900 that Tiffany produced his glass vases in red (a difficult color, technically) whose forms clearly imitated Chinese vases and whose color imitated *sang de boeuf* glazes. In these same years he introduced the feathered pattern known, appropriately enough, as "the Egyptian collar". And then there were the scores of desk sets in the *Byzantine, Chinese, American Indian, Ninth Century, Louis XVI,* and *Adam* styles. The latter formal styles were extended to Tiffany Studios' lighting fixtures, Aubusson rugs and complete suites of Adam, Hepplewhite and Queen Anne furniture.[75]

These borrowings could occasionally strike a positive note. For example, in his lava glass, the molten cascades of glass are so bold and the forms so free, that we may overlook the frequent resemblances to Japanese ceramic water containers. If for a moment we turn back to Gallé, we might note that he too occasionally reverted to such historicizing elements, even late in his career. His *Gentian* vase, for example, despite its floral allusion, is clearly based on an ancient Chinese bronze form, and some of his late *marqueterie de verre* bowls are clearly based on Japanese tea bowls and ivories.[76]

For the main part, Tiffany's historicism revealed an artist whose artistic career belonged to the late nineteenth century. One might be tempted to say that such historicizing designs were made solely in response to the conservative nature of his American carriage-trade clientele, but we need only turn to Laurelton Hall to realize that it was Tiffany's taste as well. That house has come in for a great amount of unwarranted praise in recent years. At the time of the first Tiffany retrospective, Robert Koch called it "the finest example of mature Art Nouveau architecture in the United States," and this sentiment has been repeated by many critics.[77] But far from having anything to do with the High Art Nouveau architecture of Horta or Guimard, it is wholeheartedly and unabashedly an exercise in the Neo-Islamic mode. Tiffany himself did not call it Art Nouveau or modern; he termed it "Persian."[78] Indeed, it had cusped horseshoe arches, a power generating station disguised as a minaret, walls stenciled with designs from Topkapi Palace, and the chief feature of the interior was a channeled spring that emerged in the central court which, as Tiffany himself explained, followed the Near Eastern tradition of venerating water.

Not all the rooms at Laurelton Hall were Near Eastern. The dining room's accent was Chinese, and a number of rooms displayed Tiffany's collections of Japanese and American Indian objects with a Victorian *horror vacui*. To me, the building seems the late expression of an artist who thirty years earlier had been decorating interiors with the same exotic and historicizing features.

There were, of course, saving graces at Laurelton Hall. What makes so many of the architectural elements charming is not their archaeological accuracy but, rather, the way in which Tiffany introduced colorful floral elements, as in the glass flowers he used atop the

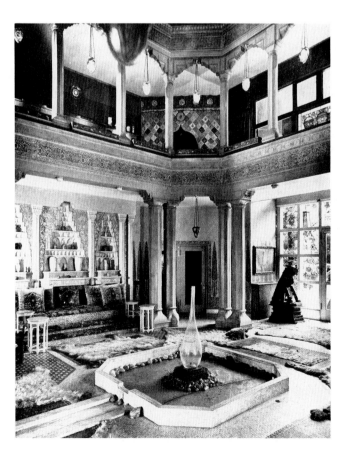

The central court of Tiffany's Long Island mansion, Laurelton Hall, 1902-05. (Photo courtesy of private collector)

Moorish arches of the portico. Likewise, one of the major terraces, despite its imported Algerian ceiling and niches, was built around a live pear tree, and glass tiles with a pear motif surrounded the opening, just as bunches of glass daffodils adorned the many columns. Nature and glass were where Tiffany found his forte.

Tiffany's close association with flowers is clearly registered in the portrait commissioned from Sorolla in 1911. The sixty-three-year-old Tiffany is shown in his garden, posed as a painter. Perhaps unwittingly, this portrait echoes a type which became very popular at the end of the nineteenth century — the artist inspired by the muse of Nature. And there is no better example of a predecessor than the one Victor Prouvé painted of Gallé. It shows Gallé as a divinely inspired modern evangelist, a halo of light surrounding him as he intently studies various examples of flora and fauna. By comparison, Sorolla's portrait of Tiffany is far more mundane; there is none of the mystical or programmatic nature of Prouvé's work. But clearly, this is the way that Tiffany saw himself — in his garden, trying to capture the fleeting beauty of Nature. It is this portrait which was chosen to serve as the frontispiece of the biography, *The Art Work of Louis C. Tiffany*, commissioned at the same time from Charles De Kay.

The publication of this biography suggests a retrospective mood and perhaps Tiffany's own recognition of the approaching end of his artistic career. He was already sixty-six years old and the most innovative portion of his work had come to an end some years earlier. It was not that much different for Gallé; his career had come to a premature end in 1904 when he was felled by leukemia. Those years just before and after 1900 had been the period of their greatest creativity. It was then that each brought his art to full maturity, an art which had been stimulated by the achievements of the past and by the beauty of Nature.

Victor Prouvé's portrait of Emile Gallé, 1892.

The portrait of Louis Comfort Tiffany by Joaquin Sorolla, 1911. (Photo courtesy of the Hispanic Society of America, New York)

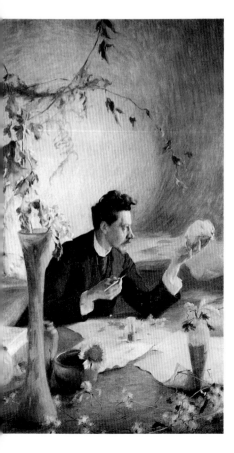

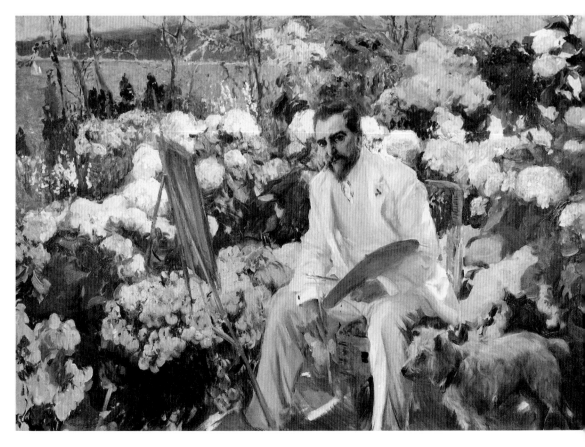

# NOTES

1. Some of this material has been presented in the form of speeches over the last decade, and I perhaps owe as much to those who held opposing viewpoints as to my supporters, for their challenges led me to pursue the subject even further. I hope that my arguments have been strengthened. On this occasion I am especially thankful to Alastair Duncan for his generous sharing of documentation with me, and I am indebted to Ellen Davidson for her skill and patience in typing my manuscript.

2. On the exceptional occasion when Alfred D.F. Hamlin ("Style in Architecture," *The Craftsman*, 8 [1905], 331), hailed "the emancipating influences of the so-called 'Art Nouveau' (whereof Tiffany and Sullivan are the first true prophets)," he used the term "Art Nouveau" in its widest, most generic meaning of "modern" style. In fact, Hamlin specifically separated Sullivan and Tiffany from what he described as "the architectural nightmares to which it [Art Nouveau] has given rise in France, Germany and Belgium." Hamlin rejected the essence of High Art Nouveau style and clearly did not see Tiffany as part of that movement. Since most American critics were wary of European Art Nouveau (howsoever they understood the name) but were enthusiastic about Tiffany, their separation of the style and the artist has this second significance as well.

3. Philip Johnson, "Decorative Art a Generation Ago," *Creative Art*, 12 (April 1933), 297-99. To keep things in proper chronological perspective we should note that Tiffany had just died on January 17 of that very same year.

4. "L'Art Nouveau," *Interiors*, 101 (March 1942), 42.

5. *Um 1900, Art Nouveau und Jugendstil* (Zurich: Kunstgewerbemuseum, 1952) 12, 39, pl. 24.

6. Thomas S. Tibbs in Robert Koch, *Louis Comfort Tiffany* (New York: Museum of Contemporary Crafts, 1958), 5.

7. Peter Selz and Mildred Constantine, eds., *Art Nouveau* (New York: Museum of Modern Art, 1960), 105-6, 182.

8. Mario Amaya, "The Taste for Tiffany," *Apollo*, 81 (February 1965), 102, and *idem, Tiffany Glass* (New York 1967), 7.

9. *Tiffany's Tiffany* (Corning: Corning Museum of Glass, 1980), foreword.

10. Diane Chalmers Johnson, *American Art Nouveau* (New York 1979), 37.

11. S. Bing, "L'Art Nouveau," *Architectural Record*, 12 (June 1902), 280-81.

12. On this change of direction see Martin Eidelberg, *E. Colonna* (Dayton: Dayton Art Institute, 1983), 30-53.

13. Even then, the chronological conjoining of Guimard and Gallé poses great problems. Although both men were at the peaks of their careers in the years just before and after 1900, Guimard's style had just evolved in the mid-1890s, whereas Gallé had been at work for several decades and, as we shall see, his vision belongs to an earlier generation and an earlier period.

14. *19th-Century America* (New York: The Metropolitan Museum of Art, 1970), nos. 269, 272, 284. Apropos of the lamp base, it was described as showing "no recognizable plant form." However, the name of this model proves to be *Bird Skeleton*. In that it thus has an identifiable and natural motif, one wonders how the authors of the catalogue would now describe its style.

15. Robert Koch, *Rebel in Glass* (New York 1964), 158; *idem, Louis C. Tiffany's Glass-Bronzes-Lamps* (New York 1971), 100.

16. Ellen P. and Bert R. Denkers in Wendy Kaplan *et al, "The Art that is Life:" The Arts and Crafts Movement in America, 1875-1920* (Boston: Museum of Fine Arts, 1987), 153. It should be noted that this vase appears under the category "Art Nouveau." For further discussion of the style of this vase, see below (n. 61).

17. Robert Schmutzler, *Art Nouveau* (New York 1964), 14.

18. I am thinking of the type of Japanese water and air patterns that were copied on Japoniste objects, and that could also be transformed, especially in the 1880s, into ornamental calligraphy. The relation and disjuncture between this phase and High Art Nouveau is recorded in the famous photograph of Van de Velde's wife modeling an Art Nouveau dress. While her costume has the modern type of "Belgian-line" design, the organic type of Japanese pattern can be seen in the pictures on the wall behind her; presumably Japanese, one is of carp and the other is of flying birds, both set against swirling, linear patterns. The relation between Eastern patterns and the new Western tradition was often noted at the turn of the century. See, for example, Marcel Bing, "Japan," in Richard Graul, ed., *Die Krisis in Kunstgewerbe* (Leipzig 1901), 87.

19. Thérèse Charpentier, "La clientèle étrangère de Gallé, *21st International Congress of the History of Art* (Berlin 1967) 3 vols., 1:258.

20. Normally one takes great pains to separate Louis C. Tiffany's operations from Tiffany and Company, since the bond of the family name has often created confusion. However, it might be equally useful to study their possible interaction. There is a commonality of thought between the styles they favored: the Japanesque,

Saracenic, Celtic, American Indian and even Naturalistic. The type of jeweled flower that Tiffany and Company produced foreshadows the later art jewelry designed by Louis Tiffany. Unfortunately, limitations of space prevent further discussion at this time.

21. A.R. de Liesville, "La Céramique au Champ de Mars," *Gazette des Beaux-Arts*, s.2, 18 (1878), 687.

22. *Idem*, "La Verrerie au Champ de Mars," *Gazette des Beaux-Arts*, s.2, 18 (1878), 701.

23. Adrien Dubouché, "Poteries décoratives," in Victor de Luynes, ed., *Rapport du jury international. Classe 20. Rapport sur la cèramique* (Paris 1882), 103.

24. Lucien Falize [under the pseudonym of "M. Josse"], "L'art japonais," *Revue des arts décoratifs*, 3 (1882-3), 300-31.

25. Ary Renan, "Hokusai's 'Man-gwa,'" *Artistic Japan*, 2 (1889), 103.

26. For example, see Eugène Grasset's introduction to Maurice P. Verneuil, *L'Animal dans la décoration* (Paris 1897), III: "L'Extrême-Orient nous a également montré quelles peuvent être les resources qu'offrent les formes animales bien traitées, aussi bien dans les bronzes, fers ciselés . . .; oeuvres d'art dans toute l'acception du mot, dignes de toute admiration et de constante étude, non pour les copier, mais pour y trouver le secret du style."

27. Some of Gallé's scientific writings are conveniently brought together in *Ecrits pour l'art* (1908; Marseille: Lafitte Reprìnts, 1980). As his widow pointed out in her apology for including these essays together with those on art, "Si Emile Gallé a renouvelé l'art décoratif, c'est pour avoir étudié la plante, l'arbre, la fleur à la fois en artiste et en savant; see *ibid.*, vi.

28. Edmond Bazire, "La Verrerie et la Cristallerie," *Revue des arts décoratifs*, 5 (1884-85), 193.

29. For some of the history of this project see Lucien Falize, "Une Exposition de la plante," *Revue des arts décoratifs*, 11 (1890-91), 1-7; Victor Champier, "L'Exposition de la Plante," *ibid.*, 351-52; Falize, "Histoire d'une exposition ajournée," *ibid.*, 12 (1891-92), 225-42; E. Gallé, "Encore l'Exposition de la Plante," *ibid.*, 377-80. Repercussions of the aborted project could still be felt after the turn of the century; see *Art et décoration*, 13 (May 1903), supplement, 1-4.

30. Emile Gallé, "La Table aux Herbes potagères," *Revue des arts décoratifs*, 12 (1891-92), 381-83. Falize told how he wanted to create a silver tea service with a similar decor of kitchen vegetables but he was defeated by Bouilhet who modified its design to a more "proper" Louis XV style.

31. A similar thought, "Ma racine est au fond des bois," had appeared already on a Gallé vase of 1889; this was pointed out by Thérèse Charpentier, "L'art de Gallé a-t-il été influencé par Baudelaire?," *Gazette des Beaux Arts*, s.6, 61 (1963), 370.

32. For one of Gallé's most detailed accounts, see his "Le mobilier contemporain orné d'après la nature," *Revue des arts décoratifs*, 20 (1900), 333-41, 365-77.

33. Emile Gallé, "Chemins d'automne," *Revue des arts décoratifs*, 13 (1892-93), 332-35.

34. The influence of Baudelaire on Gallé was challenged by Charpentier, "L'art de Gallé a-t-il été influencé par Baudelaire?," 367-74. However, Charpentier's thesis is short-sighted; it is not a statistical issue of how many times Gallé used poetic inscriptions, much less specific phrases from Baudelaire, or how infrequently Gallé directly "illustrated" Baudelaire's themes. The important issue is how Gallé interpreted the poetic intent of Baudelaire and the Symbolists.

35. Lucien Falize, "A propos de la ciselure," *Revue des arts décoratifs*, 3 (1882-3), 311.

36. For the designer, see Gustave Soulier, "Edme Couty," *Art et décoration*, 5 (January 1899), 1-15. The program of deriving a new decorative vocabulary from natural forms was a longstanding and almost academic one, and designs like Couty's could well be compared to those offered in Victor Marie Charles Ruprich-Robert, *Flore ornementale* (Paris 1866-76).

37. Robert Koch, "Tiffany's Abstractions in Glass," *Antiques*, 105 (June 1974), 1290-94, claims that the artist was "a master of abstraction," and repeats Mario Amaya's contention that Tiffany glass contained "the seeds of American abstract-expressionist painting. . . ." Such arguments not only misread the nature of Tiffany's art but are also taking a thesis popular in the 1950s—that the decorative arts from the turn of the century need to be justified as "early Modern"—and pushing it to what I believe is an extreme and unwarranted conclusion. Nonetheless, it has become imbedded in popular thought; see Tessa Paul, *The Art of Louis Comfort Tiffany* (New York 1987), 124.

38. Such statistics are offered only as a general—not an exact mathematical—indication. First not all the windows were of recent vintage. The *Eggplant* window was apparently the one from c. 1879 which was Tiffany's duplicate of the window installed in the Kemp house. One of the cartoons was for the 1885 window with flowers and bowls of goldfish made for Mary Elizabeth Garrett; the two replicas are illustrated in Horace Townsend, "American and French Applied Art at the Grafton Galleries," *Studio*, 8 (July 1899), 39. More importantly, though, most of Tiffany's ecclesiastical and allegorical windows were of a large scale and not as easily transportable to such expositions. Thus, major commissions such as that for St. Michael's Church were represented by cartoons or studio presentation drawings.

39. The Smithsonian Institution acquired a large group of thirty-eight items made in 1894. Henry Havemeyer presented fifty-six examples to the Metropolitan Museum of Art in New York in 1896, and the Cincinnati Art Museum acquired twenty-eight pieces in 1897. A number of European museums bought Tiffany glass early on, most notably the Victoria and Albert Museum in London, the Musée des arts décoratifs and the Musée de Luxembourg in Paris, the Kunstgewerbe Museum in Berlin, and the Österreichisches Museum für angewandte Kunst in Vienna. Also, some were illustrated in the firm's early advertisements. The uniformity of types of glass and of systems of markings, be it paper labels or etched registry numbers, is manifest throughout these documented examples. This warns us against accepting a theory advanced by Hugh F. McKean, *The "Lost" Treasures of Louis Comfort Tiffany* (Garden City 1980), 150-51, 162, 281, that a number of pieces bearing an etched "TGC" monogram (standing for the Tiffany Glass Co.) represent a still earlier and hitherto unknown phase of Tiffany's entry into the field of blown glass vessels. As I hope to show on a future occasion, the etched marks are spurious, recent additions. Some of this glass may have been made by Tiffany or his competition, but after 1900, and I believe that at least one example may be of relatively recent manufacture.

40. *Tiffany Favrile Glass* (New York: Tiffany Studios, 1898).

41. As early as 1878 Tiffany and Company was selling "Facsimiles of the Trojan Iridescent Bronze Glass exhumed by Dr. Schliemann." See Mary Louise McLaughlin, *China Painting* (Cincinnati 1878), advertisement at end of book. Was this perhaps *Bronze Glass* made by Thomas Webb & Sons? See Victor Arwas, *Glass, Art Nouveau to Art Deco* (New York 1977), 244.

42. One type of ornament was a threaded overlay resembling the wire cages into which some of the glass was blown for lamp bases. Occasionally it misled a hapless editor; thus the photo of such a vase in Gardner C. Teall, "The Art of Things," *Brush and Pencil*, 4 (September 1899), 302, is misidentified as "vase in glass, blown through metal binding. . . ." While some may want to view this type of orientalizing configuration as Art Nouveau or Proto Art Nouveau, it is, rather, symmetrical and typical of the way that Tiffany could exploit one tradition or medium to create another. Similarly, a wave-like pattern which Tiffany liked and exploited as a stock-in-trade pattern was known as "Damascene" because of its resemblance to the pattern found in mixed metals (Damascene swords, Japanese *mokume*) and which Tiffany and Company had likewise imitated, but in the original materials.

43. Charpentier, "La clientèle étrangère de Gallé," 259, 261-62.

44. It should be recalled that Tiffany's plant manager, Arthur J. Nash, had previously been a manager of the Thomas Webb Glasshouse, and had proposed that Tiffany's factory be baptised "The Stourbridge Glass Works

of Corona." See Koch, *Tiffany's Glass-Bronzes-Lamps*, 63, n.2.

45. One is illustrated in the firm's publicity brochure, *Tiffany Favrile Glass* (1896); reproduced in Koch, *Tiffany's Glass-Bronzes-Lamps*, 43. Another is in W.R. Bradshaw, "Favrile Glass," *The House Beautiful*, 7 (April 1900), 279.

46. Some early lamps are illustrated in an early publicity brochure: *Tiffany Favrile Glass-Lamps* (New York: Tiffany Studios, 1898). Part of it is reproduced in Koch, *Tiffany's Glass-Bronzes-Lamps*, 120-21. Also see "Moderne Beleuchtungskörper," *Dekorative Kunst*, 1 (1898), 11-12; Cecilia Waern, "The Industrial Arts of America: II," *Studio*, 14 (July 1898) 20; "L.C. Tiffany," *Dekorative Kunst*, 3 (1899), 113-15; Egon Neustadt, *The Lamps of Tiffany* (New York 1970), 141. Few of these have stayed intact; see William Feldstein, Jr. and Alastair Duncan, *The Lamps of Tiffany Studios* (New York and London 1983), 64-65. Tiffany Studios later paired these early bases with floral shades; see Neustadt, *The Lamps of Tiffany*, 141.

47. *Exhibition of L'Art Nouveau, S. Bing, Paris* (London: Grafton Galleries, 1899), 22: "Lamps and Metal Work . . . 8. Portable oil lamp in silver plate and glass with crab-feet." One such lamp with a crab base and a metal filigree shade is illustrated by W.R. Bradshaw, "Favrile Glass," *The House Beautiful*, 7 (April 1900), 278. For another lamp with a crab base but with a leaf-patterned blown glass shade (unlike most of the early blown shades which had more abstract "feathering"), see Alastair Duncan, *Tiffany at Auction* (New York 1981), 117, no. 317. Also, some later variants have crab bases paired with leaded shades of geometric or floral patterns; see Duncan, *Tiffany at Auction*, 77, 96; Feldstein and Duncan, *The Lamps of Tiffany Studios*, 70, 71; Neustadt, *The Lamps of Tiffany*, 97.

48. *Exhibition of L'Art Nouveau, S. Bing, Paris*, 22: "7. Portable oil lamp in green bronze and glass with leaded shade, dragon-fly shade." It would seem that this was the lamp model which was exhibited at Paris in 1900 and in Turin in 1902, and whose design is attributed to Clara Driscoll. It is illustrated, e.g., "Die Sektion Amerika," *Dekorative Kunst*, 11 (November 1902), 57. Recent publications have confused the matter by identifying several variants of dragonfly shades on all sorts of bases as the lamp designed by Driscoll.

49. The lamp's early date is assured by a photo of it in Teall, "The Art of Things," 309.

50. *Exhibition of L'Art Nouveau, S. Bing*, "Lamps and Metal Work," 32-35. Such a flowered inkwell (the dahlia?) is illustrated in Teall, "The Art of Things," 311.

51. Interview between the author and Julia Munson Sherman on December 8, 1969. Mrs. Sherman later took charge of the enameling and jewelry departments as well. Although in her mid-nineties, she had precise recall regarding certain aspects of Tiffany's and her work.

52. This explanation was apparently voiced often and thus is repeated by reporters such as Alfred Wechsler (under the pseudonym of A.W. Fred), "Glas und Keramik auf der Pariser Weltausstellung," *Kunst und Kunsthandwerk*, 3 (1900), 388; *idem*, "Interieur von L.C. Tiffany," *Dekorative Kunst*, 9 (December 1901), 114.

53. See Gardner Teall, "Artistic American Wares at Expositions," *Brush and Pencil*, 6 (July 1900), 179-80; Samuel Howe, "Enamel as a Decorative Agent," *The Craftsman*, 2 (May 1902), opp. 61, 62; James L. Harvey, "Source of Beauty in Favrile Glass," *Brush and Pencil*, 9 (January 1902), 175; "Die Sektion Amerika," *Dekorative Kunst*, 11 (November 1902), 55; Gabriel Weisberg, *Art Nouveau Bing* (New York 1986), 210.

54. Howe, "Enamel As a Decorative Agent," 66. While this anecdote is often repeated, a related remark has been overlooked. A few years later Howe recalled this experiment and suggested that it should have been conducted in Tiffany's garden at The Briars, because "Beautiful flowers have supplied a standard of measurement by which the colors of opalescent glass, enamel, aniline and dyes can be adjusted and their true importance determined." See Howe, "One Source of Color Values," *House and Garden*, 10 (September 1906), 110.

55. For the origins of this department see Martin Eidelberg, "Tiffany Favrile Pottery," *Connoisseur*, 166 (September 1968), 57-61; and *idem*, "American Ceramics and International Styles, 1876-1916," Princeton University Art Museum *Record*, 34, no. 2 (1975), 17-19.

56. See "Louis C. Tiffany and his Work in Artistic Jewelry," *International Studio*, 30 (December 1906), xxxii-xlii; also the photograph albums in the archives of Tiffany and Company.

57. Also germane is Tiffany and Company's practice of mounting Favrile glass vases with precious metals and stones; see "The Tiffany Display at Paris," *The Art Interchange*, 44 (May 1900), 112-13. The mounted vases were exhibited by Tiffany and Company, not by Tiffany Studios, but the two groups had adjoining displays in the one stand.

58. Interview with J.M. Sherman.

59. See Gary A. Reynolds, *Louis Comfort Tiffany: The Paintings* (New York: New York University, Grey Art Gallery, 1979), 43, 51-2, 59-60; McKean, *"Lost" Treasures*, 251-4. I would also point out that at the turn of the century Tiffany maintained a photographic darkroom in the water tower at The Briars; see Howe, "One Source of Color Values," 111.

60. I am indebted to Alastair Duncan for this information.

61. Albert Christian Revi, *American Art Nouveau Glass* (Nashville 1968), 87-89, wrote apropos of certain ceramics, including a version of this form, that specimen plants were sprayed with shellac until they became rigid, were then electroplated with copper, and plaster molds were then made. While technically possible (Christofle had specialized in such extravagances at mid-century), if there is any foundation to Revi's story it would be apropos of Tiffany's original enameled copper vases and more appropriate in terms of the metallic medium. The same sort of supposition regarding casts from life was raised by Ellen P. and Bert R. Denker; see Kaplan *et al.*, *"The Art that is Life,"* 153. Ironically, they raise that issue while discussing the very same ceramic jack-in-the-pulpit vase but, apparently unaware of Revi's statement, they refute the idea that this vase could have been cast from life and, on the other hand, contend that a ceramic vase decorated with Queen Anne's lace "appears to be based on an actual bouquet that has been frozen in plaster."

62. There are interesting parallels between Scandinavian porcelains and many of Tiffany's enamels and ceramics. One relatively close correspondence is between a Tiffany ceramic form and a Bing & Gröndahl pierced vase with a snake curled among plants; illustrated in Martin Eidelberg, ed., *From Our Native Clay* (New York 1987), 20, no. 141, and *Art et Décoration*, 8 (1900), 191, respectively. This can be explained not only because Scandinavia had been influenced by the same cult of Nature which had arisen in France, but also because the chief Tiffany designer for those things may have been a Danish woman, as per an interview between the author and Julia Munson Sherman on March 28, 1969. Supposedly she also did some sculptures of animals recalling those done at the Royal Copenhagen factory, but Tiffany did not like them. Mrs. Sherman could not remember her name, but recalled that her fiancé was a Danish married man who had problems divorcing his wife. Once he accomplished this, the Danish woman returned to her native land.

63. Louis C. Tiffany, "Color and Its Kinship to Sound," *The Art World*, 2 (May 1917), 142. This thought would seem to be one which Tiffany expressed earlier in his career. Teall, "The Art of Things," 302, used the same idea, perhaps after speaking with the artist: "It is an old saying that everything in nature is beautiful and that nature cannot err."

64. Howe, "One Source of Color Values," 105-13.

65. See Samuel Howe, "The Garden of Mr. Louis Comfort Tiffany," *The House Beautiful*, 35 (January 1914), 40-42; also Martha Wren Briggs, "A Reconstruction of the Gardens of Louis Comfort Tiffany," *Long Island Estate Gardens* (Greenvale, New York: Hilwood Art Gallery, Long Island University, 1985), 4-13.

66. Howe, "One Source of Color Values," 107.

67. See especially Howe, "The Garden of Mr. Louis Comfort Tiffany."

68. Samuel Howe, "The Use of Ornament in the House," *The Craftsman*, 3 (November 1902), 91.

69.  "An Interview with Mr. Louis C. Tiffany," *The House Beautiful*, 34 (November 1913), 179.

70.  "'Modern Art' Not Art at All, Says Mr. L.C. Tiffany," *Evening Telegram*, February 30, 1916.

71.  *A Synopsis of the Exhibit of the Tiffany Glass and Decorating Company in the American Section of the Manufacture and Liberal Arts Building at the World's Fair* (New York: Tiffany Glass and Decorating Company, 1893), 8.

72.  *Ibid.*

73.  "A New Era in Domestic Glass," *Arts and Decoration*, 3 (June 1913), 288.

74.  When Tiffany showed his painting, *Egyptian Water Carriers*, at the 1873 Cincinnati Industrial Exposition, the catalogue for that exhibition (*Exhibition of Paintings, Engraving, Drawings, Aquarelles and Works of Household Art*, 26, no. 208) bore the simple editorial comment "Very realistic."

75.  For example, see *Character and Individuality in Decorations and Furnishings* (New York: Tiffany Studios, 1913).

76.  For a revealing comparison of one of Gallé's vases and the actual Japanese ivory prototype see Thérèse Charpentier, *Emile Gallé* (Nancy: Université de Nancy II, n.d.), 109.

77.  Koch, *Louis Comfort Tiffany* (1958), 14; see also Koch, *Rebel in Glass*, 142: "an almost Expressionist combination of simplified Art Nouveau forms with Islamic overtones;" McKean, *"Lost" Treasures*, 6: "the only major Art Nouveau residence built in America."

78.  See, for example, Samuel Howe, "The Silent Fountains of Laurelton Hall," *Arts and Decoration*, 3 (September 1913), 377-9, where not only is the analogy with a Moorish palace maintained, but also the locale of Cold Spring Harbor is likened to Palestine. The same accent upon the East – India, Persia, China and Japan – was emphasized at this time apropos of Tiffany's apartment in New York City; see Charles De Kay, "A Western Setting for the Beauty of the Orient," *Arts and Decoration*, 12 (October 1911), 468-72.

27.  Flowerform Vase, Favrile glass, 13" high, Tiffany Studios, New York, *c.* 1900

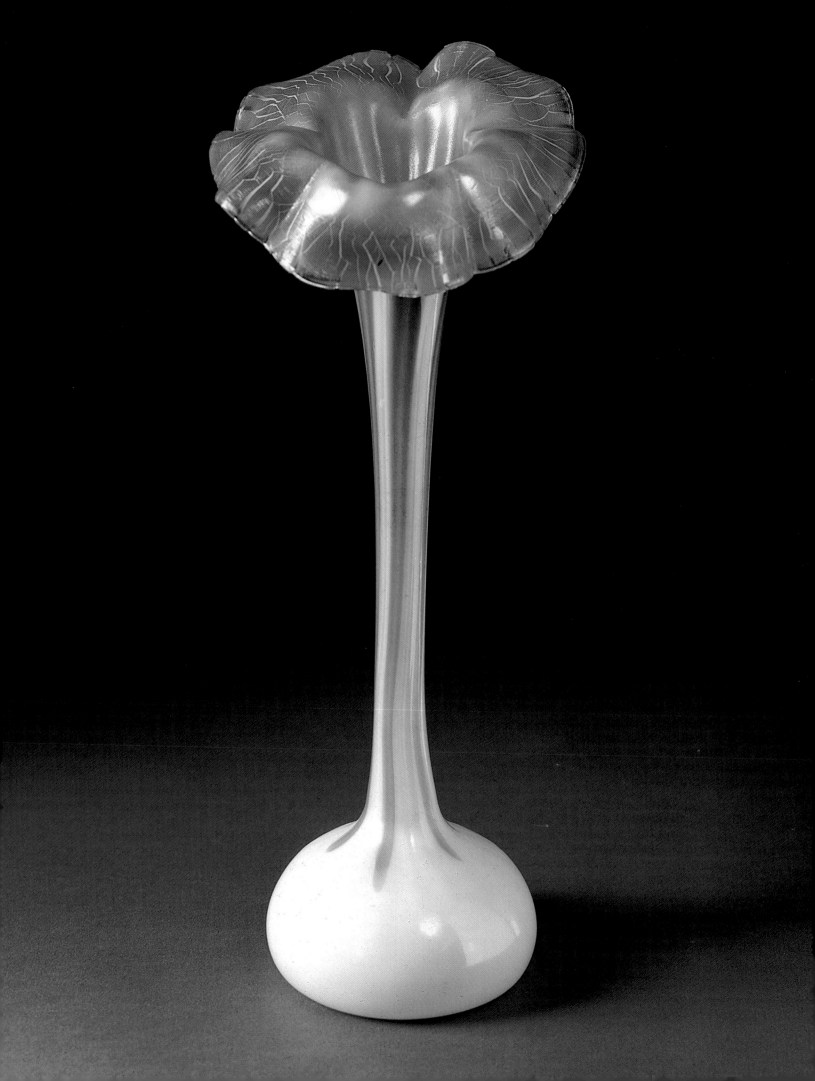

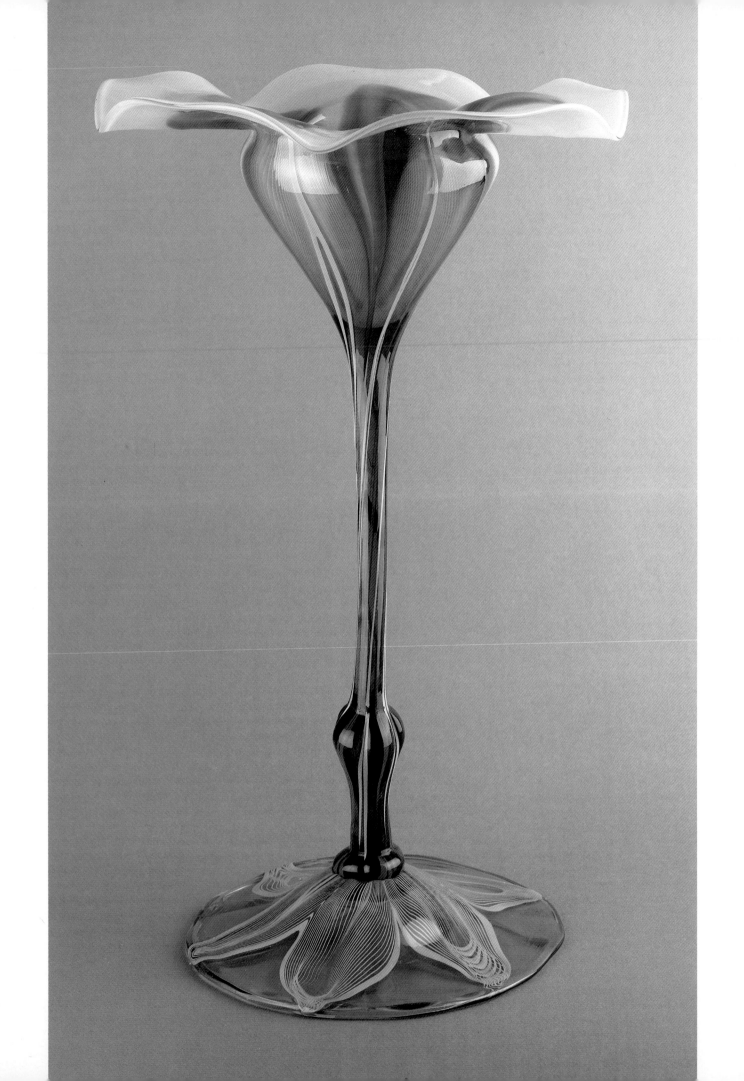

28. Flowerform Vase, Favrile glass,
14¼″ high, 6½″ diameter of base,
Tiffany Studios, New York, 1900-05

29. Reactive Paperweight Vase, Favrile
glass, 5⅞″ high, Tiffany Studios, New
York, 1900-05

30. Aquamarine Vase, Favrile glass,
15″ high, Tiffany Studios, New York,
1910-15

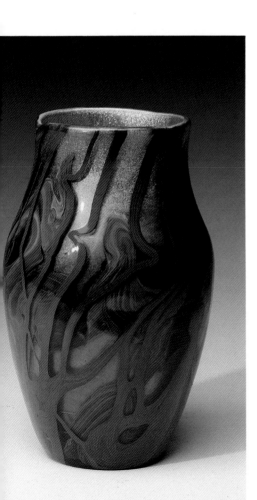

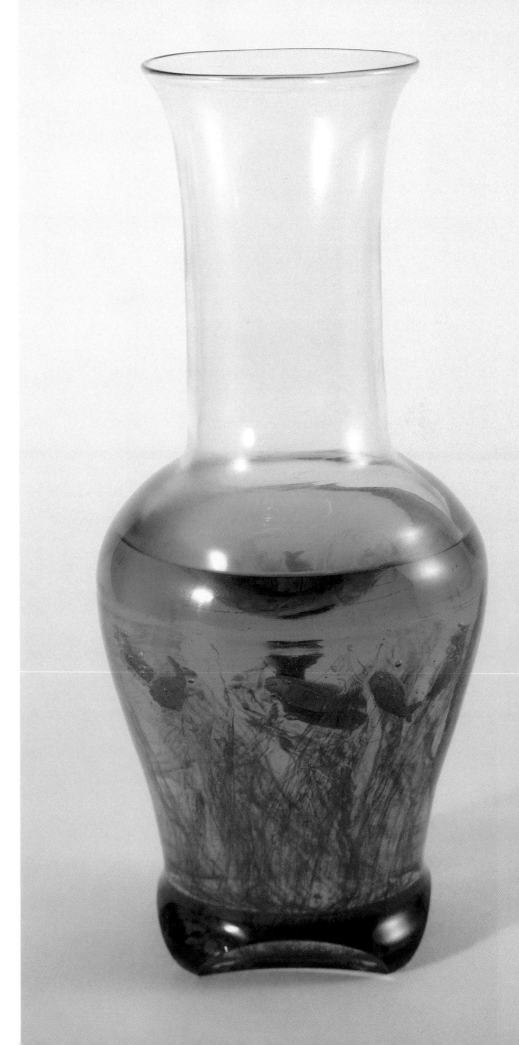

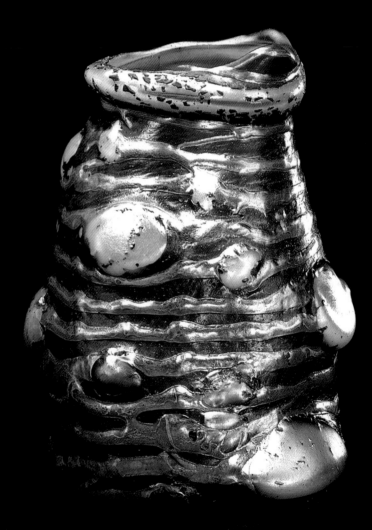

31. Lava Vase, Favrile glass, 5½″ high,
Tiffany Studios, New York, 1900-10

32. Lava Vase, Favrile lava glass, 14¾″
high, Tiffany Studios, New York, c. 1908

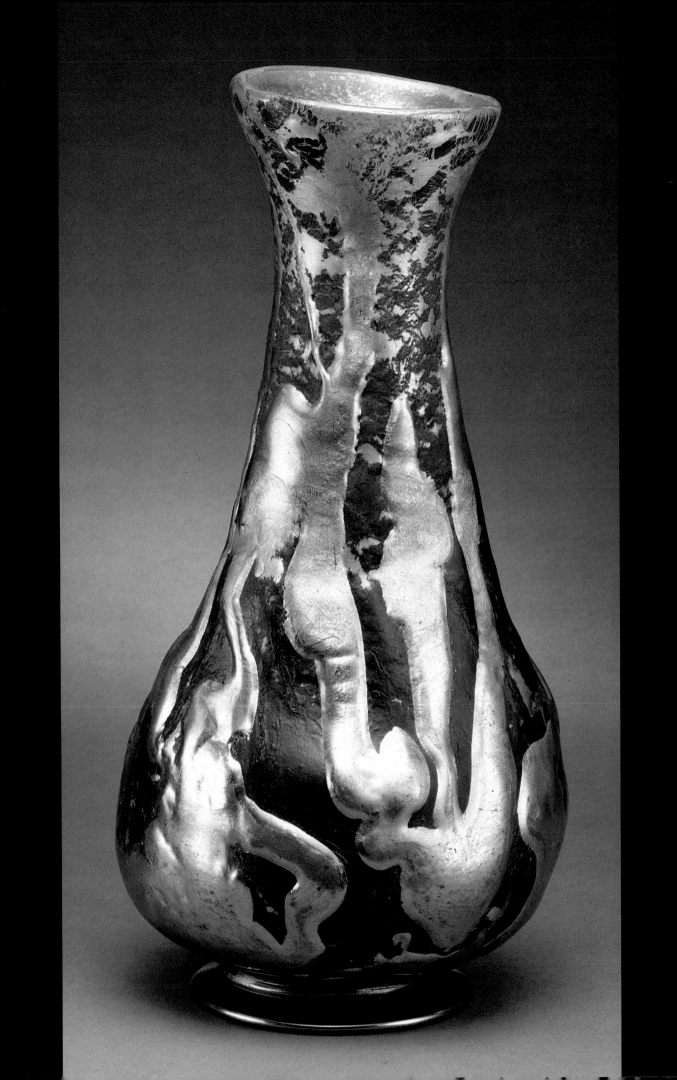

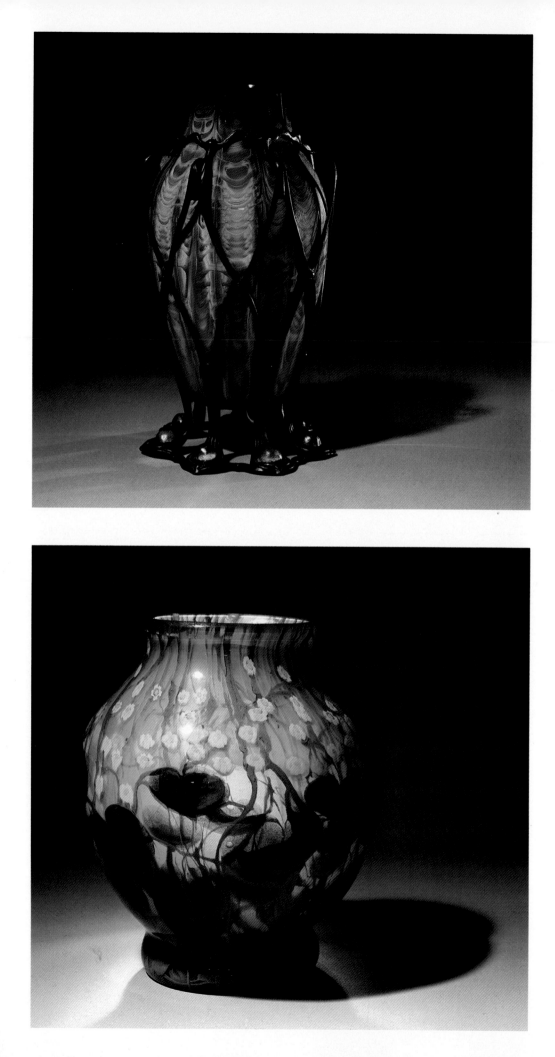

33. Mounted Agate Vase, Favrile glass with jeweled bronze mount, 10″ high, Tiffany Studios, New York, 1900-10

34. Millefiore Glass Vase, Favrile glass, 11¼″ high, Tiffany Studios, New York, 1895-1910

35. Cypriote Vase, Favrile glass, 9⁷⁄₁₆″ high, Tiffany Studios, New York, c. 1900

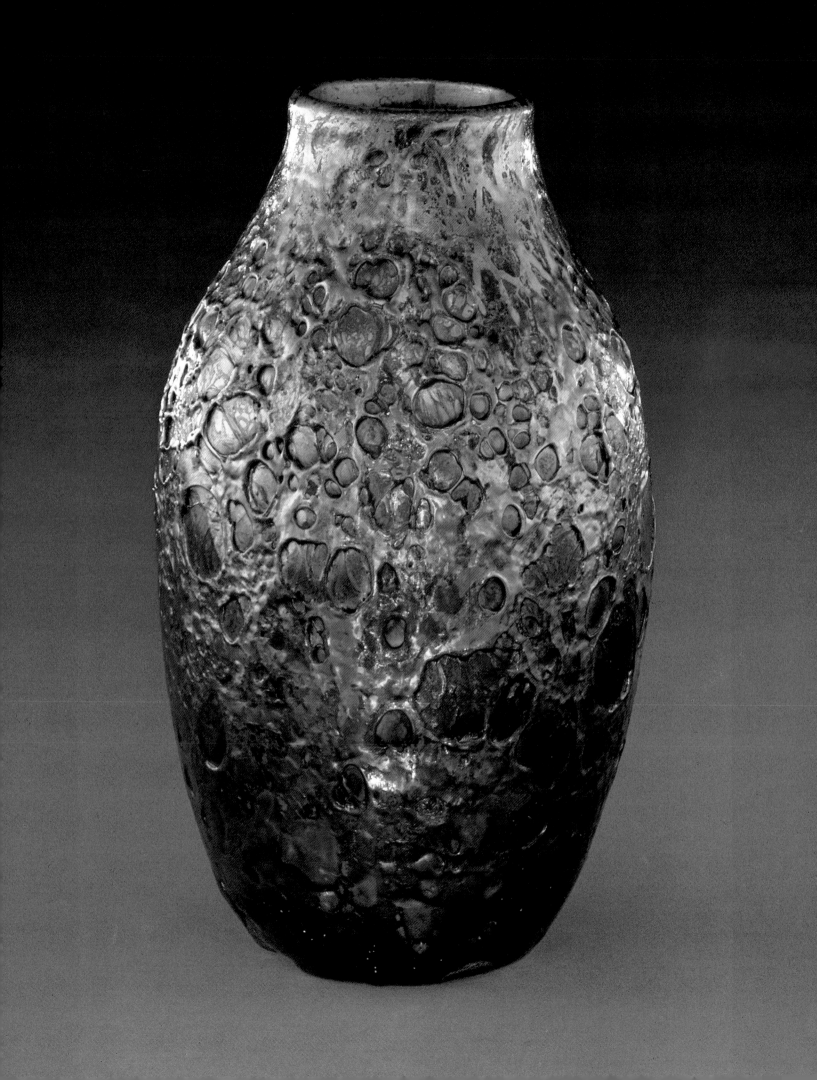

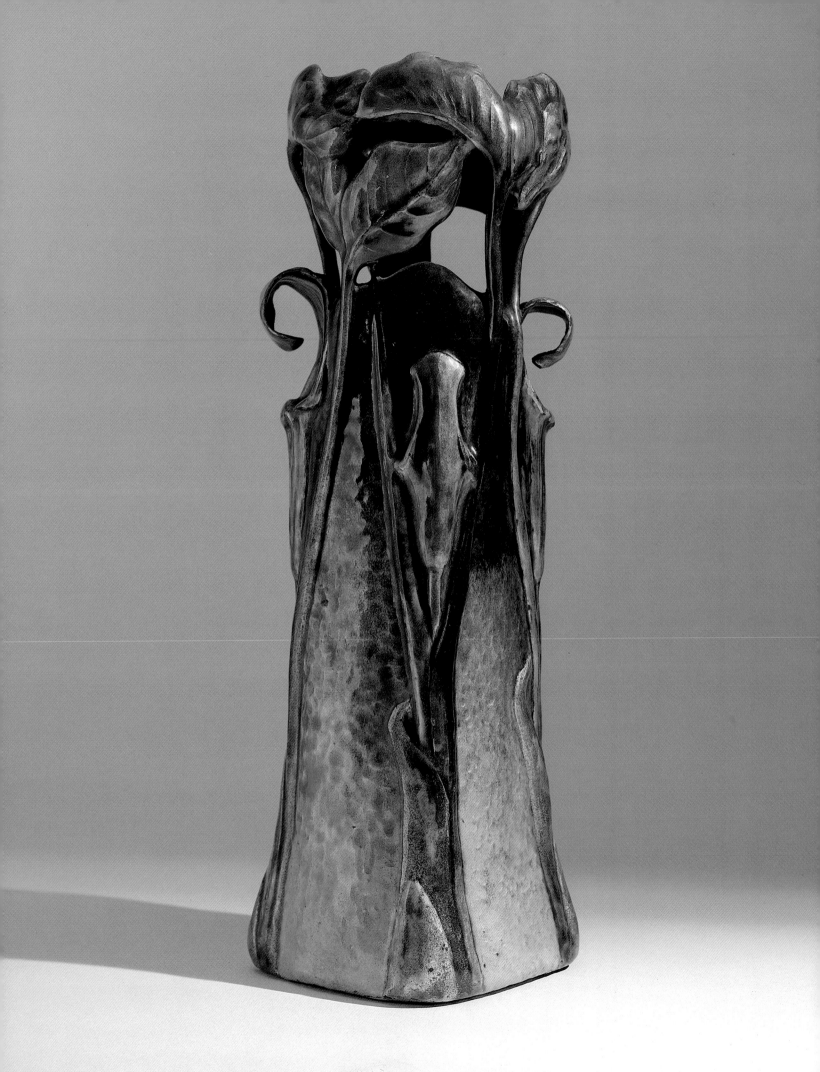

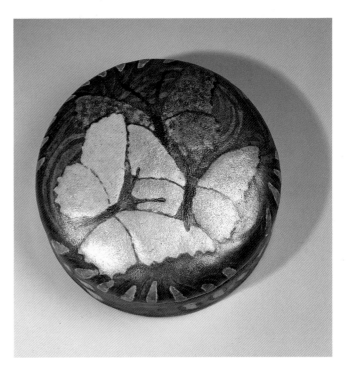

36. Jack-in-the-pulpit Vase, enamel on copper, 13⅛″ high, 4¼″ diameter, Tiffany Studios, New York, c. 1905-10

37. Enameled Box with Butterfly Design, enamel on copper, 1⅞″ x 4⅛″, Tiffany Studios, New York, c. 1902

38. Vase with handles, enamel on copper, 9¾″ high, 10½″ diameter of base, 6⅜″ diameter of liner, Tiffany Studios, New York, 1900-10

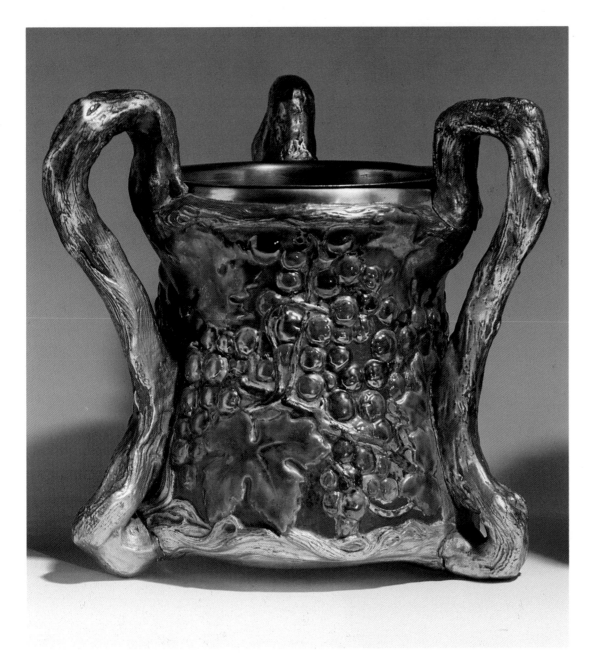

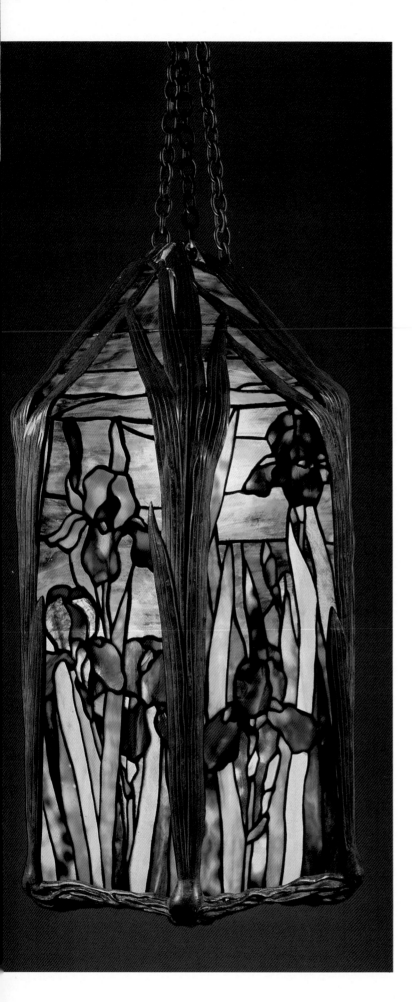

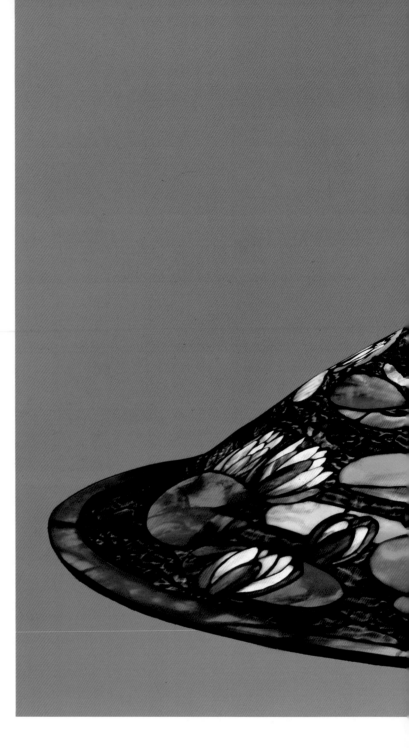

39. Iris Lantern, leaded Favrile glass and bronze, 23¼" x 13½", Tiffany Studios, New York, c. 1900-10

40. Pond Lily Chandelier, leaded Favrile glass and bronze, 36" diameter of shade, Tiffany Studios, New York, 1900-10

41. Dragonfly Chandelier, leaded Favrile glass and bronze, 28" diameter, Tiffany Studios, New York, 1900-10

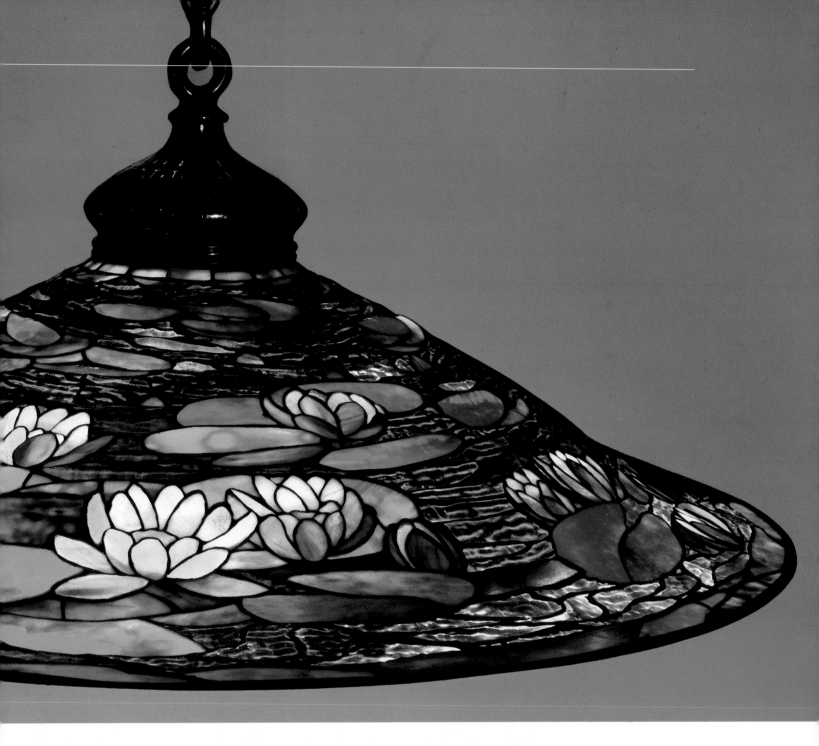

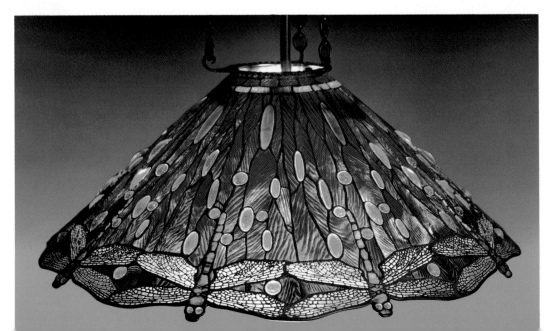

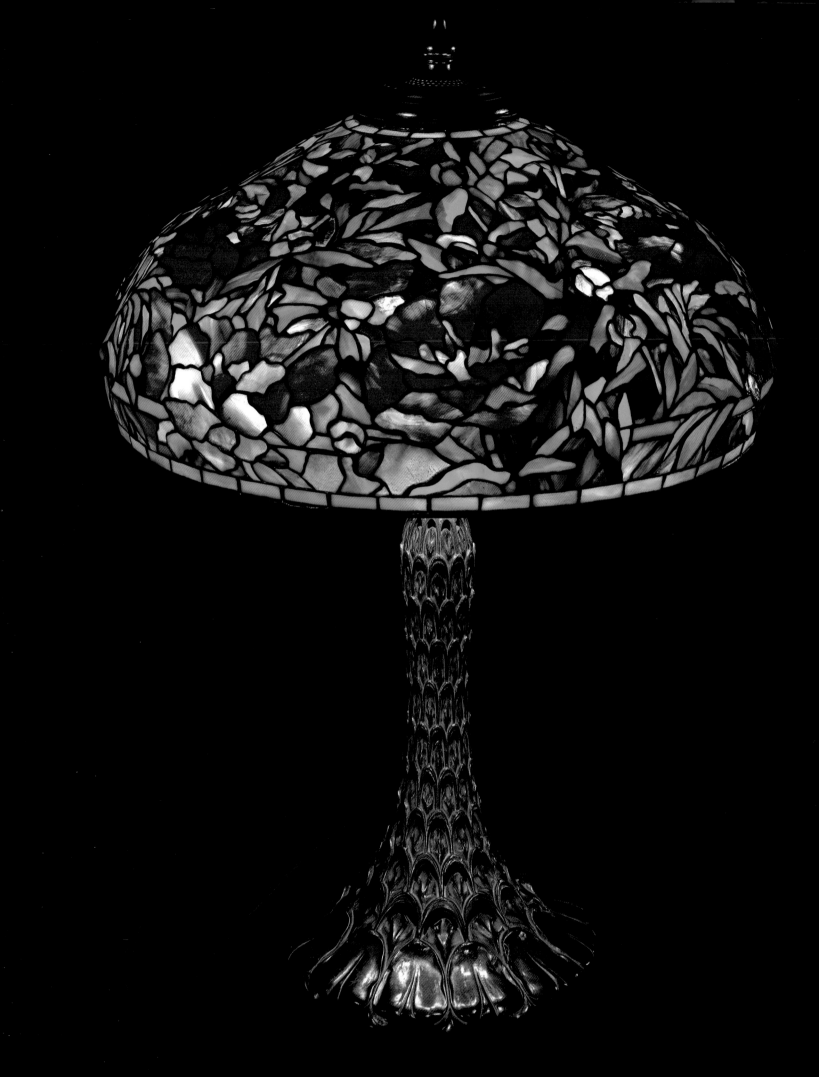

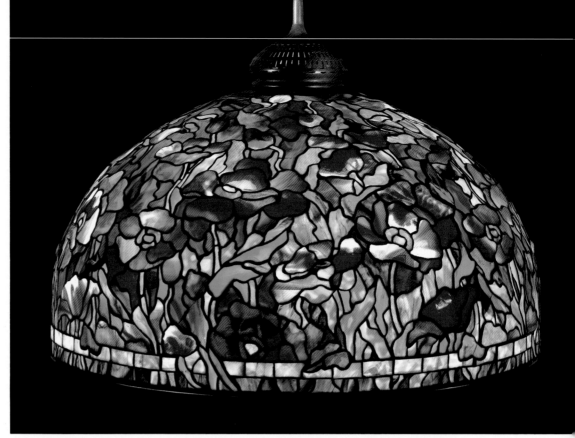

42. Elaborate Peony Table Lamp, leaded
Favrile glass and bronze, 30″ high,
22″ diameter of shade, Tiffany Studios,
New York, 1906-10

43. Oriental Poppy Floor Lamp, leaded
Favrile glass and bronze, 76″ high,
30″ diameter of shade, Tiffany Studios,
New York, c. 1900-10

44. Floral Chandelier, leaded Favrile
glass, with bronze chains, 10½″ high,
25″ diameter of shade, Tiffany Studios,
New York, 1900-10

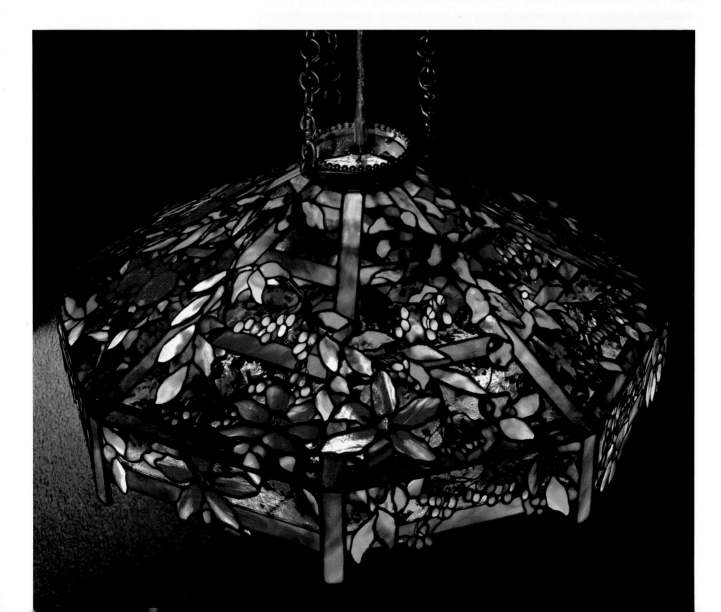

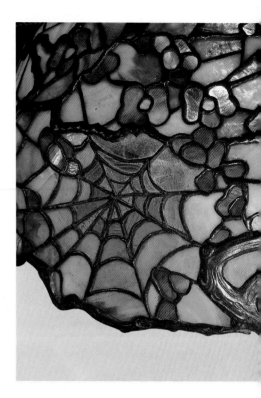

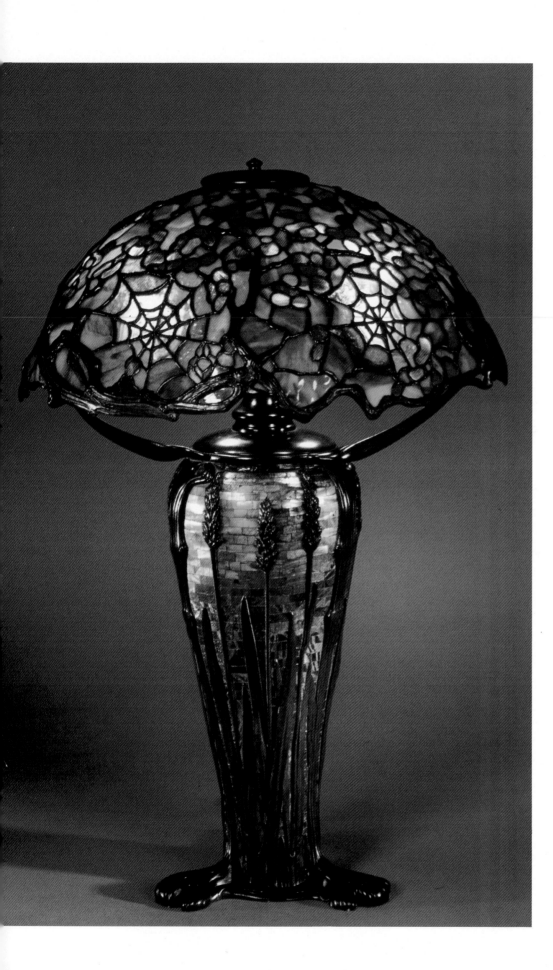

45, 46.  Cobweb Table Lamp, leaded
Favrile glass and bronze, 25½ high,
17½" diameter of shade, Tiffany Studios,
New York, 1900-05

47.  Cobweb Table Lamp, leaded Favrile
glass, mosaic, and bronze, 30¼" high,
19" diameter of shade, Tiffany Studios,
New York, 1900-05

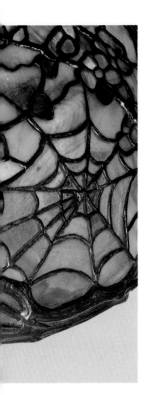
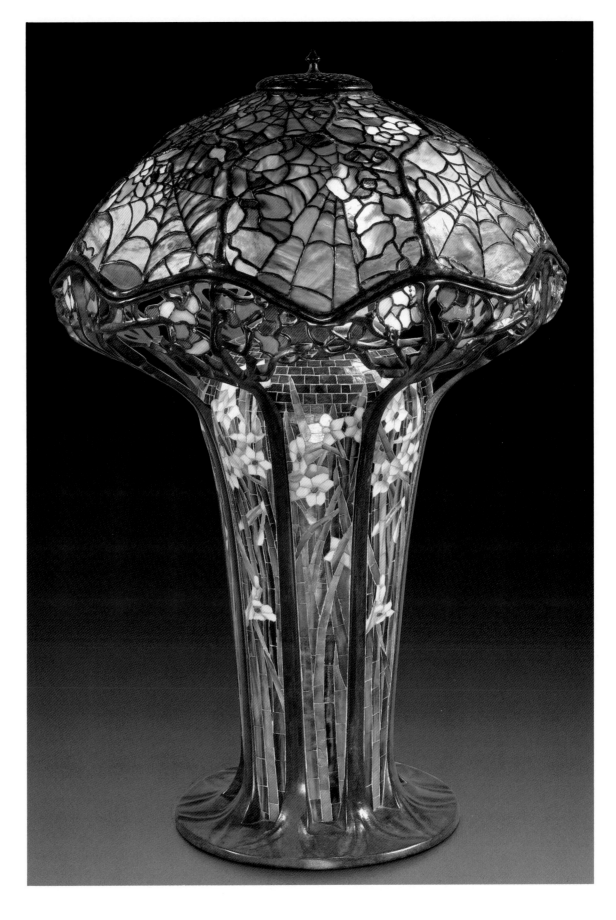

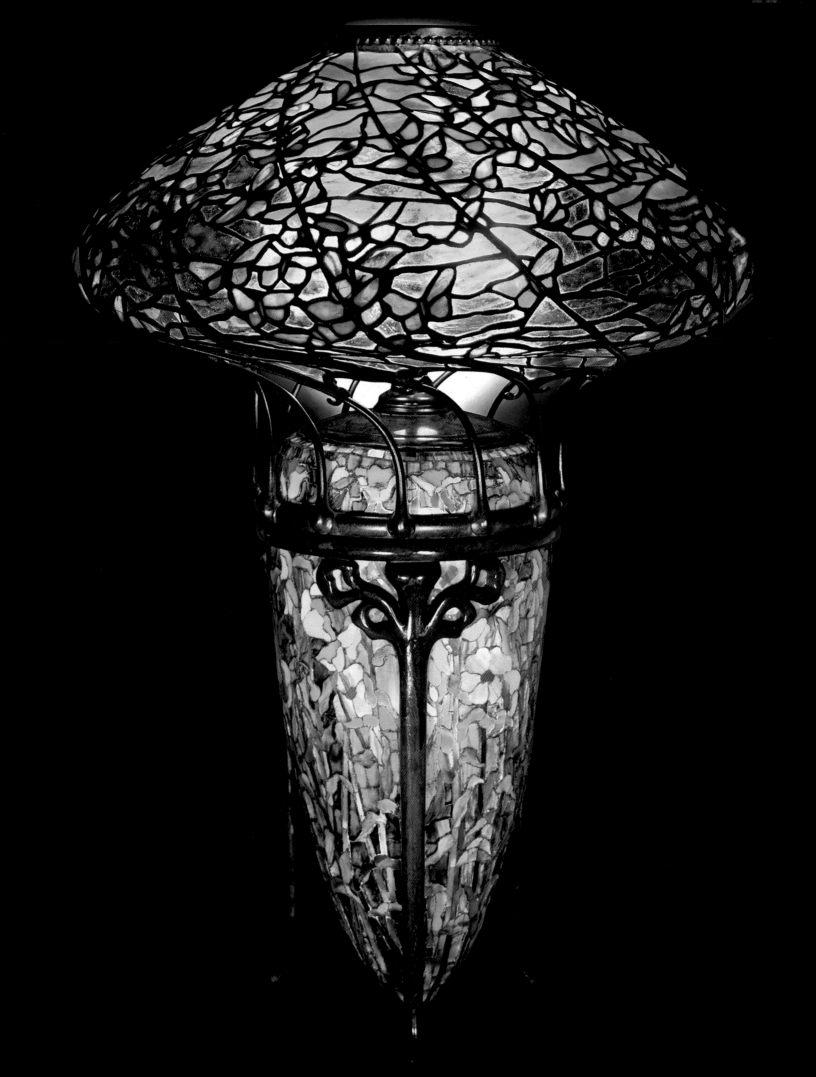

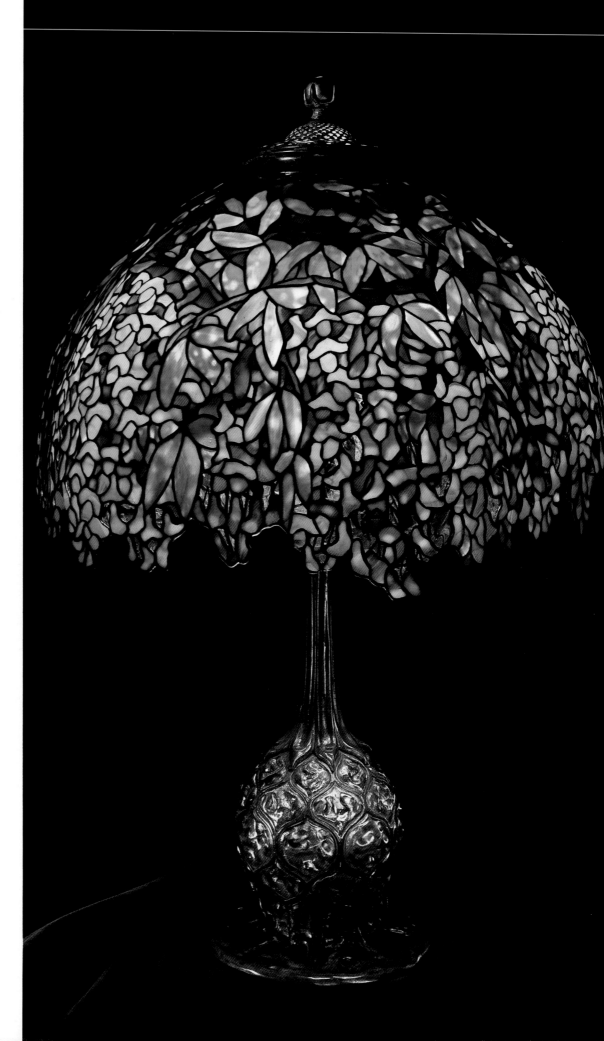

48. Butterfly Table Lamp, leaded Favrile glass, mosaic, and bronze, 26½" high, 18" diameter of shade, Tiffany Studios, New York, 1899-1905

49. Laburnum Table Lamp, leaded Favrile glass and bronze, 27½" high, 24" diameter of shade, Tiffany Studios, New York, 1900-10

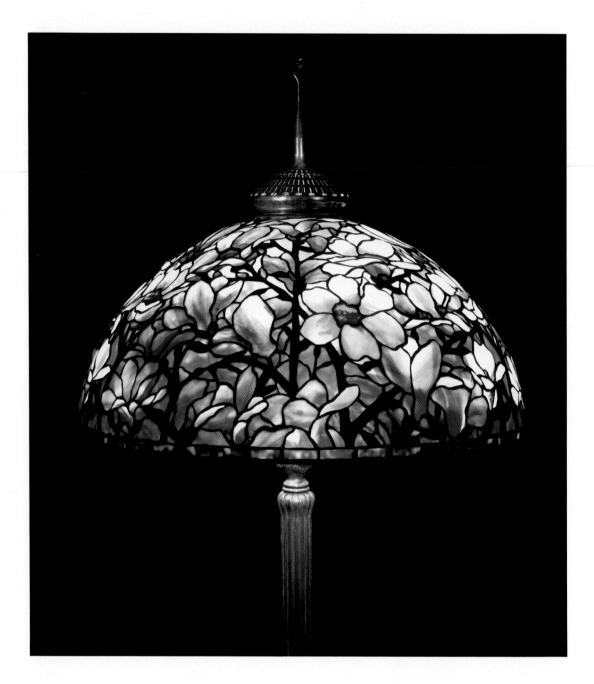

50. Magnolia Floor Lamp, leaded Favrile
glass and bronze, 79″ high, 28″ diameter
of shade, Tiffany Studios, New York,
c. 1906-10

51. Dragonfly Table Lamp, leaded
Favrile glass and bronze, 32″ high,
22″ diameter of shade, Tiffany Studios,
New York, 1900-10

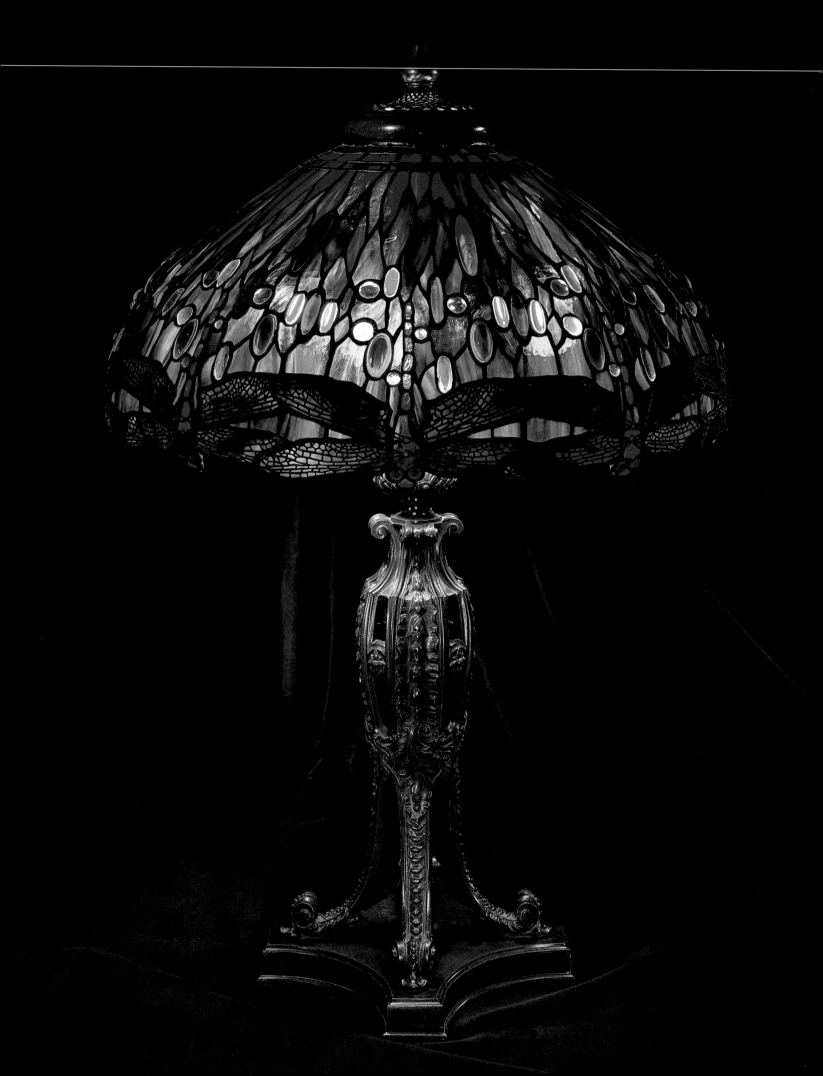

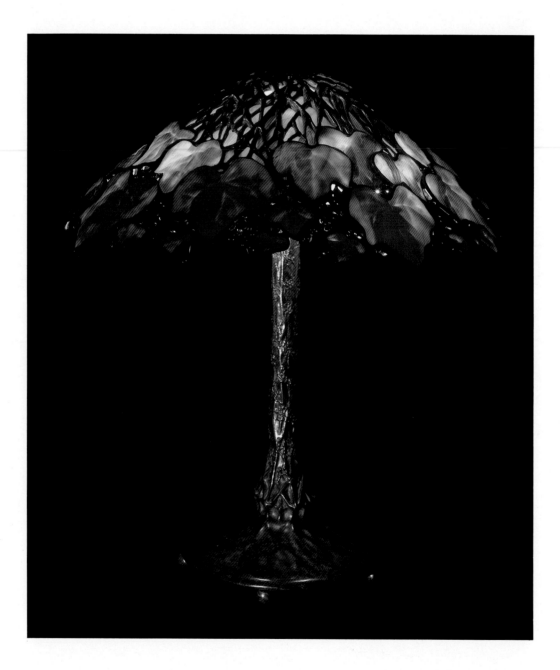

52. Maple Leaf Table Lamp, leaded
Favrile glass and bronze, 18½" high,
17" diameter of shade, Tiffany Studios,
New York, 1900-05

53. Lotus Table Lamp, leaded Favrile
glass and mosaic glass, and bronze,
34¾" high, 28" diameter of shade,
Tiffany Studios, New York, 1900-10

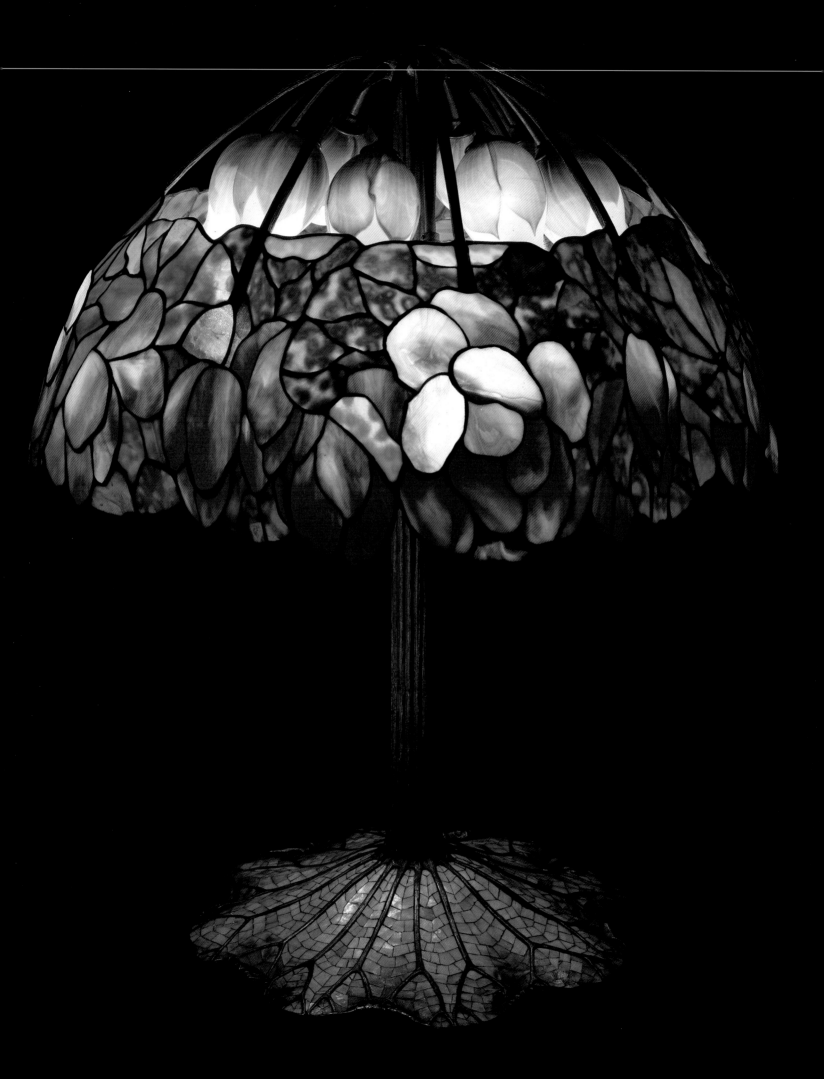

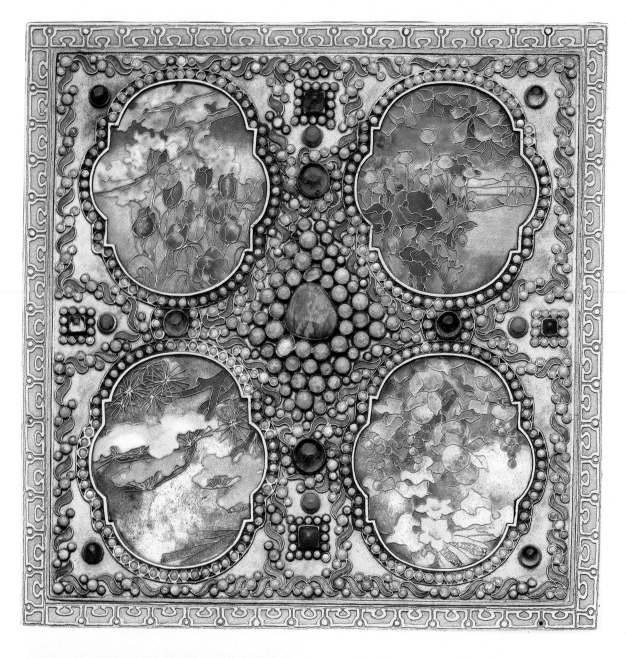

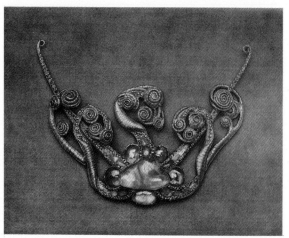

54. "Four Seasons" Jeweled Gold Box, gold, enamel, opals, tourmalines, sapphires, and chrysoprases, 6″ x 6″ x 2″ approximately, Tiffany & Co., New York, 1914

55. Medusa Brooch, gold, opal, and olivines, Louis Comfort Tiffany, *c.* 1902-04

56. Necklace with Grape and Vine motifs, gold, enamel, and opals, 18″ long, Louis Comfort Tiffany, *c.* 1904

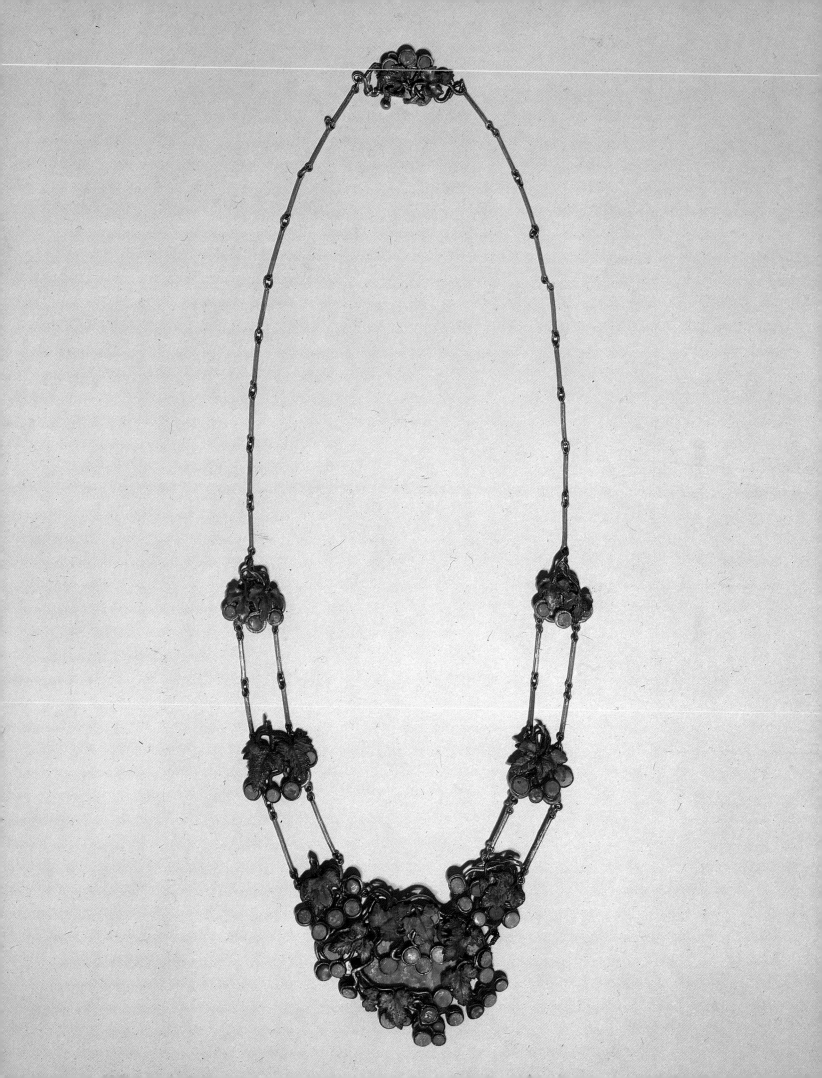

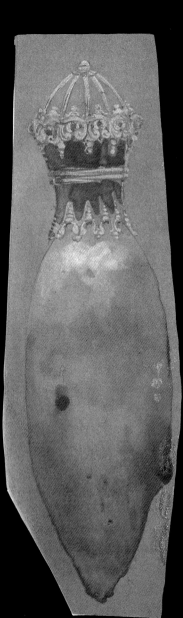

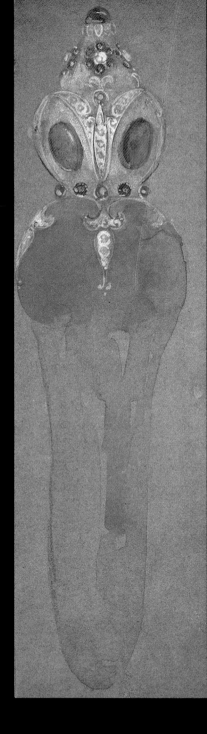

57.  Sketches for Vinaigrettes with
Favrile glass bodies, executed by Tiffany
& Co., *c.* 1900

58.  Vinaigrette, Favrile glass, enameled
gold, Mexican opals, diamonds, rubies,
and emeralds, 5¼″ long, Tiffany & Co.,
New York, 1900

# STAINED GLASS:
## SECULAR WINDOWS AND
## ECCLESIASTICAL SETTINGS

Alastair Duncan

The explosion of Church activity in the United States after the Civil War provided the newly founded American School of Glass with an undiscriminating flood of commissions, which helped to nurture it through its infancy. As the nation adopted the rapid technological advances of the Industrial Revolution, its population shifted westward in search of the raw materials needed to fuel mass-production. New towns were formed near mineral and oil deposits, at railheads, and at ports along the Great Lakes. The penalty in human terms of this economic growth was similar to that suffered earlier by the parent movement in Victorian England: overcrowding, poverty, ignorance, misery, and their common denominator, crime. Christian activity increased as the population began to concentrate in urban communities and suffered the deprivations of cramped, inadequate housing. Contemporary journals, such as *The Churchman* and *The Congregationalist*, charted the country's shift to urban living. In 1800 the number of American cities with a population of 8,000 or more was given as six; by 1886 this figure had risen to 286, representing 22.5 per cent of the nation's total population. God's message to His ministers was clear and urgent: "Go ye into all the world, and preach the gospel to every creature."[1] Dioceses and parishes were formed with bewildering speed to save mankind by remedying the evils of modern civilization. By 1888 the number of church buildings under construction was listed at 4,000.[2]

What was left to be resolved was the issue of how to share the spoils. On this there was apparently no divine guidance, and the various churches quickly joined in genteel, but earnest, spiritual battle. An 1886 editorial in *The Church* magazine traced the initial scramble for recruits, "While sometimes interfering with and restricting each other's work, the denominations have, on the whole, stimulated each other to incessant zeal. The great activity of the one has necessitated the greater activity of another, if it would maintain its relative position. . . . in the struggle for existence everywhere going on among the churches, the fittest will surely survive."[3]

All appeared, in fact, to have done so, providing the country with the rich diversity of religious choice that exists today: Methodists, Presbyterians, Episcopalians, Baptists, Unitarians, Universalists, Lutherans, Roman Catholics, Congregationalists, etc.

The American School of Glass constituted a loosely knit group of stained glass artists who were drawn together in the 1870s to protest the general *malaise* of their craft, which, after four hundred years of persistent decline, had reached its nadir at the end of the eighteenth century in the heavily enameled and transparent paintings-on-glass of the English portraitist, Sir Joshua Reynolds. Both the glass itself and the techniques used to ornament it flaunted the medium's glorious legacy in the Gothic cathedrals of Chartres, Bourges, Angers, Poitiers, Le Mans, and Canterbury.

The most eminent members of the new American School of Glass were John La Farge and Louis Comfort Tiffany, two ex-painters respected for their skills as landscapists and colorists, behind whom a host of kindred spirits, including Maitland Armstrong, F. D. Millet, Francis Lathrop, R. Geissler, E. H. Blashfield, Elihu Vedder, G. W. Maynard, Frederick Crowninshield, J. & R. Lamb, and Miss Tillinghast, set out to revitalize the craft and at the same time to establish their own identifiable decorative style.[4]

Various characteristics identify the movement, particularly the use of opalescent sheet glass in which variegated colors were blended to provide an infinite range of tonal effects; the elimination of all painting and staining from windows, except where necessary to provide the flesh details in figural compositions; the use of plating (more than one layer of glass) to achieve depths of nuances of color unachievable in a single sheet; and the use of lead lines as an integral feature of design. The resulting style of window, generally called "pictorial", represented the renaissance claimed for it by its exponents; but to many the cure was worse than the disease. The School frequently translated into glass a range of Italian Old Master paintings and canvases by contemporary Romantic and PreRaphaelite painters in a style which pursued naturalistic modeled effects and perspective.[5] This drew sharp criticism from purists who felt that stained glass artists should aim for effects that exploited its main quality, that of transmitted light, rather than base their work on the dissimilar field of painting on canvas.[6]

In all this endeavor, Tiffany was variously an indefatigable experimentalist, an innovator, and a transgressor in the nearly twenty years between the mid-1870s and early 1890s, a lengthy period of germination which came to fruition in his display at the 1893 Columbian Exposition. Until this point, his achievements in glass can be judged on balance to have been largely successful, but clearly less so than those of his principal rival, La Farge, whose windows in the same period showed a more refined sensitivity to the medium.

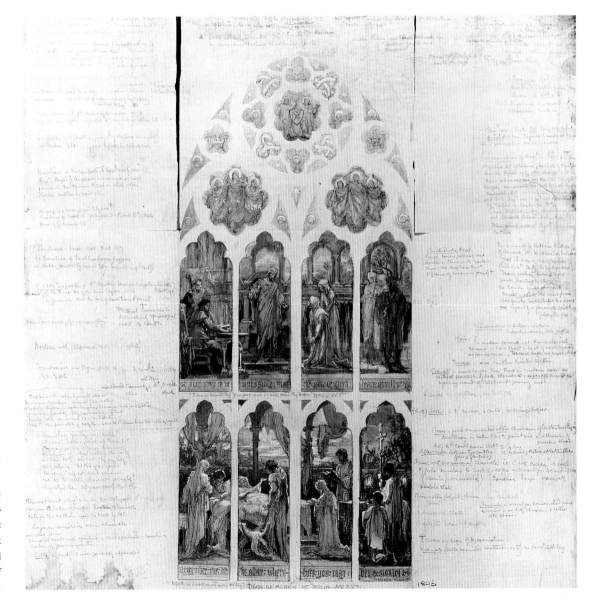

A working drawing for an ecclesiastical window, 1896, designed by Frederick Wilson with notations by Wilson or Louis Comfort Tiffany (or both). The window's conventional Gothic structure was particularly suited to pictorial religious themes of this type.

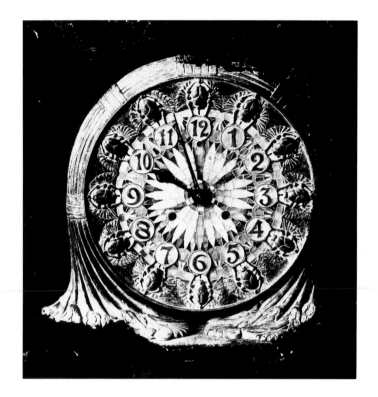

Mosaic and bronze mantel clock
with scarab decoration,
designed by Tiffany.

From 1893, after the accolades received by his Byzantine chapel at the Exposition, to which more than a million visitors flocked in awe, Tiffany leapt to international attention, passing La Farge on his way up as the latter, dogged increasingly by the financial crisis which punctuated his career, fell into decline. By this time, however, Tiffany must have been aware of the limitations of traditional ecclesiastical art for his purposes and of his own inadequacies in its pursuit. For one matter, he did not have a natural affinity for it. For another, portraiture was not his forte as an artist. In the case of a designer of religious figure windows, which by convention were filled with an endless retinue of biblical personages and angels, this was a major and obvious liability. Tiffany was also not a biblical scholar, a field in which traditional glass artists were thoroughly tutored during their apprenticeships to ensure their complete conversancy with Christian iconography.

To offset these personal shortcomings, Tiffany began early in his career to assemble an experienced team of designers proficient in ecclesiastical window design, including Frederick Wilson, Edward Peck Sperry, Joseph Lauber, Will H. Low, Henry Keck, and Jacob Adolphe Holzer. Of these, Wilson emerged as the most gifted, prolific, and long-serving.[7] Though Tiffany personally designed a number of figural windows, he increasingly turned such commissions over to his staff as the firm expanded. This allowed him time to build the business and – clearly his favorite pursuits – to experiment with glass and to design domestic windows.

Even Tiffany's inimitable glass, shot through with infinite tones and densities of color, could not save the firm's religious figural windows from charges that they were undistinguished and often overly sentimental. His church clients, both clergy and laity, were set in their preference for a traditional interpretation of Christian iconography, which denied him the opportunity to incorporate in his commissions for them the renderings of nature – both panoramas and floral studies – for which he had distinguished himself as a painter. And to make matters bleaker, he was, like all glass studios, dependent on the church for the majority of his commissions, as the

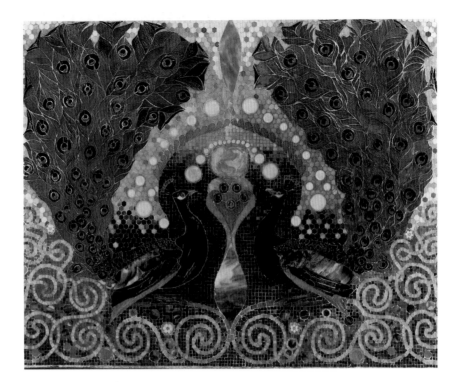

Peacock mosaic panel of Favrile glass, pottery and plaster, designed by Tiffany for the Henry O. Havemeyer house in New York. (Photo courtesy of the University of Michigan Museum of Art, Ann Arbor)

market for domestic windows was relatively small and sporadic, and could certainly not sustain him professionally. Thus the church represented his primary source of business, and would continue to do as long as the boom in church construction across the country maintained its pace.[8]

The opening in 1893 of Tiffany's glass furnaces in Corona, New York, and the subsequent introduction to the market of his Favrile glassware – handblown items such as vases, stemware, and globes for lamps – provided Tiffany with an awkward, if not painful, reminder of how his religious windows were perceived.[9] The public was mesmerized by the novel magical qualities of iridescence and the symphony of evanescent hues fused on to the surface of his new wares, and the critics were quick to praise them at the expense of his ecclesiastical windows. Suddenly the latter, the focus of his efforts in glass over two decades, were seen as the weak suite in his repertoire, despite the fact that they constituted a more noble art form than the decorative household glassware which was now capturing the headlines.[10] Tiffany was forced, as he approached the age of fifty, to assess his career as a window artist. His glass was the most spectacular in the history of the medium, yet its impact was largely neutralized in the religious figural compositions to which he was bound by convention.

The praise voiced by the critics for the small selection of secular windows Tiffany displayed at the 1893 Columbian Exposition in Chicago, the 1895 Salon at the Champs-de-Mars pavilion in Paris, and at the Salon of La Libre Esthétique in Brussels in 1897, must have encouraged him to proceed with his plans to introduce a similar range of non-figural windows into ecclesiastical settings.[11] Yet the enormity of the challenge must have daunted even Tiffany. Pictorial windows representing Christ, His Apostles, and scenes from the Scriptures were a fundamental and essential element in the iconography of Christian stained glass, the only true means to edify and elevate the congregation, and a tradition which after nearly two millennia appeared entrenched and inviolate. To attempt to alter this in any way was likely to outrage

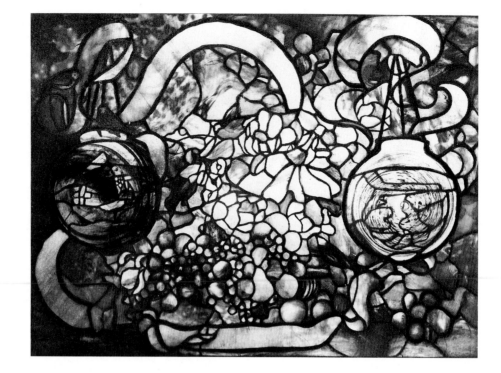

"Flower, Fish and Fruit," window designed by Tiffany in 1885 for Miss Mary Elizabeth Garrett's Baltimore home, where it was installed as part of the transom in the dining room. Clearly a favorite early commission, Tiffany exhibited the original cartoon at his 1899 show in the Grafton Gallery, London, and later made a duplicate of the window for Laurelton Hall. The Garrett window is now in the Baltimore Museum of Art.

Opposite: A view of the five-panel magnolia and wisteria window designed around 1885 by Tiffany in his 72nd Street home (see p.32). Three of the panels are now in the Charles Hosmer Morse Museum of American Art, Winter Park, Florida.

most, if not all, of the religious community, and invite charges of desecration or even heresy. Extreme prudence and diplomacy were therefore required if such an incursion into Christendom's rich artistic legacy were to stand any chance of success, even on a small scale.

Tiffany's production of secular windows had played a secondary role in his window department since its modest formation in the second half of the 1870s. His first recorded domestic commission was for a pair of "Eggplant" and "Squash" transom overdoor panels for the house which Associated Artists furnished for the pharmaceutical supplier, George Kemp, at 720 Fifth Avenue, New York, in 1879. These, depicting the two vegetables entwined on identical trelliswork, appear today as predictably stiff compositions from Tiffany's earliest days as a window designer.[12] The 1885 commission for Mary Elizabeth Garrett of Baltimore, however, proved to be a far more progressive, and clearly evolutionary, step in Tiffany's search for a domestic window style. Its design of flowers, fish bowls, fruit and scrolled ribbons, anticipated some of the most successful floral windows of his mature period (1900-15) in a compact and vigorous composition which allowed the introduction of a kaleidoscope of delicately blended colors.[13]

At roughly the same time, Tiffany created a monumental "Butterfly" panel for his own mansion at 72nd Street and Madison Avenue, New York. The panel exemplifies the mania for Orientalism which swept Europe and the Unites States at the time. In addition to a most appealing composition in which a central Japanese paper lantern draws a swarm of yellow-orange butterflies to its light against a background of further butterflies and jeweled blossoms rendered in a matching palette of yellow and orange, the window's construction provides clear evidence of Tiffany's search for startling new lighting effects in its mixture of both translucent and fully opaque pieces of glass, and sections of abalone shells and sculpted lead cames.[14] For the lounge in his 72nd Street residence, Tiffany later also designed a five-panel bay window in which flowering pale gray magnolias were set in clear glass beneath an upper tracery of pendant wisteria sprays, a highly realistic way in which to draw the building's exterior into its interior.[15]

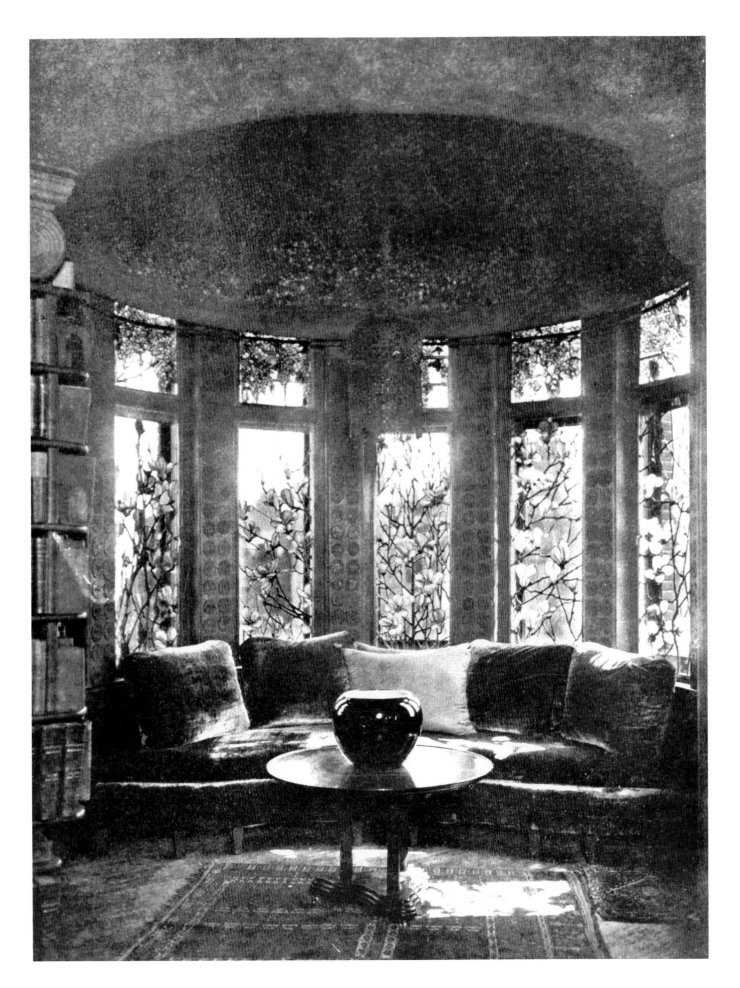

The absence of any reference to these domestic works from all contemporary literature – both in the press and in the firm's literature – implies strongly that they were executed either for Tiffany's personal use or for special friends and a narrow circle of clients. They constituted an on-going form of experimentation in his search for technical refinement beyond the field of his ecclesiastical commissions, which formed the basis of his expanding business and its steady source of revenue. Within three years of the Garrett commission, however, Tiffany had completed at least one other important domestic commission, for a Mr. William A. Slater of Norwich, Connecticut. The window, designed as a triptych with a large central panel flanked by narrower lancets, incorporated several of the decorative themes which came to characterize Tiffany's finest domestic landscape windows: a pergola of flowering wisteria, dhow-like boats sailing on a distant stretch of water, and, in the foreground, vases filled with large summer blooms, a ploy which enabled Tiffany to introduce concentrated blocks of color into his window compositions.[16]

The inauguration of the Corona glass furnaces in 1893 was celebrated with the creation of several other secular windows, including "Feeding the Flamingoes," "Autumn," and a panel depicting birds perched around a fish-bowl, that were displayed at the Columbian Exposition.[17] The three provided irrefutable and spectacular evidence for Tiffany's boast that his windows were now made entirely with his own Favrile glass.[18]

Tiffany's production of domestic windows can therefore be seen to have kept pace with his ecclesiastical work from the start, but on a modest scale. Unfortunately, as practically all these commissions were either for himself or private clients, information on individual works remained confidential, a policy to which the firm adhered fairly rigidly throughout its existence. Only in special instances after 1900 was a press release issued on a domestic commission, to invite the public to view it briefly at the Studios showroom prior to shipment to the client. Unlike its public and ecclesiastical commissions, for which three exhaustive and updated lists were published between 1893 and 1910, the firm omitted domestic windows from its literature.[19]

The first success in Tiffany's attempt to place non-figural secular windows into church settings occurred in the late 1890s. Surviving ledgers of the firm's press clippings – salvaged from the trash by an ardent Tiffany collector after the firm filed for bankruptcy in 1933 and its inventory began to be dispersed or discarded – accurately tabulate the first placement of his non-figural windows into churches.[20] These consisted primarily of flowers or landscapes, the latter placing clusters of flowers within broader outdoor panoramas. An article in the *New York Commercial Advertiser* in early 1898 reviewed the recently installed Galbraith Ward memorial window, comprising three panels decorated with different flora, in the Saint James Episcopal Church at 71st Street and Madison Avenue, New York, as "simply a mass of rich color, without the attempt to portray figures or emblems. The idea is unique in church decoration, and opens up the question of the possibility of a devotional side to the contemplation of pure color without the association of sacred emblems or inscriptions."[21]

To deflect the inevitable outburst from both the church hierarchy and other rigid traditionalists, which he expected to follow the installation of this and subsequent non-figural ecclesiastical compositions, Tiffany issued a press release which stressed the evangelical symbolism of the Saint James memorial. His argument was persuasive, linking its subject directly to the Creator. The window was an attempt to draw on "the endless wealth of precept and suggestion that lies around us in air and water and earth, in all the vast teeming bosom of Nature."[22] Far from being sacrilegious, the floral theme was in fact pantheistic, drawing its inspiration directly from God's work.

Tiffany refined this argument continually during the next decade, often choosing flowers which had a direct religious symbolism. Of these, Easter lilies and vines (emblematic, respectively, of purity and the Annunciation, and the Eucharist) were the most appropriate for church memorial windows, while poppies and lilies, to symbolize death and the Resurrection, were frequently incorporated into mausoleum windows. Other flowers served to provide variety. Tulips, irises, and goldenrod, for example, were emblematic of spring, summer and autumn, while cedars and cypress trees were described invariably in the Studios' press releases as symbols of majesty and spiritual growth.[23]

Tiffany's cause was advanced in early 1899 through the acceptance by St. John's Episcopal Church in Troy, New York, of his proposed design for a five-lancet memorial window to Charles B. Knight. Designed by Agnes Northrop and entitled "St. John's Vision of the Holy City," the window took its theme from the Book of Revelations in its depiction of the vision revealed to the Apostle during his sojourn on the Isle of Patmos.[24] Above a colorful vista of red poppies and palm fronds, there is a glimpse of a spectacular tiered and turreted celestial city beyond banks of parting opalescent clouds. In the same year, Miss Northrop designed a smaller window incorporating a similar composition of poppies and palms for the Robert Baker memorial window in the Reformed Church in Flushing, Long Island, where she was a regular communicant.[25]

The Troy commission received considerable press attention, and signaled Tiffany's break with convention. An editorial in the *New York Times* noted its historic significance: "it has generally been supposed that all stained glass windows representing a subject capable of coherent interpretation, at least in the serious domain of religious art, must be filled with human figures. The presentation windows of cathedral chapels contain portraits of people engaged in some religious act towards Christ and the saints. The great choir and clerestory windows of French cathedrals are filled with all the legendary and miraculous details in the life of saints and martyrs. . . [but] there have been several attempts in recent years to combine in the effect of stained glass and landscape pure and simple, unrelieved by the figure. . . one has just been completed. . . the subject represents a vision of the New Jerusalem as revealed to St. John. . . the idea of the landscape artist in stained glass work is here seriously put forward."[26] The *Troy Daily Press* similarly noted the novelty of the commission: "it may be quite possible that the Tiffany company, in such windows as that in St. John's Church, may be inaugurating a new movement in church art which shall revolutionize the conventional practice of the past and gain in truth as well as in devotion by a full and bold portrayal of inanimate nature under its sublimest and most thrilling aspects."[27]

No doubt buoyed by these supportive editorials, which were clipped and filed by his staff to be used to rebuff the stiff resistance he knew he would continue to face from the clergy, Tiffany proceeded immediately with other church landscape and floral window commissions. One of these, its location unidentified, was described in the *New York Sun* as an abstract floral composition "suggestive of a tangled mass of foliage, grapes, and wisteria."[28]

Tiffany's progress was eased further in these years by his careful choice of passages from the Scriptures to justify his choice of non-figural themes to portray religious ones. The chosen

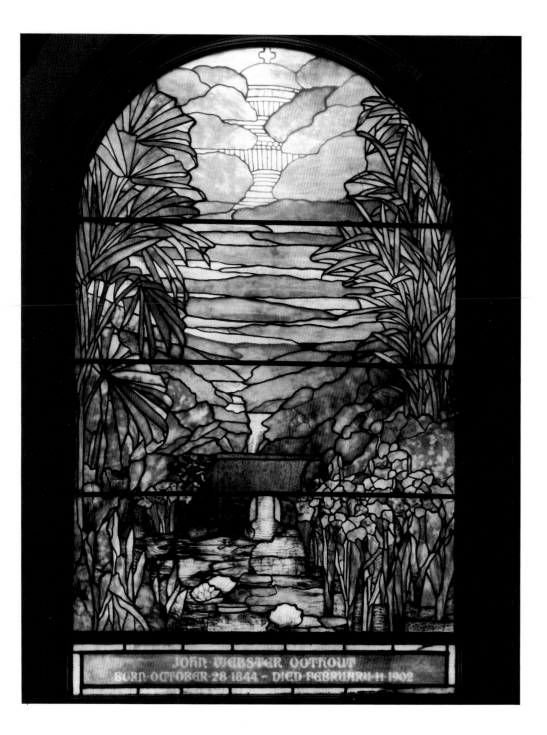

"Holy City," the John Webster Oothout Memorial designed by Tiffany c. 1902 and installed in the Third Presbyterian Church in Rochester, New York.

passage was often inscribed on, or beneath, the window to ensure that the viewer would fully comprehend its significance. Such a large selection of sayings appeared on the Studios' church landscape windows through the years, in fact, that it is reasonable to assume that at some point Tiffany ordered a member of his staff to scour both the New and Old Testaments for apppropriate texts, which were held on file and used as required. Several were used more than once, such as "The Earth is the Lord's and the Fullness thereof," or "I will lift up mine eyes to the hills, from whence cometh my help. My help cometh from the Lord, which made heaven and earth," or, a perennial favorite for vistas that included a lake, "He maketh me to lie down in green pastures, He leadeth me beside the still waters." Where there was a shortage of space on or beneath the window, these extracts were contracted (e.g. "Green pastures and still waters").

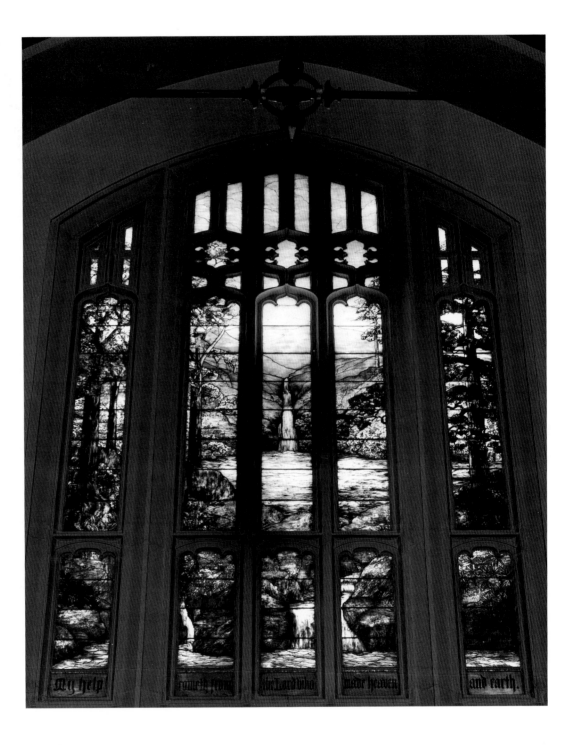

This landscape window, the largest commission of its kind undertaken by Tiffany Studios, was presented by Mrs. Frederick W. Hartwell to the Central Baptist Church in Providence, Rhode Island, as a memorial to her late husband. Its lack of any religious figures aroused fierce controversy among the congregation.

Variants for dusk landscapes — to symbolize either the end of a perfect day or of an earthly life — included "At eveningtime shall be light" and "He giveth His beloved sleep."[29]

Commissions for mausoleum memorial windows gave Tiffany the opportunity — and an exceedingly lucrative one — to extend the pantheist landscape theme beyond the church itself into adjacent Sunday School buildings or the neighboring cemetery. Many of these memorials were designed around a central stream that flowed toward the foreground from a line of distant hills. Generally called "The River of Life," this vista symbolized man's path through life, from the cradle to the grave. More ambitious projects were entitled "He showed me a pure river of water of life, clear as crystal, proceeding out of the throne of God and of the Lamb." Tiffany used a spectacular variant of the standard landscape window-with-stream for one major

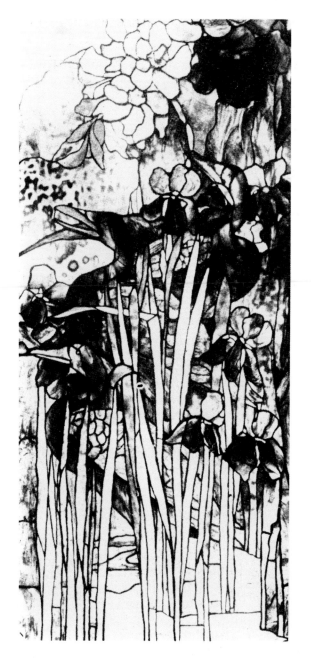

Tiffany showed this "Ducks and Fleur de Lys" window at the Paris Exposition Universelle in 1900. Its present whereabouts are unknown.

domestic commission – that of Miss Helen Gould – which incorporated a fawn drinking from a pool at the base of the stream. The appropriate passage from the Psalms accompanied this uplifting vision when it was selected for either mausoleum or church memorials, "As the hart panteth after the water brooks, so panteth my soul after thee, O God."[30]

At the 1900 Exposition Universelle in Paris, following on the general acclaim for his Favrile vases and windows at the Grafton Gallery exhibition in London the preceding year, Tiffany received a mixed reception.[31] The majesty of his inimitable iridescent Favrile glass, exemplified for most of the critics in the selection of vases and punch bowl he displayed, even took precedence over his windows, which Tiffany had chosen most carefully to prove his skills as a designer of domestic stained glass.[32] Included among these were several floral panels – most particularly the giant "Four Seasons" window, and others depicting magnolia, snowballs, and contained on a triptych screen trellised wisteria, fruiting gourd plants, and clematis[33] – all awash with shimmering colors which dazzled viewers with their deep radiant tones. Other panels, including ducks and fish in their natural habitat, underlined Tiffany's preoccupation with nature and color.

Pride of place, however, was reserved for the two monumental windows chosen to flank the entrance to the United States pavilion; to the left Tiffany's now famous "Four Seasons" window, and to the right, the "Flight of Souls" window which had been recently completed for the Wade family chapel in Lakeview Cemetery, Cleveland. Tiffany clearly felt that the latter would best represent the ecclesiastical side of his business as he made a special request to the Wade family to display it in Paris before it was installed in their chapel.[34] As his persistent supervision of the Cleveland commission — specifically, to achieve subtle artistic effects not comprehended, or deemed necessary, by either the family or their architects — had strained relations

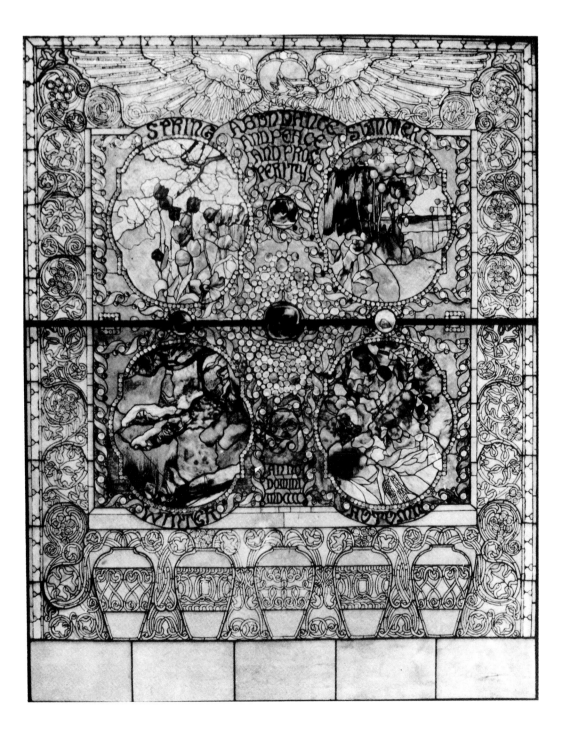

This "Four Seasons" window was shown in Paris in 1900 at the Exposition Universelle. Tiffany later installed the four panels separately in an alcove in Laurelton Hall.

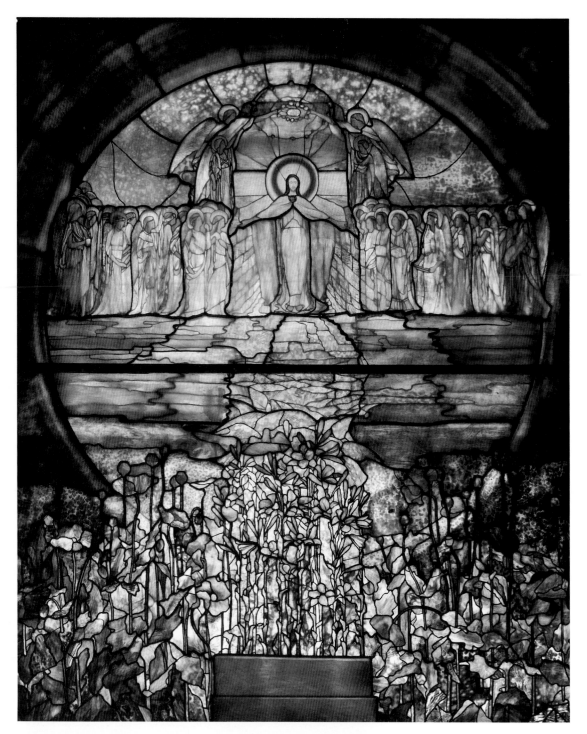

"Consummation of the Divine Promise in the Passing of the Goal from the Earthly Abode to the Heavenly Home." The window was designed by Tiffany and installed at the entrance to the United States Pavilion at the Paris Exposition Universelle of 1900. It is now in the Jeptha H. Wade Memorial Chapel in Lakeview Cemetery, Cleveland.

A pencil sketch for a mosaic mural in the Wade Memorial Chapel, Lakeview Cemetery, Cleveland, designed by Federick Wilson in 1899.

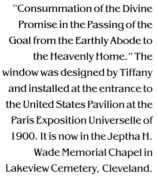

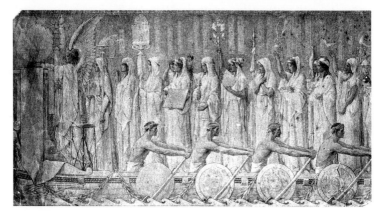

to the point where they were delighted to see the last of him, Tiffany must have had no doubt that the "Flight of Souls" represented the pinnacle of his work in church art. The critics at the Exposition, however, were almost unanimous in their censure which must have disappointed him deeply, even though the reasons given were similar to those which had been voiced intermittently by the art community in the United States during the past two decades. One French writer summed up precisely the general sense of disapproval by dividing the window into two parts. The upper, which depicted the central figure of Christ with figures of souls veering toward him, he found "froid, triste, obscur," even though it was made of Tiffany's justly famous Favrile glass. The lower part, however, which was taken up by bushes of flowers that served merely as a pretext to introduce elements of color, showed Tiffany to much greater advantage because it did not try to serve ideas or sentiments, but allowed the magic of the material to speak in its own right. If nothing else, Tiffany was reminded by this criticism that his two constituencies — those for ecclesiastical and domestic windows — required very separate audiences if he was to maintain their respective loyalties.

Whether because he felt that he had nothing further to achieve in glass or that he had in Paris attained the level of celebrity necessary to secure future commissions, or simply because he was by now inundated with new commissions, Tiffany did not display his windows in Europe again after the 1900 Exposition. Apart from the Exposition the following year in Buffalo, where records indicate that the firm's display included a selection of its Paris windows plus cartoons for others then under execution in New York, he limited his participation at international expositions increasingly to household items such as Favrile glassware, enamels, and, in small number, lamps.[35] The battle with church traditionalists remained a priority, however, and to this Tiffany turned his attention increasingly as the earlier resistance began to erode. The war was being won slowly, almost surreptitiously, as landscape and floral panels were placed piecemeal in churches of all denominations across the country.

In fact, the battle was practically won by 1910. Press releases from Tiffany Studios after 1900 were full of information on non-figural memorial commissions. In those instances where a traditional portrayal of Christ and His Disciples was retained, the figures were now often placed in the central of three or five panels, the outer panels serving simply to extend the landscape in which they were pictured. The emphasis was on the window's background rather than on its pictorial representation of a biblical event. By this adroit twist, the viewer was no longer asked, as he had previously been, to perceive these windows as figures within a landscape, but as landscapes which included figures. Refinements were continually forthcoming: in new memorial windows based on the theme of St. John's Vision of the Holy City designed during this period — the same theme as that used in St. Paul's Church, Troy, in 1899 — the vision of Jerusalem through the parting clouds was often omitted, its presence only *suggested* in the Studios' press releases.[36]

To add a personal touch to landscape memorials produced during these later years, Tiffany often incorporated a view of the neighboring countryside into the window under commission. It is common to learn, on viewing a window in a regional church, library, or old age home, that the window is a direct translation into glass of the valleys or range of mountains beyond the town. To ensure accuracy in such instances, a photograph was often requested by the Studios' window department to ensure accuracy in its preparation of the cartoon for the commission.[37]

The year 1910 marked the beginning of Tiffany's most fertile period of secular window production. Certainly many of the windows which the Studios represented as true master-pieces – such as those for Helen Gould (1910), Captain DeLamar (1912), the Sumner Memorial window for the First Church of Albany (1912), and The Bathers, intended for display at the 1915 Pan Pacific Exposition in San Francisco but installed instead directly in Laurelton Hall (1914), were executed between then and 1915.[38] High on a list of his own personal favorites was another from this period, the Russell Sage Memorial window installed in the First Presbyte-rian Church in Far Rockaway, Long Island, in 1910. Tiffany was immeasurably proud of the Sage window, and for good reason: it was the largest landscape window ever executed, and it depicted a glorious panorama rendered in deep natural tones that were startling in their realism, even by his own high standards. He described the window's religious symbolism in the church's dedicatory booklet, "It is the symbol of Life; the soft meadows from which the tree has its birth, representing the earliest stages of life. Then as the roots and trunk grow, they reach out over the rocks of the side hill and the trunks become gnarled with age. But all through life it is lifting it branches toward the sky – the Land of Promise."[39]

Omitted from Tiffany's explanation of the window was a justification of why he had placed a landscape scene within the strict constraints of a neo-Gothic window frame replete with broad oak mullions, spandrels, and an elaborate arched upper tracery. Perfected in the twelfth and thirteenth centuries to accommodate one or more registers of pictorial panels, each por-traying a scene from the Scriptures or parables which the clergy used as teaching aids for their illiterate congregations, the Gothic window aperture had been faithfully revived in the nineteenth century during the wave of Gothicism that overtook first English and then American architecture.[40] That its heavy web of wood supports – accounting for roughly a fifth of its total volume – was totally unsuited to frame a continuous summer landscape, must have been as obvious to Tiffany in 1910 as it is to today's observer, yet he persuaded Mrs. Sage and her church ministers of its aesthetic and symbolic merits. In his defense, it can be assumed that the church's architectural style was determined by Mrs. Sage and her architects long before any decision was made about who would design the building's secondary elements, such as its windows. Mrs. Sage, the wealthy widow of the railway magnate and a philanthropist with a high profile in New York's social circles, was a most desirable client whom Tiffany could not afford to lose. Anxious not to offend her, therefore, he probably accepted the commission without advising her that the building's Gothic style of fenestrations was quite unsuited to the type of window for which he was now famous and for which she was no doubt initially drawn to him. There is no suggestion in the surviving records of either Tiffany Studios or the First Presbyte-rian Church that any consideration was given initially to produce a thirteenth-century-style medallion window compatible with the architecture of the building in which it was to be housed. Tiffany simply went ahead and did what he did best within the constraints of the commission at hand.

If Mrs. Sage was persuaded, others were not, particularly Ralph Adams Cram, a partner in the architectural firm of Cram, Goodhue, & Ferguson, which had designed the church.[41] Cram was an ardent and self-righteous traditionalist who took every opportunity to assail Tiffany and his colleagues in the American School of Glass for what he considered a flagrant transgression against good taste and an exalted art form. The Sage memorial, in particular, was a personal affront since it was situated in *his* church, and he railed for many years against what he

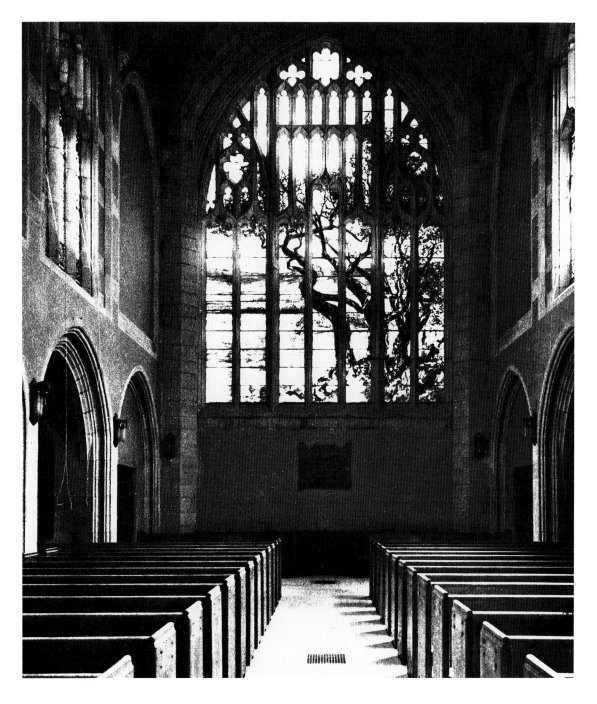

Tiffany's Russell Sage Memorial window in the First Presbyterian Church, Far Rockaway, Long Island (c. 1905), commissioned by Sage's widow, was one of Tiffany Studios' finest and largest commissions.

perceived as Tiffany's opportunism in this matter. In Cram's opinion the window was quite simply irreligious and unworthy of the building in which it was placed.

Within the glass community, Cram's neo-Gothic sympathies drew support from members of long-established studios, such as Charles Connick who, in a 1924 article deploring the continuing preoccupation among his stained glass colleagues with pictorial windows, wrote that the Sage memorial had "resulted in the feeling among glass men that architecture need not be greatly respected, and very often where windows in Gothic architecture were divided into narrow lancets by wide mullions, those mullions have been entirely ignored as in the famous memorial chapel at Far Rockaway . . ."[42] Tiffany's action did draw support, however, especially from a long-term promoter of his achievements, the critic Edith Syford, who presented the opposite view to that of Connick, "Suppose a church has features suggestive of some old cathedral's architecture. There is no more reason for filling it with stiff painted or antique glass to imitate its model than to demand that the pew holders dress in mediaeval style and that the musty odor of the cathedral be reproduced. It seems to take Americans a long time to realize that sincerity is the only road to progress in art . . . ."[43]

Today's historian can review the Sage window with the dispassion that time affords. Whereas Cram's grievance remains valid, it is easier now to comprehend the predicament which faced Tiffany in an age when all types of architectural revivalism — particularly the Gothic and Romanesque — remained firmly in favor for church buildings. Yet the year 1910 fell within the modern era, when technological progress had provided architecture with the two materials necessary to revolutionize its methods: steel and reinforced concrete. These rendered obsolete the structural devices basic to Gothic architecture: vaulted ceilings, flying buttresses, and solid granite exterior walls. The new building materials, in theory at least, even eliminated the need for walls. These advances, in turn, provided the modern stained glass artist with the opportunity to determine the shapes and size of his window aperture without having to concern himself with the disunity created by the mullions and traceries of medieval architecture. Tiffany no doubt felt stifled by the traditionalism which dominated church architecture at a time when progress was evident in practically all other areas of the building industry. In the commercial sector, numerous buildings had by 1910 attained a height of ten stories or more, and there was talk of others soon to come which would "scrape the skies." Yet church architects, on whom he was dependent for much of his work, persisted in designing churches "to look like churches." Clearly it was Cram, rather than he, who was at fault, for his buildings constituted an anachronism in the modern age.

Tiffany's church landscape and floral windows continued to be in demand during this period. After the initial success in New York, interest spread in roughly concentric circles to other States. The Studios reported on April 3, 1909, the installation of its first ecclesiastical landscape window in Ohio, in the First Presbyterian Church, Akron,[44] and others began to be placed at roughly the same time in Illinois, Pennsylvania, and Minnesota. There were still pockets of fierce resistance, however, as was graphically illustrated some years later in a brouhaha that erupted when the Pittsburgh tycoon Andrew Carnegie attempted to donate a Tiffany landscape window to the cathedral in Dunfermline, the city in Scotland where he had been born. The event illustrates again that Tiffany was often the target of criticism, but it also shows that he was not insensitive to his critics, and that he tried in many instances to accommodate them.[45]

In 1913, Carnegie's wealth and success were already legendary, so his request for a memorial window for Dunfermline was evidence of the esteem in which he held Tiffany and his window-making skills. For Tiffany, the commission provided a great opportunity to establish the industrialist as a treasured client from whose association other commissions would certainly follow. In other words, Carnegie was not a client he was likely to alienate.

The *New York Sun* recorded the events surrounding the Dunfermline commission.[46] On visiting Tiffany Studios with his wife, Carnegie requested a memorial window to his parents and dead brother and sister, which would represent an idealized view of the Pittencrieff glen near Dunfermline. A typical Tiffany landscape was prepared, which included a view of distant hills through pine trees with a profusion of flowering rhododendron bushes in the foreground.[47] At this point the Studios warned Carnegie that since the cathedral in Dunferm-

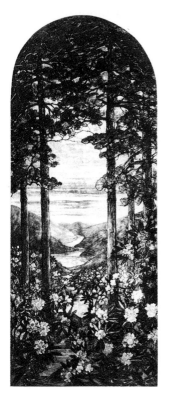

The landscape window commissioned by the tycoon Andrew Carnegie for Dunfermline Abbey, Scotland, as a memorial to his parents.

line was more than 800 years old, a modern non-figural theme, such as the proposed landscape, would be stylistically inappropriate. What was required was a reinterpretation of a period window incorporating a series of biblical figures or emblems within medallion-type borders. Carnegie agreed to consider an alternate design based on this suggestion (which Mrs. Carnegie strongly endorsed), but advised one of the Studios' staff in secret not to draw the Gothic-style figures too well since he did not want his wife to approve of it. On seeing the two completed cartoons, Carnegie could not be swayed from his initial decision, and ordered the Studios to proceed with the landscape, stating, "I want something new, something American. I don't want any of these old style windows with the figures of bible prophets and crosses and that sort of thing. I want an outdoor scene. God is in that sunset. God is in all the great outdoors. I want a window just like that."

The window was executed and delivered to the Dunfermline cathedral, where it was promptly rejected by the church council for the very reasons which Tiffany had expressed: it was totally out of keeping with the building's Anglo-Norman architecture. Advised of the cathedral's decision, Carnegie arranged for it to be placed in the town's public library, which he selected as an appropriate alternative venue, as his father had instituted the region's first circulating library many years earlier. He explained his choice, "It will have a better even if a less historic and sacred setting, but it's something of a joke on the Tiffany people, isn't it?"

This statement, published in the daily press, generated an immediate response from Tiffany Studios, issued through its general manager, Edwin George Stanton. Responding that "The joke isn't on us, it's on Mr. Carnegie," Stanton traced the history of the commission, even publishing the cartoon of the intended medallion window as a means to repudiate Carnegie's account. Clearly voicing Tiffany's sensitivity to similar issues that had arisen in the past, Stanton ended his press statement by comparing this event with others which preceded it, "Mr. Carnegie does us an injustice by his little joke. It is not the first time we have so suffered. We designed a Renaissance chapel for the World's Fair in Chicago in 1893. It was never intended for sale, but one woman insisted that we set a price on it, and when we had done so took our breath away by purchasing it. Then she did not know what to do with the chapel. After we had stored it for her for many years she finally gave it to the cathedral of St. John the Divine. I do not know why the cathedral authorities were so rash as to accept it, but they did, and as we had sold it we could do nothing. The result is that it now stands in the crypt of the cathedral, and persons of fine taste, seeing a Renaissance chapel lost in a Gothic cathedral, cry out against the Tiffany Studios for designing such a misfit. Yet it is not our fault. But what are you to do with persons who will have their own way though they break every law of art and taste?"

The above statement is important in a historical context as it provides the only recorded defense by the Studios against accusations of bad taste among more than a thousand press clippings of its work which the firm filed between 1897 and 1927. Loyalty to its customers remained a high priority, even to the extent of remaining silent when they made outrageous artistic demands that would expose it to later charges against which it could not retaliate. It is therefore reassuring to read that the firm was both aware of, and concerned about, the placement of the Chicago chapel in the Cathedral of St. John the Divine, as its presence there obviously violated established tenets of artistic good sense.

It implies, also, that there were similar mitigating factors in those instances where one finds a Tiffany landscape window in a church where both the building itself and all the other windows conform to another architectural style. The obvious discord which the solitary Tiffany land-scape panel imposes on an otherwise unified interior forces the question of why he would have wanted to be guilty of such artistic disharmony. This, in turn, raises the more fundamental issue of who should have been the final arbiter of taste in such matters if the artists could not be relied upon to discipline themselves. Whose responsibility was it to monitor the stampede among late-nineteenth-century American churches to embellish their new structures?

Surprisingly, perhaps, Tiffany survived any real condemnation on this issue, even though, as he was by far the most prolific window manufacturer of his era, examples of his work were involved in many unhappy mixtures of artistic styles. Traditionalists turned their frustration rather to the clergy on their own opportunistic ambitions: in the race to win converts and to erect edifices which would establish their credentials as spiritual leaders in a highly competi-tive field, they acceded readily both to the wishes of the donors of memorial windows and to the suggestions of stained glass studios.[48] The inevitable result was a medley of styles, as memorials were added piecemeal until all window spaces were filled. Offenders were warned to no avail against the "picture mania of the day": churches were not art galleries where the works of different painters could be juxtaposed as in an exhibition.[49]

The ever-vigilant Cram traced the original problem in a 1927 article, "The old days when a completely untrained bishop or priest employed whatever firm approached him with the most dynamic super-salesmanship, or permitted a valued parishioner to make his own choice, both of subject-matter and of manufacturer are happily gone forever — at least in most sections of the country . . ."[50] Another traditionalist, Charles Collens, admonished his readers that, "like fire, stained glass is a good servant but a bad master."[51] The lack of a common policy among church administrators concerning window styles worked to Tiffany's advantage, often allow-ing him to proceed unimpeded in his goal to introduce non-figural windows whenever the opportunity arose, the installation of each making easier that of the next.

For most, the issue was dead by the late 1910s, when the spate of church building had abated and interiors had already acquired their patchwork appearance. Today, as one views a glorious Tiffany landscape of floral composition in isolation, far from its original setting in a now defunct church, it is hard to understand the controversy that often surrounded its original unveiling.

# NOTES

1. Hamilton M. Bartlett, "The Work of the Church in Cities," *The Church* (July 1886), 95 ff. See also Rev. Daniel Addison, "The City Church," *The Churchman* (September 24, 1904), 268.

2. Will H. Low, "Old Glass in New Windows," *Scribner's*, iv (1888), 675.

3. *The Church* (note 1), 95.

4. For a comprehensive article on the American School of Glass, which was founded around 1875, see Charles H. Caffin, "Decorated Windows," *The Craftsman*, III (March, 1903), 350-60. See also Clement Heaton, "Memorial Windows: An Analysis," *The American Architect*, CXI (May 16, 1917), 301-6; Harry Eldredge Goodhue, "Stained Glass in Private Houses," *The Architectural Record*, XVII (1905), 347-54; and Mary Martin, "Stained, Leaded and Painted Glass," *Arts and Decoration*, 28 (April 1928), 73, 112. For Tiffany's own account of the School, see "Art Glass supreme in Colored Glass," *Forum*, XV (1893), 621-8.

5. Like his colleagues in the American School of Glass, Tiffany drew readily on the field of Old Master paintings for the themes of many of his ecclesiastical windows. Particular favorites, often translated directly into glass, included works by Prockhurst (e.g., Christ Blessing Little Children, The Ascension, and Magdalene), Raphael (The Transfiguration), Ingres (The Apotheosis of Homer), Murillo (The Annunciation), Perugino (The Ascension), Correggio (Holy Night), Carracci (The Holy Family), Dürer (Resurrection of Christ), Fra Angelico, Botticelli (Madonna and Child), Giotto, and Lippi. Nineteenth-century artists provided similar inspiration, especially Heinrich Hoffman (Christ and the Doctors, Christ at Gethsemane, and The Adoration of the Magi), Gustave Doré (Christ Leaving the Praetorium), Holman Hunt (Christ Knocking at the Door), Bouguereau (The Adoration of the Shepherds), Jules Lefebvre, and the PreRaphaelite, Edward Burne-Jones.

6. Sir Joshua Reynolds summed up as well as any the disappointment which most painters experienced on trying to capture on glass the effects they achieved on canvas. "I had frequently pleased myself with reflecting, after I had produced what I thought a brilliant effect of light and shadow on my canvas, how greatly that effect would be heightened by the transparency which the painting on glass would be sure to introduce. It turned out quite the reverse." (quoted in Charles H. Caffin [note 4], 35).

7. Frederick Wilson (1858-1932) was a highly versatile artist who provided Tiffany with a ceaseless output of figural window and mosaic compositions for more than thirty years. In 1927 he retired to pursue an independent career as a stained glass designer. In addition to his ecclesiastical work, he was responsible for many of the Studios' historical window themes, such as Charlemagne and Alcuin, Sir Galahad, the Argonauts, and library memorials to early printers and typographers such as Gutenberg, Caxton, Manutius, and Plantin.

8. Church construction in the United States continued to accelerate beyond the turn of the century. In 1904, an article in *The Churchman* (December 31) estimated the number of parishes and missions at roughly 6,927, a gain of 2 per cent over the previous year.

9. Tiffany's Favrile glassware was dispatched to retail stores across the country, such as John L. Earll in Utica, New York (see the Utica *Herald*, November 25, 1899), Fischer's department store in Washington, D.C. (the Washington *Star*, November 26, 1898), and I. R. Brayton in Buffalo (the Buffalo *Commercial*, December 13, 1899).

10. The initial response by the critics to Tiffany's Favrile glassware was immensely favorable, particularly when compared to his windows. Charles H. Caffin, for example, wrote in the New York *Evening Post* (February 15, 1899) of an exhibition at the Tiffany showroom at 331-341 Madison Avenue, "Included in this exhibit are several important windows. They are handsome enough. It would be hard with such material to produce a result that is not handsome. But they have not the deep artistic feeling that is exhibited in the vases . . ." In December of the same year, Otto von Bentheim wrote in *Dekorative Kunst* (December 1899), 178, "Tiffany's talent is almost entirely limited to color . . . but entirely free and above all criticism are his vases. These we cannot admire enough. The difference between them and the other items is so 'jumping' that it is hard to believe that one hand only was active here . . . In these apparently free-form decorations one finds ornamental designs of the deepest originality, and the effects of color reaches here a unique and in every way perfect splendor . . ."

11. Included among these secular windows at the 1893 Exposition were "Feeding the Flamingoes," "Autumn" (designed by Lydia Emmett), and "Birds and Fish-bowl"; at the 1895 Salon du Champ-de-Mars and the inaugural exhibition at S. Bing's Salon de l'Art Nouveau in Paris in the same year, the windows Tiffany displayed were not from his designs, but by noted European artists whom Bing had commissioned. These included Paul Ranson (two examples), Roussel, Pierre Bonnard, Ibels, Vuillard, Toulouse-Lautrec, Félix Vallaton, Eugène Grasset, Serusier, Maurice Denis, P.-A. Isaacs, and Albert Besnard; at the 1897 Salon of Le Libre Esthétique, Tiffany exhibited his own "Deep Sea" window, which was reviewed in the Brussels *La Gazette* (March 1898).

12. The original windows, now in the collection of the Morse Gallery of Art, Winter Park, Florida, are illustrated in Hugh McKean, *The "Lost" Treasures of Louis Comfort Tiffany* (Garden City 1980), 56-7.

13. The Garrett commission, entitled "Flowers, Fish and Fruit" in some contemporary literature, was installed as part of a transom in Miss Garrett's dining-room. Tiffany included the cartoon for the window in his 1899 exhibition at the Grafton Gallery in London; a duplicate panel was made and installed in the living-room at Laurelton Hall. It must be presumed that the 1885 example for Miss Garrett, now in the collection of the Baltimore Museum of Art, is comprised entirely of non-Tiffany glass made under his supervision at one of New York's commercial glasshouses, while the later example, which is believed to have been destroyed in the fire which swept Laurelton Hall in 1956, would have been comprised entirely of glass manufactured at Tiffany's Corona furnaces.

14. The Butterfly window, now in the collection of the Morse Gallery of Art, Winter Park, incorporates many features of Tiffany's on-going experimentation in window production: milled lead cames, translucent non-glass materials, and a search for novel contrasting lighting effects through the juxtaposition of translucent and reflecting glass surfaces.

15. The realistic effect achieved here by Tiffany, in which the wisteria and magnolia sprays appear to hang against the outside of the windows and therefore to draw the exterior into the room itself, was a theme developed further by Frank Lloyd Wright shortly after the turn of the century. Wright provided a sharply modernistic interpretation of Tiffany's flowers in his application of abstract geometric floral compositions to the windows in his Prairie School residences.

16. Illustrated in Will H. Low (note 2), 678.

17. The fact that Tiffany's display at the 1893 Exposition appears to have included only the three secular windows listed here, among a giant display of liturgical objects that centered on an entire Byzantine chapel, indicates Tiffany's perception of the relative balance in the market for a producer of stained glass windows and mosaics.

18. Several early references, including Charles De Kay's book, *The Art Work of Louis C. Tiffany* (Garden City 1914), list the date of Tiffany's monumental "Four Seasons" panel as 1893, the year of the Columbian Exposition. It appears with hindsight that this is incorrect. Not only is the quality of the glass in the "Four Seasons" window of such technical complexity that it is unlikely to have been among the first creations of the furnaces he established in Corona in that year, but the window, when shown at the 1900 Exposition Universelle in Paris, included the date 1900 in roman numerals. The additional fact that the window is not referred to or illustrated in any surviving literature on Tiffany's exhibitions between 1893 and 1899 strongly suggests that the ascribed date of 1893 is incorrect. Tiffany retained the "Four Seasons" window for display purposes until after the 1901 Pan-American Exposition in Buffalo (see *The Jewelers' Review*, July 24, 1901), after which it was disassembled and the four panels of the seasons installed individually in Laurelton Hall. The entire window, largely complete but lacking sections of its urn border and jeweled center, is in the

collection of the Morse Gallery of Art, Winter Park, where it has recently been reassembled in the new warehouse.

19. The only known lists of Tiffany windows include the Addendum to the 1893 Exposition catalogue, an updated version published in 1897, and an extensive list entitled "A partial List of Windows" distributed around 1910. Curiously, this does not include all the windows given in the two earlier listings.

20. The ledgers, which comprise thousands of press cuttings from the period from both American and European newspapers and magazines, also include copies of press releases issued by the Studios to newspapers across the United States to announce the completion of new window commissions in their regions.

21. The *New York Commercial Advertiser*, February 16, 1898. It is significant that the Ward memorial window is not in the main body of the church, but in a side corridor, where it is hidden from the congregation.

22. This description was included in several press releases issued by the Studios around 1900 (see note 20).

23. The William Goddard memorial in St. Luke's Church, East Greenwich, Rhode Island, provides an example of tulips, irises, and goldenrod used to depict the seasons.

24. For a color illustration of the window, see Alastair Duncan, *Tiffany Windows* (New York and London 1980), pl. 39.

25. For a discussion of the Robert Baker memorial, see the *Brooklyn Eagle* (March 30, 1899).

26. The *New York Times* (April 8, 1899) See also reviews of the window in the Philadelphia *Item* (May 8, 1899); the Troy *Budget* (April 23, 1899); the New York *Evening Post* (April 8, 1899); and the *Troy Daily Press* (April 8, 1899).

27. The *Troy Daily Press* (note 26).

28. The *New York Sun* (January 16, 1898).

29. Appropriate passages from the Scriptures were also included wherever possible by the Studios in the releases which it issued to the press to announce the completion of new church commissions.

30. For an example of a mausoleum window that incorporates a variation on the theme of the fawn in the Gould commission, see Alastair Duncan, *Tiffany Windows*, col. pl. 75.

31. The Grafton Gallery exhibition, on Brook Street, London, opened on May 16, 1899, and was reviewed, among others, by *The Illustrated London News* (June 24), 92, and *The World* (May 24), 28. The latter provided a typically mixed review in its criticism of the Baptism of Christ window, designed by Frank Brangwyn, finding it garish in comparison to Tiffany's Favrile glassware, which was "a blaze of color, shot through with ruby lights and metallic lustres."

32. For reviews of Tiffany's display at the 1900 Exposition Universelle, see the New York *Mail & Express* (March 13); the Pittsburgh *Dispatch* (March 14); the Kansas City (Mo.) *Journal* (March 17); *The China Decorator*, (April 1900), and *The New York Times* (April 20).

33. The whereabouts of the magnolia panel, designed by Agnes Northrop, is now unknown. The Snowball panel was purchased at the Exposition by Mr. Kaier of Oslo, and has remained in his family. The triptych screen was discovered some years ago by Mr. Paul Nassau, of the Lillian Nassau Gallery in New York, in a New England collection, and was lent by him to *The Folding Image* exhibition in 1984.

34. Tiffany decided to include the "Flight of Souls" window in his exhibit at the 1900 Exposition as early as 1898 (see the Cleveland *Plain Dealer*, December 25, 1898). For a color illustration of the window, see Alastair Duncan, *Tiffany Windows* (note 24), col. pl. 5.

35. The Pan-American Exposition in Buffalo was the last event in which Tiffany showed a comprehensive range of his wares. Many, such as "The Four Seasons" window and the Havemeyer punch bowl, had been in Paris the previous year. Included in Buffalo was a selection of ecclesiastical and secular windows and window cartoons; Favrile glassware; enamels; blown and leaded glass lamps, including the prototype for the Gould peacock lamp; and a large illuminated and tiered glass fountain. See *The Jewelers' Review* (note 18).

36. Variations on the St. John's Vision of the Holy City window in St. Paul's, Troy, which only *suggest*, rather than depict, the celestial city, include the William Stoddard memorial in St. Luke's Church, East Greenwich, Rhode Island, and the Margaret Standart Watson memorial in the Central Presbyterian Church (now the Westminster Presbyterian Church), Auburn, New York.

37. Documented examples of surviving Tiffany windows that depict specific landscapes include the John Henry Livingston memorial in St. Paul's Church, Troy (the neighboring countryside); the Kingsbury memorial in the First Presbyterian Church, Albany (a view of Lake Luzerne); the Cole memorial in the Aftenro Old Age Home in Duluth (the hills beyond the town); and the three Proctor diptych memorials in the Union Church, Proctor, Vermont (views of the neighboring valley, Pico Peak, etc.).

38. Windows executed in the 1910-15 period also show a remarkably high level of technical expertise, especially in the quality of their copper-foil leading, the elimination of conventional reinforcing bars, and the application of delicate etched detailing to the back layers of glass. By 1920 much of this quality had disappeared as the production of windows at the Studios became increasingly commercial. In the 1920s, only one window, that commissioned by Mr. Towle and designed by Tiffany himself, approached in its selection of glass the artistic level attained in the earlier years. The Towle window, which was given in 1925 by William De Forest to the Metropolitan Museum of Art, New York, is now on display in the Sculpture Garden of the Museum's new American wing. For reviews of the window, see *The Christian Science Monitor*, Boston, January 15, 1926, and *The Herald Tribune*, New York, December 7, 1925.

39. Tiffany's quotation on the windows was included in the Church's dedicatory booklet, published in 1910. See also *The New York Observer* (May 19, 1910), 618.

40. The American preoccupation with Gothic-style church architecture and the subsequent impact of this on window styles has been reviewed frequently since the 1880s. See, for example, Ralph Adams Cram, "Church Building: Decoration and Stained Glass," *The Churchman* (August 18, 1900), 207-12; Anne Webb Karnaghan, "Three Workers in Stained Glass," *The American Magazine of Art*, XIX (November 1928), 389-96; Charles J. Connick, "Modern Glass – A Review," *International Studio*, 80 (October 1924), 40-53; Orin E. Skinner, "The Decorative Elements in Stained Glass," *The American Architect*, CXXIX (February 5, 1926), 215-20; and Helen Jackson Zakin, "American Neo-Gothic Stained Glass," *Henry Keck Stained Glass Studios 1913-74* (Syracuse, 1985), ch. 3.

41. A narrow and dogmatic traditionalist, Cram was blinded by the glory of Europe's Gothic age. He wrote and spoke out constantly against the American School of Glass, believing specifically that a church window is merely a piece of translucent colored decoration and therefore subordinate to its architectural environment. His account of a recent Tiffany commission, published in *The Churchman* (August 18, 1900), 212, reveals his abhorrence of the pictorial style of window practiced by Tiffany and others. "To show the false position the art of glass-training occupies nowadays, let me speak of an incredible occurrence I know of. Certain people who were proposing to give a memorial window and who had a liking for the painter Millet, asked a certain firm of glass-stainers to make a window representing 'The Sower', and, instead of refusing the commission, it was accepted with alacrity. Now no subject could possibly be chosen which was less adaptable to stained glass than this particular picture, and yet the work was cheerfully undertaken, without the least regard to the absurdity of the idea. Not only this; but, at the instigation of the donors, the glass makers copied the well-known picture, and because the man in whose memory the window was to be erected wore a full beard, they showed this full beard on Millet's figure. Could anything be more preposterous and more disheartening? Yet this is an example of what is asked for and what is gotten at this time, and it shows how totally false is the attitude of the public and the makers of glass toward this most noble and exalted form of religious art."

42. Charles J. Connick (note 40), 46.

43. Edith Syford, "Examples of Recent Work from the Studios of Louis C. Tiffany," reprint, *New England Magazine*, September 1911, unpaginated.

44. A Studios' press release on April 3, 1909, listed the W. B. Fisher memorial in the First Presbyterian Church,

Akron, as the first landscape to be installed in an Ohio church.

45. Tiffany did, however, impose his own taste over those of the clergy and donors of memorial windows on occasions when it suited him. His mastery of his field and increasing celebrity allowed him a measure of freedom to insert whatever style of window he wished. Elderly communicants of two Midwest churches who were interviewed in 1980 recalled separate instances when Tiffany and the church authorities differed on what type of window should be chosen. In both cases, Tiffany's preference prevailed.

46. The *New York Sun*, December 13 and 14, 1913.

47. The completed window was illustrated in the *Sun* on December 14; *Memorials in Glass and Stone*, Tiffany Studios booklet, New York, 1913; and Alastair Duncan, *Tiffany Windows*, 166.

48. Tiffany did on occasion design medieval medallion windows for neo-Gothic churches. Many of these, such as the John W. Stoddard memorial in the Westminster Church, Dayton, Ohio, and those in the first Church of Christ, Fairfield, Connecticut, and St. Saviour's Episcopal Church, Bar Harbor, Maine, are inspired works that incorporate the mosaic principles and primary colors of the Gothic originals with breathtakingly beautiful results.

49. *The Church Standard*, January 6, 1900.

50. Ralph Adams Cram, "Stained Glass in Church Architecture," *Stained Glass* (1927), 223.

51. Charles Collens, "The Memorial Window – A Plaint," *The American Architect*, CXI (March 21, 1917), 182.

59. "Vase of Red Peonies" Window, leaded Favrile glass, 54" x 44", Tiffany Studios, New York, *c.* 1900

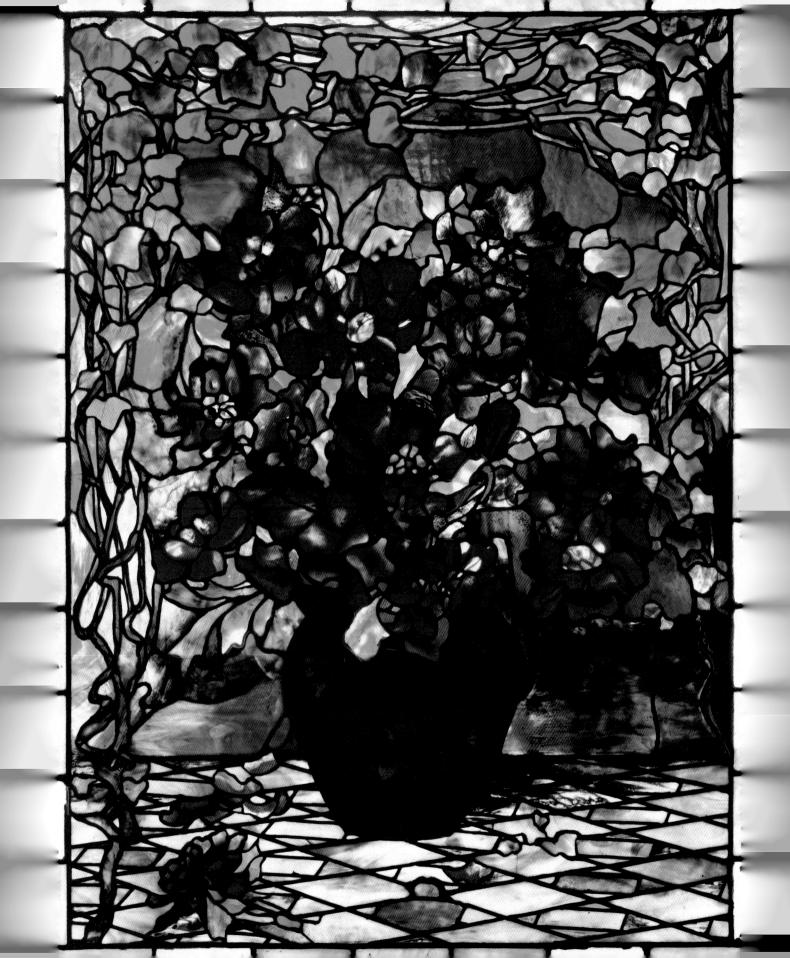

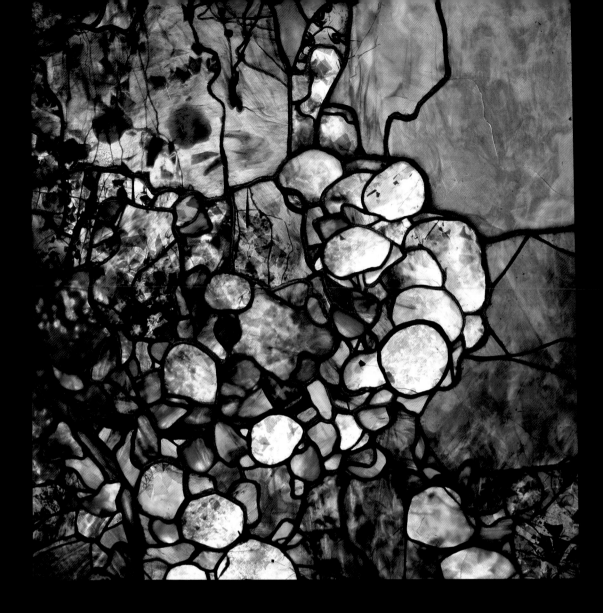

50. Exposition Snowball Window, leaded Favrile glass, 31½" x 31½", Tiffany Studios, New York, 1900

51. "Magnolia" Window, leaded Favrile glass, 16" x 48¼", Tiffany Studios, New York, c. 1905-10

52. Window with Parakeets and Gold Fish Bowl, leaded Favrile glass, 42" x 78", Tiffany Glass & Decorating Co., New York, c. 1893

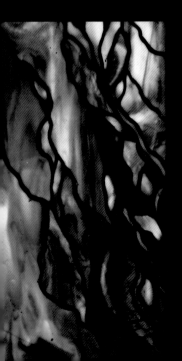

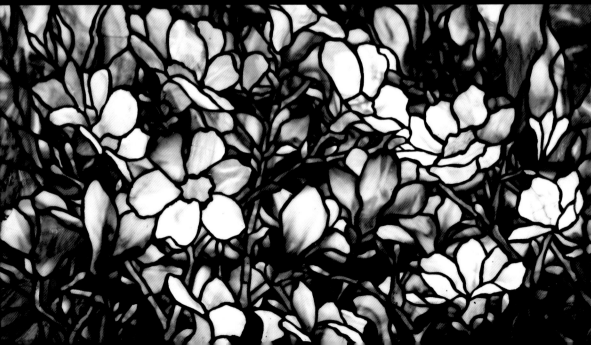

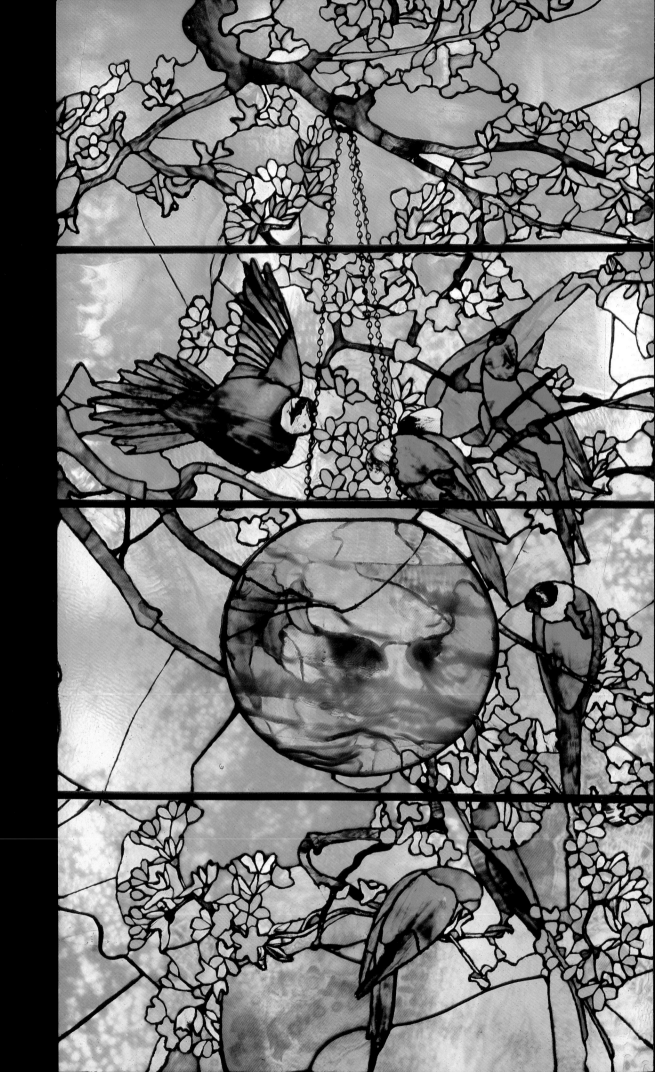

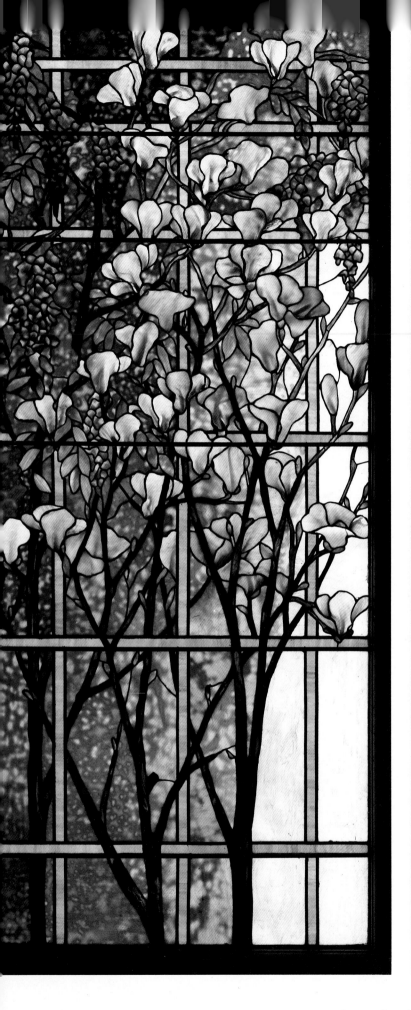
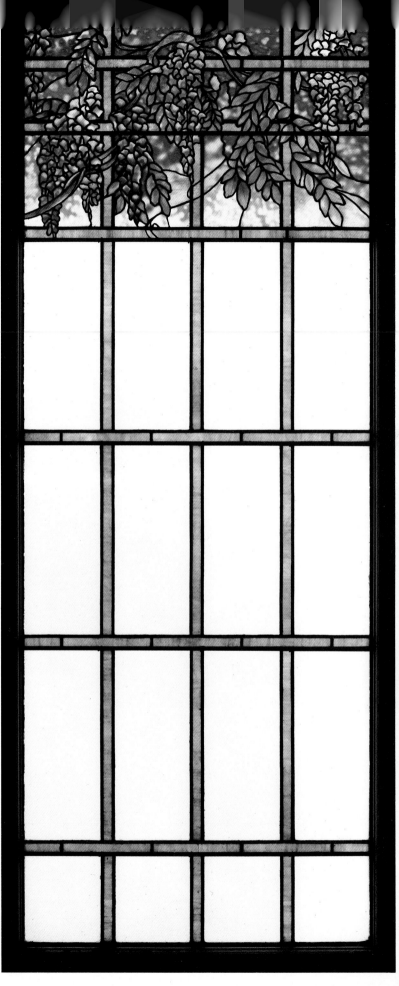

63-66.  "Magnolia and Wisteria" Window, leaded Favrile glass, four panels each 89" x 37", Tiffany Studios, New York, 1905-10

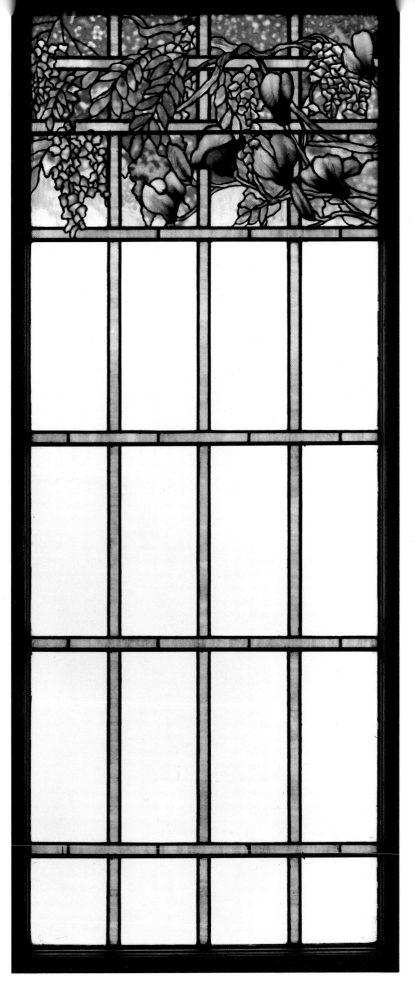
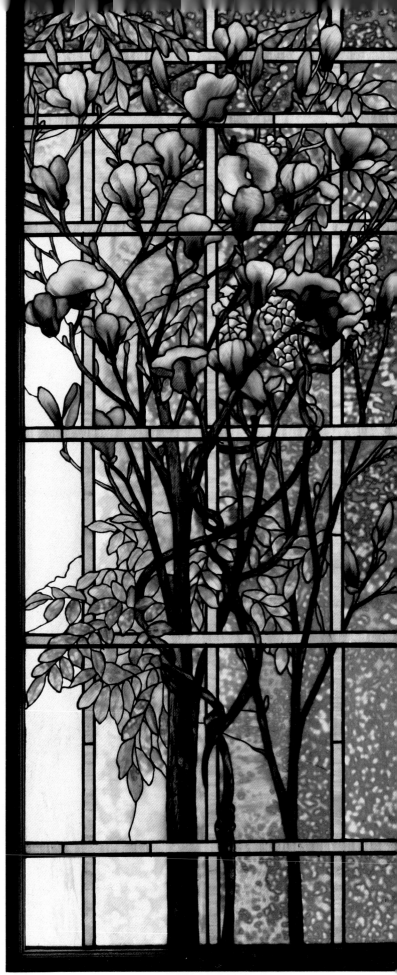

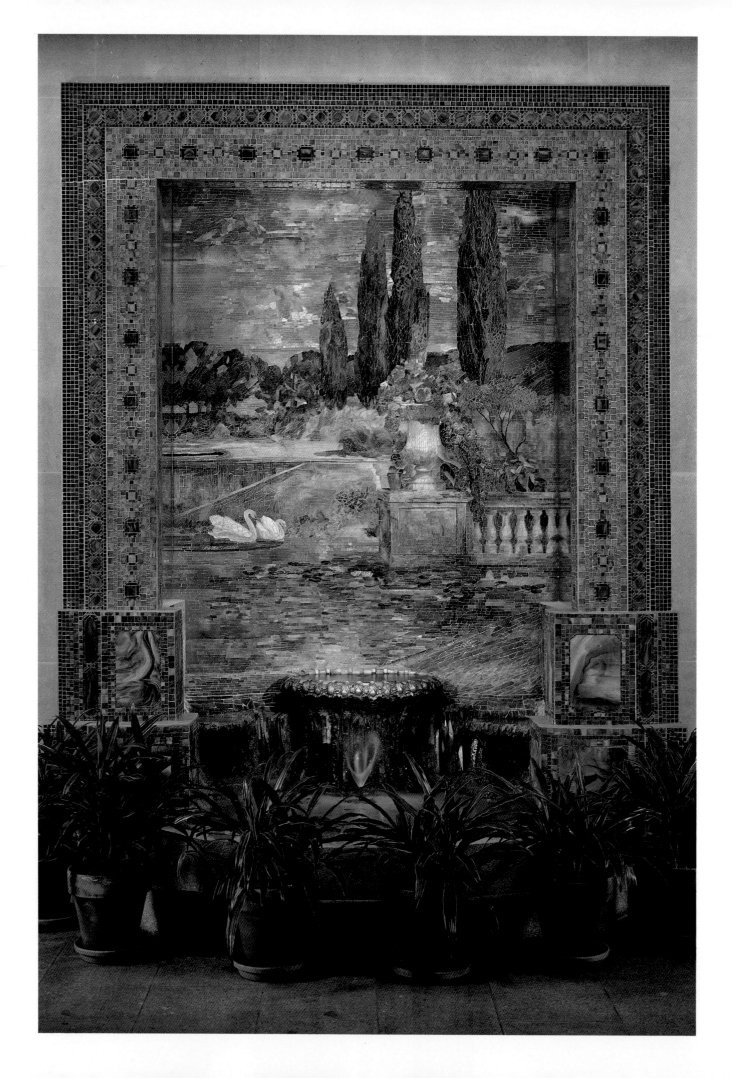

67. Mural and Fountain, Favrile glass mosaic, Tiffany Studios, New York, c. 1900-10

68. Cartoon for Mosaic Bird Bath, pencil and watercolor on paper, 13⅞″ x 11⅞″, Tiffany Studios, New York, c. 1900-10

69. Mosaic Wall Panel with Fish Design, Favrile glass mosaic, 38¼″ x 16″, Tiffany Studios, New York, c. 1906

70. "Sulphur Crested Cockatoos" Mosaic Wall Panel, Favrile glass mosaic, 22½″ x 31½″, Tiffany Studios, New York, 1908

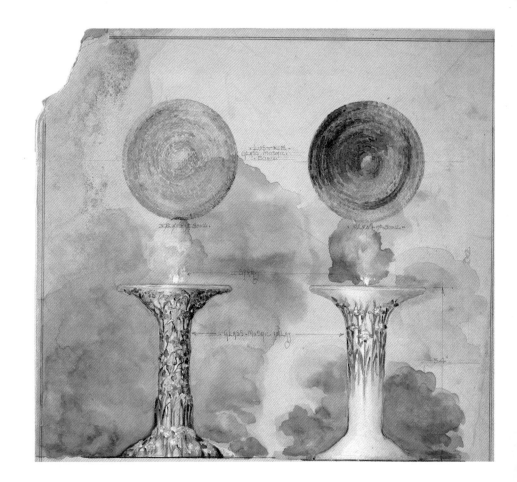

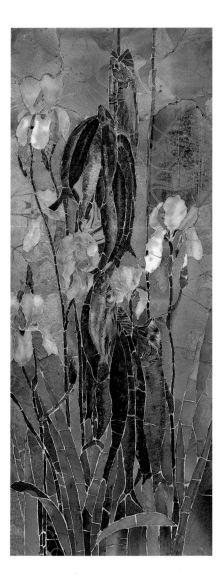

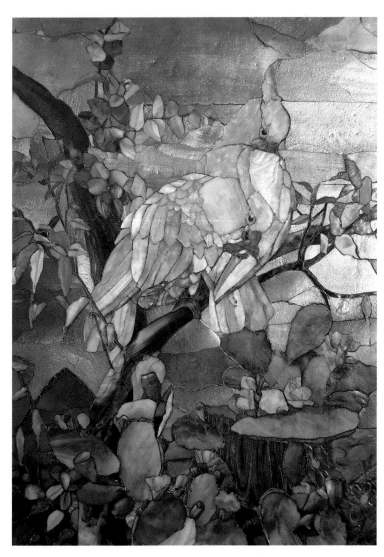

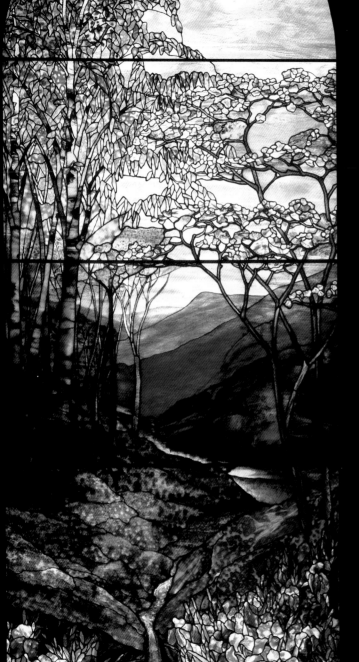

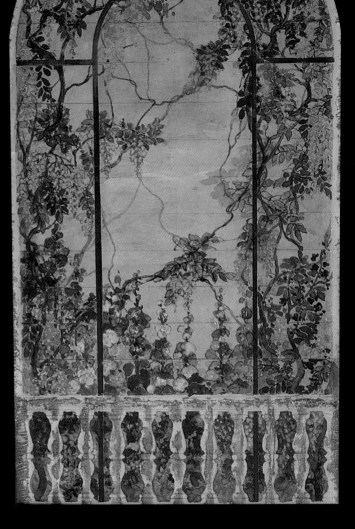

71. Sarah Fay Sumner Memorial
Window, leaded glass, 120″ x 42″, Tiffany
Studios, New York, 1912

72. Cartoon for Wisteria and Hollyhock
Window, watercolor and pencil on board,
11⅞″ x 21⅝″, Louis Comfort Tiffany,

# DETAILS OF PLATES

**1. Helen Gould Landscape Window**
Tiffany Studios, New York, 1910
Leaded Favrile glass
130" x 70" (3.30 x 1.78m.)
Unsigned
Literature: Ethel Syford, *Examples of Recent Work from the Studios of Louis C. Tiffany*, Boston 1911; Mary Martin, "Stained, Leaded and Painted Glass," *Arts and Decoration* (April 1928), 112; Alastair Duncan, *Tiffany Windows*, London/New York 1980, 171 (detail)
Provenance: Miss Helen Gould; Mr. Vito D'Agostino; Parke-Bernet (N.Y. 1969); Bruce and Adele Randall

**2, 3. Peacock Window**
Tiffany Studios, New York, c. 1912
Leaded glass
111½" x 29¾" (2.83m. x 75 cm.)
With tag impressed *TIFFANY STUDIOS NEW YORK*
Literature: *Memorials in Glass and Stone*, Tiffany Studios, New York 1913; "A New Era in Domestic Glass," *Arts and Decoration* (June 1913), 288; Alastair Duncan, *Tiffany Windows*, cover ill. and Plate 61.
Provenance: Capt. Joseph R. DeLamar; Private collection; Mr. David Bellis

**4. Cockatoo and Parakeet Window**
Tiffany Studios, New York, c. 1912
Leaded Favrile glass
109½" x 29¾" (2.78m. x 78cm.)
Unsigned
Literature: *Memorials in Glass and Stone*; "A New Era in Domestic Glass," *Arts and Decoration* (June 1913), 288; *The New York Herald Magazine* (December 1926), 12; Alastair Duncan, *Tiffany Windows*, Plate 61.
Provenance: Captain Joseph R. DeLamar; Private collection; Mr. David Bellis
Note: Commissioned by Capt. DeLamar for the Pompeian Room in his town house at Madison Ave. and 37th St., New York, the windows were later transferred to DeLamar's country estate "Pembroke" in Glen Cove, Long Island

**5. Punch Bowl with Three Ladles**
Tiffany Studios, New York, 1900
Favrile glass and gilded silver
Bowl: 14½" x 24" in diameter (37 x 61cm.)
Ladles: ½" x 3½" (1 x 9cm.)
Impressed on base *April 1900/Tiffany/ G. & D. Co.)1282*
Exhibited: Exposition Universelle, Paris 1900; Pan-American Exposition, Buffalo 1901; "Nineteenth Century America," Metropolitan Museum of Art, New York, April-September 1970; "Glass from World's Fairs, 1851-1904," Corning Museum of Glass, Corning, N.Y., 1986

Literature: Florence N. Levy, "Applied Arts at the Paris Exposition," *American Art Annual III* (New York 1900), 21; Robert Koch, *Louis C. Tiffany, Rebel in Glass*, New York 1966, Pl. ix; *Nineteenth Century America: Furniture and Other Decorative Arts*, New York 1970; S. Bing, *Artistic America, Tiffany Glass, and Art Nouveau*, Cambridge, Mass., 1970, frontispiece; Robert Koch, "Tiffany Exhibition Punch Bowl," *Arts in Virginia*, 16 (Winter/Spring 1976), 32-39; Charles H. Carpenter, Jr., "The Silver of Louis Comfort Tiffany," *Antiques* (February 1980), 393; Patricia Bayer, "Art Nouveau," *Antiques World* (October 1981), 31; Carla Cerutti, *Arti Decorative del Novecento: Liberty* (Milan 1985), 50-51; Frederick R. Brandt, *Late 19th and Early 20th Century Decorative Arts, The Sydney and Frances Lewis Collection in the Virginia Museum of Fine Arts*, Seattle 1985, 74-75; Jane Shadel Spillman, *Glass from World's Fairs*, Corning, N.Y. 1986, 49; Tessa Paul, *The Art of Louis Comfort Tiffany*, Baldock, Herts, England, 1978, 78
Provenance: Henry O. Havemeyer; Robert and Gladys Koch; Collection of the Virginia Museum of Fine Arts, Sydney and Frances Lewis Art Nouveau Fund

**6. Gould Peacock Lamp**
Tiffany Studios, New York, 1908-13
Favrile glass and enamel on copper
40½" (1.02m) high, 13" (33cm.) diameter
Base unsigned; globe inscribed *M 3460* on inside rim
Exhibited: Tiffany Studios Showroom, 1916; Dayton (Ohio) Art Institute, October-November 1966; "Louis C. Tiffany: The Laurelton Hall Years", Nassau County Museum of Fine Art, Roslyn, N.Y., August 17-October 19, 1986; Art Nouveau Gallery, Virginia Museum of Fine Arts, Richmond
Literature: Charles de Kay, *The Art Work of Louis C. Tiffany*, New York 1914, 34; *The Objects of Art of the Louis Comfort Tiffany Foundation*, Sale No. 789, Parke-Bernet Galleries, New York, September 24-28, 1946, lot 288; Gertrude Speenburgh, *The Arts of the Tiffanys*, Chicago 1956, 69-70; R. Koch, *Rebel in Glass*, 187, 206; Henry Winter, *The Dynasty of Louis Comfort Tiffany*, Boston 1971 (privately printed), 242-43; Patricia Bayer, "Art Nouveau," 24; Alastair Duncan, *Tiffany at Auction*, New York 1981, 17; William Feldstein, Jr., and Alastair Duncan, *The Lamps of Tiffany Studios*, New York/London 1983, 76-77; F. R. Brandt, *Late 19th Century and Early 20th Century*

*Decorative Arts*, 74-75; *Louis C. Tiffany: The Laurelton Hall Years*, 21; T. Paul, *The Art of Louis Comfort Tiffany*, 92
Provenance: Mr. Charles W. Gould; Louis C. Tiffany Foundation; Mr. Richard Barnett; Mr. Oscar Schroeder; Christie's (N.Y. 1978); Collection of the Virginia Museum of Fine Arts, Gift of Sydney and Frances Lewis

**7. Lotus Bowl**
Tiffany Studios, New York, c. 1905
Favrile pottery
4¾" (12cm.) high x 12½" (32cm.) long x 7³⁄₁₆" (18cm.) wide
Inscribed *L. C. T.*
Provenance: Philadelphia Museum of Art, Gift of Mr. and Mrs. Thomas E. Shipley, Jr.

**8. "Fern" Ceramic Vase**
Tiffany Studios, New York, c. 1905
Favrile pottery
12" (30cm.) high
Inscribed *L. C. T.*
Literature: Gareth Clark and Margaret Hughton, *A Century of Ceramics in the Unites States*, New York 1979, fig. 56; John Loring, *Tiffany's 150 Years*, New York 1987, 123
Provenance: Professor Martin Eidelberg

**9. "Salamander" Vase**
Tiffany Studios, New York, 1905-10
Favrile pottery
9½" (24cm.) high, 6½" (16cm.) wide
Signed *LCT* with firm's original paper label
Literature: John Loring, "American Art Pottery", *Connoisseur* (April 1979), 281
Provenance: Professor Martin Eidelberg
Note: Following the 1900 Exposition Universelle in Paris, Tiffany began his pottery experimentation in earnest. His early pieces in the medium reflected a heavy and uninspired hand. By 1906, however, after years of continual research, he produced boldly sculpted pieces of an impressive lightness and vigor. Some of them, such as this "Salamander" vase, which was designed as a cabbage with a profusion of flowers above a plant-form body, were re-created from an earlier *repoussé* enamel-on-copper model.

**10. Double Card Case**
Tiffany Studios, New York, 1905-10
Wood and Favrile glass with mother-of-pearl, abalone and enamel insets on cover
5½" (14cm.) high, 5½" (14cm.) long
Inscribed *L. C. Tiffany*
Provenance: Joseph Briggs; Mr. and Mrs. Howard Ellman

**Humidor**
Tiffany Studios, New York, 1905-10
Wood and Cypriote Favrile glass
4⁹⁄₁₆" (12cm.) high, 4½" (11cm.) long
Inscribed *A23614 L. C. T.* and (indistinctly) *207*
Provenance: Joseph Briggs; Mr. and Mrs. Howard Ellman

**Humidor with Mounted Scarab Decoration**
Tiffany Studios, New York, c. 1900
Wood and Favrile glass scarabs
5½" (14cm.) high, 6¾" (17cm.) long
Stamped on base (twice) *TIFFANY STUDIOS N. Y.* around an *L. C. T.* monogram, and inscribed *S/C 2871*
Literature: Alastair Duncan, *Fin de Siècle Masterpieces from the Silverman Collection*, New York 1989
Provenance: Mrs. Alice Osofsky; Private collection
Note: Virtually nothing is known of Tiffany's production of wood tabletop items, including humidors, playing card cases, and cigarette boxes, beyond the fact that they were offered by Tiffany & Co. in the firm's annual Blue Book catalogues around 1910.

**11. Bronze-mounted Cypriote Glass Covered Box with Salamander Decoration**
Tiffany Studios, New York, 1895-1905
Favrile glass and bronze
9¼" (23cm.) long
Unsigned
Provenance: Private collection

**12. Enameled "Gourd" Tray**
Tiffany Studios, New York, c. 1900
Enamel on copper
25½" x 14" (65 x 35cm.)
Unsigned
Literature: James L. Harvey, "Source of Beauty in Favrile Glass," *Brush & Pencil* (January 1902), 175; R. Koch, *Rebel in Glass*, 189
Provenance: Christie's (N.Y. 1985); Mr. and Mrs. Erving Wolf

**13. "Morning Glories" Sketch**
Louis Comfort Tiffany, New York, 1913
Watercolor on paper
22⅝" x 21⅜" (57 x 54cm.)
Signed *Louis C. Tiffany, October 1913*
Literature: Robert Koch, *Louis C. Tiffany's Glass, Bronze, Lamps*, New York 1971, fig. 21
Provenance: Arthur J. and Leslie H. Nash; Private collection; Sotheby's (N.Y. 1983); Bruce and Adele Randall

**14, 15. Enameled Frog Paperweight**
Tiffany Studios, New York, 1900-10
Enamel on copper
5" (13cm.) diameter
Inscribed *L. C. T.*, impressed *EL 212*
Provenance: Bruce and Adele Randall

**16. "My Family at Somesville"**
Louis Comfort Tiffany, c. 1888
Oil on canvas
24" x 36" (61 x 91cm.) Unsigned
Exhibited: "Tiffany – Louis Comfort Tiffany: The Paintings," Grey Art Gallery and Study Center, New York University, March 20, 1979, Plate 8, No. 24; "The Art of Louis Comfort Tiffany," M. H. de Young Memorial Museum, San Francisco, April 25-August 8, 1981, No. 13; "The Treasures of Tiffany," Museum of Science and Industry, Chicago, June 10-November 14, 1982, fig. 19, No. 64; "Louis C. Tiffany: The Laurelton Hall Years," 48
Literature: G. Speenburgh, *The Arts of the Tiffanys*, 39; H. F. McKean, *The "Lost" Treasures of Louis Comfort Tiffany*, New York 1980, 23
Provenance: Collection of the Artist; Charles Hosmer Morse Museum of American Art, Winter Park, FL, through the courtesy of the Charles Hosmer Morse Foundation
Note: Based on a small oil sketch, this painting depicts Tiffany's children, Charles Lewis, Mary Woodbridge, and the twins Louis Comfort and Julia de Forest, with his wife Louise and a nurse. The treatment of the surrounding Maine countryside exhibits the luminous quality that characterizes many of his best landscapes.

**17. "Family Group with Oxen"**
Louis Comfort Tiffany, c. 1888
Oil on canvas
22¾" x 35⅛" (58 x 89cm.) Unsigned
Exhibited: "The Genius of Louis C. Tiffany," Heckscher Museum, Huntington, N.Y., July 9-August 15, 1967, No. 149; "Tiffany . . . The Paintings," No. 36
Provenance: Mr. and Mrs. Charles T. Lusk

**18. "Fields of Irvington"**
Louis Comfort Tiffany, 1879
Watercolor
19" x 26" (48 x 66 cm.)
Signed *Louis C. Tiffany, '79*
Exhibited: "Louis Comfort Tiffany 1848-1933," Museum of Contemporary Crafts of the American Craftsman's Council, New York, January 24-April 6, 1958, No. 5; "The Genius of Louis C. Tiffany," No. 159; "The Laurelton Hall Years," 22, No. 2
Literature: C. de Kay, *The Art Work . . .,* 8C; R. Koch, *Rebel in Glass*, 25
Provenance: Private collection

**19. "Marketplace at Nuremberg"**
Louis Comfort Tiffany, c. 1893
Oil on canvas
30½" x 39" (77 x 99cm.)
Signed lower right, *Louis C. Tiffany*
Exhibited: "Tiffany . . . The Paintings," fig. 20; "The Laurelton Hall Years," 23, No. 3
Literature: C. de Kay, *The Art Work . . .,*

8D; R. Koch, *Rebel in Glass*, 27
Provenance: Private collection

**20. "Magnolias"**
Louis Comfort Tiffany, 1885-95
Oil on canvas
21" x 30" (53 x 76cm.)
Signed *Louis C. Tiffany*
Exhibited: "The Genius of Louis C. Tiffany," No. 148
Literature: G. Speenburgh, *The Arts of the Tiffanys*, 39
Provenance: Private collection

**21. "A Corner of My Studio"**
Louis Comfort Tiffany, 1890
Oil on canvas
30⅛" x 12¼" (76 x 31cm.) Unsigned
Exhibited: Society of American Artists, New York, 1890; "Louis Comfort Tiffany 1848-1933," No. 3; "Tiffany . . . The Paintings," fig. 19, No. 43
Literature: C. de Kay, *The Art Work . . .,* 10A; G. Speenburgh, *The Arts of the Tiffanys*, 39; R. Koch, *Rebel in Glass*, 95
Provenance: Robert Tiffany Lusk; Yale University Art Gallery, Gift of Louis Tiffany Lusk
Note: The woman depicted is thought to be Tiffany's second wife, Louise, whom he married in 1886.

**22. "Pumpkin and Beets" Window**
Tiffany Studios, New York, c. 1900
Leaded glass
46⅜" x 58" (1.17 x 1.47m.)
Unsigned
Exhibited: "The Art of Louis Comfort Tiffany," Toledo Museum of Art, November 12-December 17, 1978, No. 51; "The Treasures of Tiffany," No. 28
Literature: H. F. McKean, *The "Lost" Treasures . . .,"* 88, fig. 81; Norman Potter and Douglas Jackson, *Tiffany*, London 1988, 73
Provenance: Charles Hosmer Morse Museum of American Art, Winter Park, FL, through the courtesy of the Charles Hosmer Morse Foundation

**23. "Cathedral Steps, Morlaix, Brittany"**
Louis Comfort Tiffany, 1890
Watercolor
40" x 17" (1.01m. x 43cm.)
Signed lower/left, *Louis C. Tiffany*
Exhibited: "Lous Comfort Tiffany 1848-1933," No. 9; "The Laurelton Hall Years," 37
Literature: René de Quelin, "A Many-Sided Creator of the Beautiful," *Arts and Decoration* (July 1922), 177
Provenance: Private collection

**24. "Market Day outside the Walls of Tangier, Morocco"**
Louis Comfort Tiffany, 1873
Oil on canvas
35" x 56" (89cm. x 1.42m.)
Signed and dated lower left, *Louis C. Tiffany 73*
Exhibited: National Academy of Design, New York 1873; "Tiffany . . .

The Paintings," Plate 8, No. 14
Provenance: Private collection

**25, 26. "Four Seasons" Window**
Tiffany Glass & Decorating Co., New York, 1897
Leaded Favrile glass
78" x 45" (1.98 x 1.14m.)
Unsigned
Literature: *Tiffany Studios Memorials in Glass and Stone*; A. Duncan, *Tiffany Windows*, 158
Provenance: Mr. Walter Jennings; Private collection
Note: Commissioned by Walter Jennings in 1897 for his country residence on Long Island.

**27. Flowerform Vase**
Tiffany Studios, New York, c. 1900
Favrile glass
13" (33cm.) high
Inscribed *L. C. T. M2068* with original Tiffany Glass and Decorating Company monogram paper label
Exhibited: "The Art of Louis Comfort Tiffany," No. 51; "The Treasures of Tiffany," No. 206
Literature: H. F. McKean, *The "Lost" Treasures . . .,* 158
Provenance: Charles Hosmer Morse Museum of American Art, Winter Park, FL, through the courtesy of the Charles Hosmer Morse Foundation

**28. Flowerform Vase**
Tiffany Studios, New York, 1900-05
Favrile glass
14¼" (36cm.) high, 6½" (16cm.) diameter of base
Inscribed *02417*
Provenance: Estate of Pauline Heilman, Sotheby's (N.Y. 1982); Private coll.

**29. Reactive Paperweight Vase**
Tiffany Studios, New York, 1900-05
Favrile glass
5⅞" (15cm.) high
Inscribed *47 A-Coll L. C. Tiffany-Favrile*
Provenance: Bruce and Adele Randall

**30. Aquamarine Vase**
Tiffany Studios, New York, 1910-15
Favrile glass
15" (38cm.) high
Transcribed *1999H*
Literature: R. Koch, *Louis C. Tiffany's Art Glass*, New York 1977, No. 28; N. Potter and D. Jackson, *Tiffany*, 45
Provenance: Joseph Briggs; Haworth Art Gallery, Accrington, Lancs, England; T. Paul, *The Art of Louis Comfort Tiffany*, 80-81
Note: A similar example is illustrated in Elizabeth Lounsbery, "Aquamarine Glass," *American Homes and Gardens* (December 1913), 419

**31. Lava Vase**
Tiffany Studios, New York, 1900-10
Favrile glass
5½" (14cm.) high
Inscribed *L. C. Tiffany Favrile 6904B*, with firm's original paper label
Provenance: Mr. David Bellis

**32. Lava Vase**
Tiffany Studios, New York, c. 1908
Favrile lava glass
14¾" (37cm.) high
Inscribed *L. C. Tiffany Favrile 2563C*
Literature: A. Duncan, *Fin de Siècle Masterpieces . . .*
Provenance: Private collection; Sotheby's (N.Y. 1988); Private collection

**33. Mounted Agate Vase**
Tiffany Studios, New York, 1900-10
Favrile glass with jeweled bronze mount
10" (25cm.) high
Inscribed *Louis C. Tiffany – Favrile – 546D*
Literature: A. Duncan, *Tiffany at Auction*, 40, ill. 109
Provenance: Mrs. Lillian Nassau; Eugene and Eleanor Gluck; Christie's (N.Y. 1979); Mrs. Lillian Nassau; Mr. David Geffen; Christie's (N.Y. 1984); Team Antiques

**34. Millefiore Glass Vase**
Tiffany Studios, New York, 1895-1910
Favrile glass
11¼" (29cm.) high
Inscribed *Louis C. Tiffany R2385*
Literature: *New York Times Magazine* (March 19, 1979), 92; *Architectural Digest* (June 1983), 155
Provenance: Mrs. Lillian Nassau; Mr. David Geffen; Christie's (N.Y. 1984); Team Antiques

**35. Cypriote Vase**
Tiffany Studios, New York, c. 1900
Favrile glass
9⁷⁄₁₆" (24cm.) high
Inscribed *Louis C. Tiffany L. C. T. 1779*
Exhibited: Paris Exposition, 1900
Provenance: Philadelphia Museum of Art

**36. Jack-in-the-pulpit Vase**
Tiffany Studios, New York, c. 1905-10
Enamel on copper
13⅛" (33cm.) high, 4¼" (11cm.) diameter
Inscribed *Louis C. Tiffany*, impressed *SG101*
Literature: N. Potter and D. Jackson, *Tiffany*, 96; A. Duncan, *Fin de Siècle Masterpieces . . .*
Provenance: Barry Toombs; Sothebys (N.Y. 1984); Private collection
Note: Tiffany appears to have set up an enamel department in 1898 as an adjunct to the Studios' newly established metal furnaces, in time to include several enameled items in his selection for the Paris 1900 exhibition. The critic Samuel Howe traced Tiffany's technique in the April 1902 issue of *The Craftsman*. After 1904 there were no specific references to the enameling department in the firm's literature. It appears to have closed as quietly as it began, probably around 1910, although it reopened in 1921 when Tiffany Furnaces, the successor to

Tiffany Studios, introduced a new line of enamelware, mainly to desk sets.

**37. Enameled Box with Butterfly Design**
Tiffany Studios, New York, c. 1902
Enamel on copper
1⅞" x 4⅛" (5 x 10cm.)
Inscribed *C D 9041 8, Louis C. Tiffany, July 28, 1902, N.F. McG to C.B.*
Provenance: Bruce and Adele Randall

**38. Vase with Handles**
Tiffany Studios, New York, 1900-10
Enamel on copper
9¾" (25cm.) high, 10½" (27cm.) diameter of base, 6⅜" (16cm.) diameter of liner
Impressed *TIFFANY STUDIOS NEW YORK S1285* with Tiffany Glass Decorating Co. logo
Exhibited: "The Laurelton Hall Years"
Literature: C. de Kay, *The Art Work . . .,* 34; G. Speenburgh, *The Arts of the Tiffanys,* 76; R. Koch, *Rebel in Glass,* 189; Henry Winter, *The Supplement,* Back Bay Annex, Boston 1967, 46
Provenance: Parke-Bernet (N.Y. 1946); Private collection; Team Antiques

**39. Iris Lantern**
Tiffany Studios, New York, c. 1900-10
Leaded Favrile glass and bronze
23¼" x 13½" (59 x 34cm.)
Unsigned
Literature: W. Feldstein, Jr., and A. Duncan, *The Lamps of Tiffany Studios,* 38-39
Provenance: Private collection

**40. Pond Lily Chandelier**
Tiffany Studios, New York, 1900-10
Leaded Favrile glass and bronze
36" (91cm.) diameter of shade
Unsigned
Literature: W. Feldstein, Jr., and A. Duncan, *The Lamps of Tiffany Studios,* 84-87
Provenance: Private collection, Oak Park, IL., Mr. John Belger, Sr.

**41. Dragonfly Chandelier**
Tiffany Studios, New York, 1900-10
Leaded Favrile glass and bronze
28" (71cm.) diameter
Impressed *TIFFANY STUDIOS NEW YORK*
Provenance: Private collection

**42. Elaborate Peony Table Lamp**
Tiffany Studios, New York, 1906-10
Leaded Favrile glass and bronze
30" (76cm.) high, 22" (56cm.) diameter of shade
Shade: Impressed *TIFFANY STUDIOS NEW YORK*
Base: Impressed *TIFFANY STUDIOS 542*
Literature: W. Feldstein, Jr., and A. Duncan, *The Lamps of Tiffany Studios,* 32-33
Provenance: Private collection; Mr. David Bellis

**43. Oriental Poppy Floor Lamp**
Tiffany Studios, New York, c. 1900-10

Leaded Favrile glass and bronze
76" (1.93m) high, 30" (76cm.) diameter
Unsigned
Literature: W. Feldstein, Jr., and A. Duncan, *The Lamps of Tiffany Studios,* 158
Provenance: Private collection

**44. Floral Chandelier**
Tiffany Studios, New York, 1900-10
Leaded Favrile glass, with bronze chains
10½" (27cm.) high, 25" (63cm.) diameter of shade
Impressed *TIFFANY STUDIOS NEW YORK*
Literature: W. Feldstein, Jr., and A. Duncan, *The Lamps of Tiffany Studios,* 174-75
Provenance: Mr. David Bellis
Note: This is one of the few Tiffany shades known to incorporate painted details, a technique used selectively on Tiffany windows, mainly for facial details. The shade is also unusual in having a non-repeating design, including trellised morning glories and clematis.

**45, 46. Cobweb Table Lamp**
Tiffany Studios, New York, 1900-05
Leaded Favrile glass and bronze
25½" (65cm.) high, 17½" (44cm.) diameter of shade
Base: The underside and font impressed *TIFFANY STUDIOS NEW YORK 2883*
Literature: *The Spinning Wheel* (May 1979), cover ill.; *Review of the Season,* Christie's Yearbook, London 1979, 355; Victor Arwas, *Tiffany,* New York 1979, Plate 35; A. Duncan, *Tiffany at Auction,* 110, No. 297; W. Feldstein, Jr., and A. Duncan, *The Lamps of Tiffany Studios,* 90-91
Provenance: Mr. Jasha Nicoyevski; Mrs. Lillian Nassau; Mr. and Mrs. Eugene Gluck; Christie's (N.Y. 1979); Mr. Joel Schur
Note: The present example is illustrated in the original Tiffany Studios photograph album to advertise model no. 151; see Egon Neustadt, *The Lamps of Tiffany,* Fairfield, Conn., 1970, 169, No. 236

**47. Cobweb Table Lamp**
Tiffany Studios, New York, 1900-05
Leaded Favrile glass, mosaic, and bronze
30¼" (77cm.) high, 19" (48cm.) diameter of shade
Base impressed *TIFFANY STUDIOS NEW YORK*
Provenance: Mr. Jeffrey Thier; Mr. and Mrs. Jack Stievelman

**48. Butterfly Table Lamp**
Tiffany Studios, New York, 1899-1905
Leaded Favrile glass, mosaic, and bronze
26½" (67cm.) high, 18" (46cm.) diameter of shade
Shade: Unsigned

Base: The font impressed *TIFFANY STUDIOS NEW YORK 25902*
Literature: W. Feldstein, Jr., and A. Duncan, *The Lamps of Tiffany Studios,* 168-69
Provenance: Mr. Ted Ingham; Mr. David Bellis

**49. Laburnum Table Lamp**
Tiffany Studios, New York, 1900-10
Leaded Favrile glass and bronze
27½" (70cm.) high, 24" (61cm.) diameter of shade
Shade: Impressed *TIFFANY STUDIOS NEW YORK 1537*
Base: Unsigned
Provenance: (shade) Christie's (N.Y. 1982); (base) Sotheby's (N.Y. 1984); Mr David Bellis

**50. Magnolia Floor Lamp**
Tiffany Studios, New York, 1906-10
Leaded Favrile glass and bronze
79" (2m.) high, 28" (71cm.) diameter of shade
Shade impressed *TIFFANY STUDIOS NEW YORK 1599*
Literature: W. Feldstein, Jr., and A. Duncan, *The Lamps of Tiffany Studios,* 74-75
Provenance: Mrs. Lillian Nassau; Mr. David Geffen; Christie's (N.Y. 1984); Private collection

**51. Dragonfly Table Lamp**
Tiffany Studios, New York, 1900-10
Leaded Favrile glass and bronze
32" (81cm.) high, 22" (56cm.) diameter of shade
Shade: Impressed *TIFFANY STUDIOS NEW YORK 1507-33*
Base impressed *TIFFANY STUDIOS NEW YORK 550*
Literature: W. Feldstein, Jr., and A. Duncan, *The Lamps of Tiffany Studios,* 168-69
Provenance: Mr. Ted Ingham; Mr. David Bellis

**52. Maple Leaf Table Lamp**
Tiffany Studios, New York, 1900-05
Leaded Favrile glass and bronze
18½" (47cm.) high, 17" (43cm.) diameter of shade
Base impressed *TIFFANY STUDIOS NEW YORK 78*
Exhibition: "Art Nouveau," Finch College Museum of Art, 1969, No. 168
Literature: W. Feldstein, Jr., and A. Duncan, *The Lamps of Tiffany Studios,* 34-35
Provenance: Mrs. Beatrice Weiss; Mr. John Mecom

**53. Lotus Table Lamp**
Tiffany Studios, New York, 1900-10
Leaded Favrile and mosaic glass, and bronze
34¾" (88cm.) high, 28" (71cm.) diameter of shade
Base impressed *TIFFANY STUDIOS NEW YORK 352*
Literature: W. Feldstein, Jr., and A. Duncan, *The Lamps of Tiffany Studios,* 78; A. Duncan, *Fin de Siècle*

*Masterpieces . . .*
Provenance: Charles Wrigley; Wrigley family (by inheritance); Mrs. Sandra van den Broek; Private collection
Note: The Lotus was the most expensive table lamp recorded in Tiffany's Studios' Price Lists between 1900 and 1913. Because of its high cost ($750), only one was made at a time, to be replaced by another example when required.

**54. "Four Seasons" Jeweled Gold Box**
Tiffany & Co., New York, 1914
Gold, enamel, opals, tourmalines, sapphires, and chrysoprases
6" x 6" x 2" (15 x 15 x 5cm.) approximately
Base stamped *TIFFANY & CO., 18397 MAKERS 6035, 18KT. GOLD,* above the letter *M* for John C. Moore, president and chairman 1907-47
Provenance: Private collection; Sotheby's (N.Y. 1987); Charles Hosmer Morse Museum of American Art, Winter Park, FL, through the courtesy of the Charles Hosmer Morse Foundation
Note: The Tiffany & Co. ledgers record this box entered April 30, 1914; the box was made at the factory, the enameling and stone-setting were done in the workshops at the store. This box was made while Louis Comfort Tiffany held the position of artistic director of Tiffany & Co. It depicts the famous Four Season stained glass panel which he exhibited at the Paris Exposition Universelle in 1900 and the following year at the Pan-American Exposition in Buffalo.

**55. Medusa Brooch**
Louis Comfort Tiffany, c. 1902-04
Gold, opals, and olivines
Inscribed *L. C. Tiffany*
Provenance: Henry Walters; Parke-Bernet (N.Y. November 22, 1943, lot no. 586); present whereabouts unknown

**56. Necklace with Grape and Vine motifs**
Louis Comfort Tiffany, c. 1904
Gold, enamel, and opals
18" (46cm.) long
Marked *Tiffany & Co.*
Exhibited: St. Louis Exposition, 1904; Paris Salon, 1906; "Louis Comfort Tiffany 1848-1933," Plate 30, No. 246
Literature: *Tiffany & Company, at the Saint Louis Exposition,* 172; R. Koch, *Rebel in Glass,* 190; S. Bing, *Artistic America . . .,* 166; R. Koch, *Louis C. Tiffany's Art Glass,* No. 118; T. Paul, *The Art of Louis Comfort Tiffany,* 96
Provenance: Sarah E. Hanley; Metropolitan Museum of Art, Gift of Sarah E. Hanley, 1946

**57. Sketches for Vinaigrettes with Favrile glass bodies, executed by Tiffany & Co.,** c. 1900
Provenance: Tiffany & Co.

155

**58. Vinaigrette**
Tiffany & Co., New York, 1900
Favrile glass, enameled gold, Mexican opals, diamonds, rubies, and emeralds
5¼″ (13cm.) long
Impressed *TIFFANY & CO* with beaver hallmark
Exhibited: Paris Exposition, 1900; Pan-American Exposition, Buffalo, 1901
Literature: Contemporary photograph, Tiffany & Co, Archives, Parsippany, N.J.
Provenance: Christie's (N.Y. 1987); Private collection

**59. "Vase of Red Peonies" Window**
Tiffany Studios, New York, c. 1900
Leaded Favrile glass
54″ x 44″ (1.37 x 1.11m.)
Unsigned
Provenance: Bruce and Adele Randall

**60. Exposition Snowball Window**
Tiffany Studios, New York, 1900
Leaded Favrile glass
31½″ x 31½″ (80 x 80cm.)
Exhibited: Paris Exposition Universelle, 1900
Provenance: Fredrik Kiaer, 1900; Kiaer family (by inheritance)

**61. "Magnolia" Window**
Tiffany Studios, New York, 1905-10
Leaded Favrile glass
16″ x 48¼″ (41cm x 1.22m.)
Unsigned
Provenance: Bruce and Adele Randall

**62. Window with Parakeets and Gold Fish Bowl**
Tiffany Glass & Decorating Co., New York, c. 1893
Leaded Favril glass
42″ x 78″ (1.06 x 1.98m.)
Unsigned
Exhibited: Columbian Exposition, Chicago 1893
Literature: *Objects at the 1893 Chicago Exposition: synopsis of the exhibition . . .*, Tiffany Glass & Decorating Company (1893), illustration p. 5, discussion p. 8; William H. Thomas, "Window Making as an Art," *Munsey's Magazine* (December 1901), 392; A. Duncan, *Tiffany Windows*, Plate 3; J. S. Spillman, *Glass from World's Fairs*, 45
Provenance: Lorenz Trust

**63-66. "Magnolia and Wisteria" Window**
Tiffany Studios, New York, 1905-10
Leaded Favrile glass
Four panels, each 89″ x 37″ (2.26m. x

94cm.)
Provenance: Bruce and Adele Randall

**67. Mural and Fountain**
Tiffany Studios, New York, c. 1900-10
Favrile glass mosaic
Provenance: Metropolitan Museum of Art, Gift of Lillian Nassau, 1976, Gift of Mrs. L. Grooves, 1978

**68. Cartoon for Mosaic Bird Bath**
Ecclesiastical Department, Tiffany Studios, New York, c. 1900-10
Pencil and watercolor on paper
13⅞″ x 11⅞″ (35 x 30cm.)
Signed *Louis C. Tiffany*
Designed for Mrs. Richardson Pratt, Brooklyn, N.Y.
Provenance: Metropolitan Museum of Art, Purchase, Walter Hoving and Julia T. Weld Gifts and Dodge Fund, 1967

**69. Wall Panel with Fish Design**
Tiffany Studios, New York, c. 1906
Favrile glass mosaic
38¼″ x 16″ (97 x 41cm.)
Unsigned
Literature: W. H. Thomas, "Glass Mosaic as Old Art with a New Distinction," *International Studio* (May 1906), LXXVII
Provenance: Private collection

**70. "Sulphur Crested Cockatoos" Wall Panel**
Tiffany Studios, New York, 1908
Favrile glass mosaic
22½″ x 31½″ (57 x 80cm.) Unsigned
Literature: Mario Amaya, *Tiffany Glass*, London 1967, 20; C. Eileen King, "Tiffany – Peacock of Glass-Makers," *The Antique Dealer and Collector's Guide* (October 1972), 82; N. Potter and D. Jackson, *Tiffany*, 114; T. Paul, *The Art of Louis Comfort Tiffany*, 56-57
Provenance: Joseph Briggs; Haworth Art Gallery, Accrington, Lancs, England

**71. Sarah Fay Sumner Memorial Window**
Tiffany Studios, New York, 1912
120″ x 42″ (3.04 x 1.06m.) Unsigned
Literature: *Memorials in Glass and Stone*; A. Duncan, *Tiffany Windows*, Plate 64
Provenance: First Reformed Church, Albany, N.Y.

**72. Cartoon for Wisteria and Hollyhock Window**
Louis Comfort Tiffany, c. 1910
Watercolor and pencil on board
11⅞″ x 21⅝″ (30 x 55cm.) Unsigned
Provenance: Mr. Vito D'Agostino; Bruce and Adele Randall

# CHRONOLOGY

| | |
|---|---|
| 1848 | Louis Comfort Tiffany born in New York on 18th February |
| 1866 | Painting tuition under George Inness |
| 1867 | Exhibition of paintings at the National Academy of Design, New York |
| 1868/9 | Studied painting in Europe under Léon Bailly; met Samuel Colman |
| 1870 | Elected a member of the Century Club, New York |
| | Visited Cairo |
| 1871 | Elected an associate member of the National Academy of Design |
| 1872 | Married Mary Woodbridge Goddard on 15th May |
| 1873 | First experiments in glass-making at New York commercial glasshouses, including Heidt, Thill, Dannenhoffer, and Leo Popper |
| | Birth of first daughter (April 3rd) |
| 1874 | Birth of first son (December 9th; died three weeks later) |
| 1876 | Exhibition of paintings at the Philadelphia Centennial Exposition, National Academy of Design and the Century Club |
| | Executed first ornamental windows |
| 1878 | Exhibition of paintings at the International Exposition, Paris |
| | First completed window commission, for St. Mark's Episcopal Church, Islip, Long Island |
| | Established residence at Bella Apartments, 48 E. 26th Street, New York |
| | Elected treasurer of the Society of American Artists |
| | Birth of son, Charles Lewis II (January 7th) |
| 1879 | Formation of his first business, L. C. Tiffany & Associated Artists, an interior decorating firm, with Samuel Colman, Lockwood de Forest, and Candace Wheeler |
| | Birth of second daughter, Hilda (August 24th) |
| | Commission for George Kemp's Fifth Avenue residence |
| 1880 | The interior decoration of the Veterans Room and Library in the Seventh Regiment Armory on Park Avenue, New York |
| | Commission for the drop curtain, Madison Square Theatre, New York |
| | First experiments with mosaics; first wallpaper designs |
| 1880/1 | Commission for the entrance stairway and halls, Union League Club, New York |
| 1881 | Registration of Tiffany's patent for opalescent window glass |
| | Elected a full member of the National Academy of Design |
| 1881/2 | Commission for the William S. Kimball residence, Rochester, New York |
| | Commission for Mark Twain residence, Hartford, Conn. |
| | Commission for Cornelius Vanderbilt II's mansion |
| | Commission for Ogden Goelet's residence, Fifth Avenue |
| | Commissions for W. H. De Forest dining room, Kingscote dining room, J. Taylor Johnston parlor, William T. Lusk dining room |

| | |
|---|---|
| 1882/3 | Commission to decorate the White House under President Arthur |
| 1883 | Termination of L. C. Tiffany & Associated Artists |
| 1884 | Death of Tiffany's first wife |
| c. 1885 | Construction of the Tiffany mansion at 72nd Street and Madison Avenue, New York, in collaboration with Stanford White |
| 1885 | Formation of his new firm, the Tiffany Glass Company |
| | Decoration of the Lyceum Theater, New York |
| 1886 | Second marriage, to Louise Wakeman Knox |
| 1888 | The Kempner Memorial window installed in St. Paul's Episcopalian Church, Milwaukee (Tiffany's largest figural window) |
| 1889 | Extensive travel through Europe |
| | Chittenden window commission for Yale University |
| 1890 | Early experiments with glass tiles |
| c. 1890 | Construction of The Briars, a country estate at Oyster Bay, Long Island |
| 1890/2 | Redecoration of Henry O. Havemeyer house |
| 1892 | Formation of the Tiffany Glass & Decorating Company and the establishment of a glass furnace in Corona, Long Island |
| 1893 | Participation in the Columbian Exposition in Chicago, including a chapel, other liturgical works, and domestic windows. Tiffany Glass & Decorating Company won 54 medals |
| c. 1893 | The division of Tiffany's glass manufacturing operation into the Stourbridge Glass Co. and the Allied Arts Co. |
| 1894 | Application with the United States Patent Office to register the trademark "Favrile" to be used on all items made by the company |
| | Exhibition of glassware at the Salon of the Société Nationale des Beaux-Arts, Paris |
| 1894/7 | First sales of Favrile glassware, including vases and lamps with blown glass shades |
| | Fifty-three pieces of Favrile glassware gifted to the Metropolitan Museum of Art by Henry O. Havemeyer |
| | Thirty-eight pieces of Favrile glassware sold to the Smithsonian Institution, Washington, D.C. |
| | Twenty-three pieces of Favrile glassware sent to the Imperial Museum of Fine Arts, Tokyo |
| 1895 | Exhibition at the Salon of the Société Nationale des Beaux-Arts, Paris, of a selection of Favrile glassware and of windows designed by Besnard (La Cascade), Bonnard (La Maternité), Roussel (Le Jardin), Ranson (La Moisson Fleurie), Isaac (Iris et Roseaux), Ibels (L'Eté), Vuillard (Les Marronniers), Denis (Une Paysage), Lautrec (Papa Chrysanthème), Vallotton (Une Parisienne), and Serusier (three untitled panels) all of which were executed by Tiffany |
| 1895/6 | Exhibition of Favril glassware and windows designed by Grasset and Serusier, at S. Bing's "L'Art Nouveau" gallery in Paris |
| 1896 | Commission for Pratt Institute library |
| 1896/7 | Exhibition of Favrile glassware at the Salon of the Société Nationales des Beaux-Arts, Paris |
| 1897 | Publication of a list of completed Tiffany window commissions |
| 1897/8 | Exhibition at the Salon of La Libre Esthétique, Brussels |
| 1898 | Opening of a Tiffany showroom at 331-341 Fourth Avenue, New York |
| | Art Institute of Chicago commission |
| 1898/9 | Exhibition of Favrile glassware and an electric lamp at S. Bing's "L'Art Nouveau" Gallery |
| | Formation of an enameling department |
| 1899 | Exhibition at the Grafton Gallery, London, of windows, lamps, and glassware |
| | First documentation of a leaded glass lamp (a butterfly model) |
| 1900 | Participation in the International Exposition, Paris, with more than 100 pieces of glassware, windows, lamps, mosaics, and enamels. Award of several Grand Prix by the Exposition Jury and the appointment as a knight of the Legion of Honour by the French State |
| | Change in the firm's use of the name from "Tiffany Glass & Decorating Company" to "Tiffany Studios" |
| | Chicago Public Library commission |
| 1901 | Participation in the Pan-American Exposition, Buffalo, and in St. Petersburg, Russia, and the award of Grand Prix at both |
| | Wisteria lamp designed by Mrs. Curtis Freschel |
| 1902 | Appointment as Design Director of Tiffany & Company on the death of his father, Charles Lewis Tiffany |
| | Re-location of Tiffany showroom to 45th Street, New York |
| | Formal adoption of the name "Tiffany Studios" for all items made at the Corona factory |
| | Participation in the Turin Exposition; the award of the Grand Prize for the lily cluster lamp model |
| | Tiffany Furnaces established |
| 1902/5 | Construction of a summer home, Laurelton Hall, near Oyster Bay on the north shore of Long Island for $2 million |
| 1904 | Death of his second wife on 9th May |
| | Exhibition at the St. Louis International Exposition |
| 1905 | Exhibition at the Salon of the Société des Artistes Français, Paris |
| 1906 | Publication of a Tiffany Studios Price List providing a comprehensive listing by model number of lamp shades, bases, candlesticks, "Fancy" goods, and desk-sets |
| | Exhibition at the Salon of the Société des Artistes Français in Paris |
| c. 1910 | Publication of "A Partial List of Windows", an updated (but incomplete) list of completed Tiffany Studios window commissions (primarily ecclesiastical) |
| 1911 | Completion of the glass mosaic curtain for the National Theater in Mexico City |
| 1912 | The peacock and cockatoo panels for Captain J.R. DeLamar installed in his Madison Avenue residence |
| 1912/14 | Construction of the mosaic murals and domes for the Roman Catholic Cathedral in St. Louis, Missouri, consisting of 30 million pieces of glass mosaic |

| 1913 | Exhibition at the Salon of the Société des Artistes Français in Paris |
| | Publication of an updated version of the 1906 Tiffany Studios Price List of lamps, bases, etc., including models introduced in the interim |
| | Egyptian Fete at Tiffany Studios showroom |
| | Visit to Nuremberg, West Germany |
| | Visit to Havana, Cuba, to oversee large domestic window commission |
| 1914 | Biography of Tiffany by Charles de Kay, entitled "The Art Work of Louis C. Tiffany" |
| | Exhibition at the Salon of the Société des Artistes Français in Paris |
| | Creation of "The Bathers" window later installed in Laurelton Hall |
| | Queen Anne's Lace design patented (February 3rd) |
| | Gala Feast at Laurelton Hall |
| 1915 | Participation in the Pan-Pacific Exposition in San Francisco |
| | Creation of the "Dream Garden" mosaic mural designed by Maxfield Parrish for the lobby of the Curtis Publishing Company building in Philadelphia |
| 1916 | Retrospective exhibition of Tiffany paintings, glassware, mosaics, enamels, and lamps, to celebrate Tiffany's 68th birthday; "Quest of Beauty" birthday party at the Tiffany Studios showroom |
| | Tiffany's mosaic chapel from the 1893 Columbian Exposition, which had been installed in 1899 in the crypt of the St. John the Divine Cathedral in New York, re-installed at Laurelton Hall |
| | Visit to Alaska |
| 1918 | Creation of the L. C. Tiffany Foundation to subsidize gifted young artists |
| 1919 | Retirement of Tiffany and the rough division of Tiffany Studios into Tiffany Furnaces, which was taken over by A. Douglas Nash for the continued production of Favrile glassware; and the Tiffany Ecclesiastical department, which continued the firm's production of windows, mosaics, leaded lamps, etc. |
| 1922 | Creation of the Te Deum Laudamus mosaic triptych for the First Methodist Church in Los Angeles |
| 1924 | L. C. Tiffany Furnaces dissolved |
| 1927 | Collection of Tiffany glass presented to Andrew Dickson White Museum of Art at Cornell University |
| 1932 | Tiffany Studios declared bankruptcy |
| 1933 | Death of L. C. Tiffany on 17th January |
| | Westminster Memorial Studios established by former employees to complete outstanding Tiffany Studios commissions |
| 1934 | First of several public auctions to dispose of the firm's inventory |
| 1946 | Contents of Laurelton Hall sold at public auction in New York |
| 1957 | Laurelton Hall partially destroyed by fire |
| 1958 | First important retrospective exhibition of Tiffany's work, The Museum of Contemporary Crafts, New York |
| 1967 | Heckscher Museum exhibition, Huntington, New York |
| 1979 | Grey Art Gallery and Study Center, New York University, paintings exhibition |

# INDEX

*(Page numbers in italic refer to illustrations)*

# ACKNOWLEDGMENTS

Neil Harris
John D'Agostino
Mr. and Mrs. Jack Stievelman
Mr. and Mrs. David Lorenz
Virginia Museum of Fine Arts: Frederick R. Brandt, Paul N. Perrot
Mr. and Mrs. Michael Lerner
First Reformed Church, Albany: Robert Akland
David Bellis
John Belger, Sr.
Dick Belger
Citibank Citicorp Center: Patrick J. Cooney
Mr. and Mrs. Howard Ellman
Mr. and Mrs. Herb Kornblum
Benedict Silverman
Joel Schur
Charles Hosmer Morse Museum of American Art, Winter Park, Florida: Hugh F. McKean, David Donaldson, Ann H. Gerken
Mr. and Mrs. Bruce Randall

Bruce Randall, Jr., Sarah Calderbank
Mr. and Mrs. John Mecom, Jr.
Mr. and Mrs. Erving Wolf
Mathew Wolf
Hessisches Landesmuseum, Darmstadt, Germany: Dr. Wolfgang Beeh, Dr. Carl Benno Heller
Haworth Art Gallery, Accrington: Norman Potter
Yale University Art Gallery: Helen Cooper, William Cuffe
Mr. and Mrs. Salvatore Migliaccio
Mr. and Mrs. Felice Minucci
Mrs. Louise Platt
Henry Platt
Martin Eidelberg
Ralph Esmerian
The Metropolitan Museum of Art: Alice Cooney Frelinghuysen, Deanna Cross
Tiffany & Company: William R. Chaney, Fernanda Gilligan, John Loring, Janet Zapata

Philadelphia Museum of Art: Anne d'Harnoncourt, Jack Lindsay
Mr. and Mrs. James Lusk
Mr. and Mrs. Charles Lusk
Fredrik Kiaer
Herbert M. Gelfand
Mr. and Mrs. Robert Kogod
Jane M. Farmer
Gary Wexler
Lillian Nassau, Ltd.
National Museum of American Art: Dr. Elizabeth Broun, Margy P. Sharpe, Lois Fink
Renwick Gallery, Smithsonian Institution: Jeremy Adamson, Michael Monroe
University of Michigan Museum of Art: Dr. Hilarie Faberman, Anne-Marie Karmazin
Isidra Pastor
Anthony Jones
Mrs. Molly Barringer
Bruce Newman

The New-York Historical Society: Wade McCann
Sotheby's, New York: Carolyn Holmes
Christopher Bancroft
Art Femmenella
Jack Cushen
Mary C. Higgens
Edward Hewett
Shawn McNally
Art Institute of Chicago: Mary Woolever

*Photography:* David Robinson, Glenn Steigelman, Townsend Photo, Bob Young, Peter Simon, Greg Heck

*Very special thanks are extended to MaryBeth McCaffrey for her research and coordination of the catalogue and exhibition and to Janet Zapata for the information she made available on Louis Comfort Tiffany's association with Tiffany & Co.*